Writing on the Edge

A Borderlands Reader · Edited by Tom Miller

Writing on the Edge

The University of Arizona Press   Tucson

The University of Arizona Press
© 2003 The Arizona Board of Regents
First printing
All rights reserved
♾ This book is printed on acid-free, archival-quality paper.
Manufactured in the United States of America

08   07   06   05   04   03   6   5   4   3   2   1

Library of Congress Cataloging-in-Publication Data
Writing on the edge : a borderlands reader / edited by Tom Miller.
p. cm.
Includes bibliographical references.
ISBN 0-8165-2241-3 (pbk. : alk. paper)
1. American literature—Southwestern States. 2. American literature—
Mexican-American Border Region. 3. Mexican-American Border
Region—Literary collections. 4. Mexican literature—Mexican-American
Border Region. 5. Mexican-American Border Region—Civilization. 6.
Southwestern States—Literary collections. 7. Southwestern States—
Civilization. I. Miller, Tom, 1947–
PS566 .W745 2003
810.8′0979—dc21
2002154866
British Library Cataloguing-in-Publication Data
A catalogue record for this book is available from the British Library.

The preparation of this book was supported in part by a grant from the the U.S.–Mexico Fund for Culture/Fideicomiso para la Cultura México/USA, whose purpose is to foster mutual understanding and cultural exchange between artistic and intellectual communities of Mexico and the United States of America.

Support also came from the Arizona Humanities Council, the Arizona Commission on the Arts, the Tucson/Pima Arts Council, and the *Tucson Citizen*.

For Chuck, Ann, John, and Mike, with love

Contents

Part 4

Part 5

Section 1

Section 2

Part 6

Part 7

Section 1

Section 2

Part 8

Acknowledgments

I'd be embarrassed to reveal how much time passed assembling this collection. Let's just say that it took more time than the United States took to seize all of Mexico's northwest in the mid-1800s. The nice part of taking my own sweet time was the luxury of continually reading literature from and about the border, uncovering bygone gems, enthusiastically recommending new literary discoveries to friends, and then repeating the process. I started by looking at the subject from the inside out, as an author who had already written extensively about the border, but I quickly saw vast shelves full of literature far beyond my own approach. So many people have shaped my broader appreciation of border literature over the years that to list them all would be impossible. I will name a few of them here. To the others who helped me, know that I wish you each *felices fronteras* and *buena lectura*.

The following are among those who helped jostle this project along, and to them I am most grateful: Ricardo Aguilar Melantzón, Juan Bruce-Novoa, the late José Antonio Burciaga, Bobby Byrd, Denise Chávez, Steve Cox, Celestino Fernández, Carlos Flores, Robert F. Gish, Jim Griffith, Margo Gutiérrez, Juan Felipe Herrera, Milton Jamail, Marco Jerez, Oscar Martínez, Larry McMurtry, Leon C. Metz, Kelley Merriam, Oscar Monroy, Carlos Morton, Harry Polkinhorn, Charles Tatum, Gabriel Trujillo Muñoz, Mark Weiss and librarians up and down the border on both sides, especially in Del Rio and El Paso, Texas. Over the years my filing system, on paper and screen, overflowed into random and disorganized piles. Fawn-Amber Montoya took on the heroic task of making sense of it all and assembling it in its proper order.

May you all find the luxury to relax in your own private borderland.

Introduction

"Dang if you ain't the unmexicanist Mexican I ever seen," Danny Shaw says to the very Anglo-looking kid who had just moved north to Brownsville, Texas. The jumble of identity—what we look like, how we sound, our body language, the clothes we wear, the food we eat—these elements wear well on the characters in James Carlos Blake's *Borderlands*, a recent and rousing contribution to border literature. Soon Blake's new kid learns to ease into both cultures. "It was the start of a lifelong habit of trying to fit in with the people around me by assuming their modes of speech, a practice reputedly common to misfits, con artists and liars of all sorts, which of course includes writers."

The illusory truths and artful pretensions that live in the thin Third Country between the United States and Mexico are admirably suited for writers. Since there was first a border to cross in the mid-1800s, observers and dreamers, liars and poets, the desperate and the hopeful have taken out their quills, ball-points, typewriters, and laptops, unfurled their parchment, opened their journals, twisted their platens, and adjusted their monitors, all with the goal of articulating the scent of a new beginning. "Sometimes," says Johnny Ten Mason after crossing into Mexico in Vance Bourjaily's *Now Playing at Canterbury,* "it takes the air of a different country to wash the crap out of a man's lungs."

The borderland bookshelf holds works ranging from romantic and gushy to harsh and precise. Writers who approach the border from the north have far different olfactory nerves from those who contemplate it from the south. The best of both groups acknowledge this and play off it in their work, as words from both countries meet in a literary everyman's land. Just as no frontier exists similar to the border between the United States and Mexico, so too is there no other literature defined by such an international line. It captures the unadulterated awe of northbound travelers before incidents and circumstances irreparably change them. For the southbound nomad, works from the border are filled with genuine curiosity and false bravado.

Among the qualities that make border literature such a rich lode are its size and breadth. It yields works that question national policies and personal values. It depicts *carrizo* cane sprouting beside the Rio Grande and cement office buildings growing in Tijuana. As a metaphor, one could hardly improve upon crossing from one country with its language, attitudes, and culture into another with a very different tongue, approach, and society. The creative writer reflects on patriotism and character, while the insightful reader gains an understanding of allegiance and mettle.

When I moved to the borderland in the late 1960s and quickly realized that speaking Spanish would enhance my personal and professional life, I wandered into a bookstore and asked for something to get me started. The clerk handed me *How to Speak Spanish with Your Servant.* I learned to say, "Do you have a health card?" "Always call me if you can't come to work," "Sweep the floor before you mop it," "Wash the refrigerator inside and out," and my favorite: "Don't take the clothes out of the machine until it stops and shuts off." This was my introduction to borderland literature.

Scholars argue all night over authenticity. Can a New Jersey physician (William Carlos Williams) portray the frontier with the same poetic intensity as a native songwriter (Flaco Jiménez)? Does a British Catholic essayist (Graham Greene) see the same border as an American feminist poet (Demetria Martínez)? A mid-twentieth-century Mexican novelist (Agustín Yáñez) as a contemporary Mexican crime writer (Paco Ignacio Taibo II)? Do traditional standards of excellence apply to an area known for raw emotions and rough language? Border Spanish and border English fertilize each other with syllables, words, and complete phrases. These sounds enrich writing within the region but often befuddle the faraway reader.

Those of us who cozy up to the border, who feel it's our homeland, will be surprised to see how many passers-by have been struck by our wedge of North America. The frontier belongs to everyone, and we can learn as much from outsiders' perspectives as they can from our homegrown outlook. "The literary space of the borderlands is full of souls," wrote professor Armando Miguélez, a Spaniard. "The borderlands writers seem to conspire with the forces of evil." Miguélez calls it "an 'I accuse' literature, born of the contemplation of injustice."

The Mexican Revolution of 1910 and the Bracero Program of 1941–1964 (an American attempt to harness cheap Mexican labor to the rural Southwest) are the defining events for twentieth-century borderland literature. Their presence, even unwitting as subtext, permeates writing on both sides. Whatever characteristic defines borderland adventure in the twenty-first century, you may be sure its foundation—whether passionate, political, or military—is already taking shape.

"We need a big border on top," says Juárez/El Paso native and professor Ricardo Aguilar, "so we don't have to directly face the United States. Mexico City thinks of the northern desert as a natural obstacle to invasion. It's considered a God-given blessing." Wrote William Burroughs in *Naked Lunch:* "Something falls off you when you cross the border into Mexico, and suddenly the landscape hits you with nothing between it, desert and mountains and vultures." It's a landscape that inspires fear, love, and a clean slate.

For writers in the Pimería Alta, the Arizona-Sonora desertland, William Burroughs's mountains and vultures are simply the backdrop to Aguilar's God-given blessing. For a while in the 1970s and '80s, borderland scribe Marco Jerez and some colleagues lived the writer's dream. They formed a literary community in Nogales, Sonora, and called it Café y Arte. "Our goal," recalled Jerez, "was to destroy as much as possible the negative intellectual centrism that corrodes Mexico. It was made up of working- and middle-class intelligentsia. We published more than twenty books. We showed movies, had a little library, exhibited art, and served coffee. We had atmosphere. You could run a tab and pay it off later. It was a place of civility." Decades after its formation, Jerez can still get excited about his border literary arts society. "We'd do on-the-spot translations, with groups sitting around different tables working on the nuance of various words. Then we'd get together to work out the difference. We traveled north to Tucson and read at cafes there and invited poets south to read at Café y Arte. We weren't smuggling drugs. We were smuggling poetry." Anthropologist Ruth Behar writes similarly of carrying words north. "Esperanza has given me her story to smuggle across the border," she notes of a Mexican compañera in *Translated Woman.* "She has chosen to be a literary wetback." As Chilean poet Vicente Huidobro once wrote, "Words should fly like airplanes over custom offices and international borders, and should land in all the fields."

The notion of literature in a region that the rest of both countries considers at best an irrelevant nuisance allows for more free-ranging creative output. With only negligible cultural attention from afar, it's easy to experiment. The movies *Mariachi* and *Desperado* gained notoriety as full-bodied parodies of the border. (In the latter, actress Salma Hayek owns Café con Libros, a border-town bookstore. "Nobody reads," she laments. "This town never had a bookstore.") To test bi-national resourcefulness, I once contemplated sending wheelbarrows full of individual words across the border to a *ma-*

quiladora where assembly-line workers would piece them together and send them back as polished short stories. The idea, which never got beyond the bar of the Hamilton Hotel in Laredo, allows us to think of maquiladora laborers as cultural workers and their product as frontier prose.

The *zona fronteriza* is not a positive totem in Mexican literature. As one study concluded, "It is as if the border were a malignant force that provoked suffering." Oscar Monroy, a native of Nogales, Sonora, and one of the founders of Café y Arte, has made a career of trying to combat this image, yet the reality of his hometown has frustrated him at every turn. "This government has a way to distribute tomatoes and green chiles but, for the love of God, not books. The power structure traffics in marijuana, prostitution, gold, and copper but not a powerful intellectual life." I was speaking with Monroy at his roomy Nogales home, La Bahía de Silencio. "Throughout Sonora there are no streets named for famous philosophers"—his voice started to rise and he began to pound the dining-room table—"only for famous drunks. *Corridos* [ballads] should be about poets, not smugglers. Freud was a borderlander!" He began to wave his arms about. "So was Jesus!" Monroy, born in 1933, has self-published scores and scores of books.

To some, the border is the world itself; to others a mere pit stop in their travels. The names Damon Runyon and Emma Goldman are etched in twentieth-century history, but seldom are they associated with the border. Runyon, though, wrote about going to the horse races in Juárez with Pancho Villa. Goldman paused in San Diego and Tijuana on her way to Mexico's interior, where she published an anarchist newspaper. "Tijuana is not Mexico," wrote Raymond Chandler in *The Long Good-Bye*, another unexpected work on the frontier bookshelf. "No bordertown is anything but a bordertown, just as no waterfront is anything but a waterfront." Likewise Sinclair Lewis's *Main Street*, whose Middle American couple, the Kennicotts, traveled west for more than three months: "They saw the Grand Canyon, the adobe walls of Santa Fe and, in a drive from El Paso into Mexico, their first foreign land."

Even more surprising than finding the Kennicotts at the border was discovering Maigret, the detective who appeared in scores of Belgian author Georges Simenon's crime books. *Maigret at the Coroner's* kept our hero trotting in and out of Nogales, trying to pin down a murder. On the U.S. side, "everything was calm and reassuring, everything uniform," Simenon wrote in another book, *The Bottom of the Bottle*, while the other side was "a swarming mysterious world" where "furtive figures prowled on every corner of darkness" and "one sensed human heat, and gestures, and whispers." In the late 1940s Simenon made his residence just north of Nogales, where he maintained three lovers, including his wife, and a ferocious writing pace of almost twenty pages a day.

A boundary, according to Ambrose Bierce in *The Devil's Dictionary*, is "an imaginary line between two nations, separating the imaginary rights of one from the imaginary rights of another." At the age of seventy, Bierce himself reached that boundary in the form of the Rio Grande and saw a "vast expanse of Mexican territory alluringly spread out and inaccessible." In Ciudad Juárez he linked up with the Villa forces as a journalist, but he carried a rifle and killed a soldier in battle. El Gringo Viejo, as the villistas called him, "was given a sombrero and questioned no more." Wrote Bierce in one of his last missives north: "To be a Gringo in Mexico— Ah, that is euthanasia!" Bierce disappeared into Mexico, never to be heard from again. Another author who entered Mexico and, like Bierce, also disappeared, was Oscar Zeta Acosta, rambunctious 1960s and '70s Chicano attorney, activist, and jackass of all trades who left behind two rousing books and a stack of unpaid bills.

Fiction encourages us to float episodic impossibilities, so I imagine a Baja California trailer park filled exclusively with foreigners who have disappeared into Mexico. The residents of the Parque Desconocido all use false names. Acosta and Bierce, wearing tank tops and Bermuda shorts, play chess daily at sunset. The game is leisurely, the table wobbly, and the two polish off a six-pack of Negra Modelo every evening. More than once, after crossing the border, I have anchored my Airstream at the Parque Desconocido for a few nights to watch and listen, hoping to sit at the same rickety table as Acosta and Bierce. The trailer court's game room has a one-shelf library maintained by a quiet fellow whose Spanish wears a slight German accent; it is B. Traven, the secretive European author who settled in Mexico and wrote brilliantly of its underclass in *The Treasure of the Sierra Madre* and other classics. Traven, shuffling about in *guarache* sandals and a straw hat, pulls out some dominoes and we sit down to play. When I prepare to leave two days later, Acosta, Bierce, and Traven each hand me some mail to post when I'm back across the border.

The El Paso–Juárez area is the literary center of the U.S.–Mexico border. *Punto.*

This may come as a surprise to those who have traveled the rest of the frontier and may startle those who know these two cities. Yet, having visited border towns from the Gulf of Mexico to the Pacific Ocean, I can assure you that the landlocked center of the Third Country also has the most fertile literary landscape. El Paso–Juárez has both river and desert, cowboy and Indian, the virtuous and the vulgar. It is both the departure point and terminus for the two universal plot lines, as the late novelist John Gardner identified them, in all literature: either you go on a journey, or a stranger comes to town.

The area is appealing because some of the most coarse and most polished writing has come from there—works by Cormac McCarthy, Benjamin Alire Sáenz, the late Tom Lea, Denise Chávez, and songwriter Tom Russell, to name a few. And also because it's the last place along the border where you can still hear energetic barroom arguments about the Mexican Revolution as if it were still in progress. Late one weekday afternoon, some writers took me to the Back Door, an El Paso bar where Brenda Lee shared the jukebox with Los Lobos. A pitcher of beer came, and a fellow to my left proclaimed Carlos Fuentes the Julio Iglesias of literature. "We used to have poetry readings with an open mike," playwright Carlos Morton recounted. "Sometimes fifteen people would line up. There were fistfights." "Did you hear?" a fellow to his right said. "West Texas State Teachers College got upgraded. Now it's East Oklahoma State Teachers College."

A Juárez *corridista*—a writer of *corridos*—suggested I look for a building across from a church on El Paso's South Oregon Street a few blocks from the bridge to Mexico. "You'll see literary history. Our literary history."

The sun had almost set by the time I reached the block the corridista had recommended. It was in a run-down area with crowded, neglected apartment houses filled with Mexicans newly arrived from the interior. A woman at a corner Laundromat pointed out the two-story tenement with literary history. An open-air hallway lined with graffiti led from the street to an interior courtyard, where twenty apartments looked out on a sagging clothesline adorned with damp white sheets and dripping blue jeans. A man in a sweat-stained straw cowboy hat rolled a bald tire past me. The rest of the courtyard was a jumble of children's bicycles, slatless wooden chairs, and disassembled swamp coolers. Two of the tenants, all of whom appeared to be marginally employed, stopped sipping beer long enough to look down at me suspiciously from the second-floor balcony. I was unknown to them and I was taking notes. One asked what I wanted.

"I'm here because of Mariano Azuela," I called up to them. They looked perplexed. Don't know him, their faces said.

"Azuela," I repeated over the din of traffic. "The plaque at the entrance." I motioned toward the street, where an engraved sign proclaimed this the building where, in 1915, the Mexican doctor and novelist Mariano Azuela finished and published his great novel of the Mexican Revolution, *Los de abajo* (The Underdogs), "The writer from the Revolution," I said. "You live in a very historic building." One of the fellows grinned. "In that case," he called down, lifting his beer can, "you are welcome."

From La Hacienda, where I lunched with Juárez writer José García a couple of days later, I could make out the University of Texas at El Paso on one side of the river and the Universidad Autónoma de Juárez on the other. García dazzled me with his abstract, deconstructionist, postmodern gibberish, especially as he applied it to the border. "I don't subscribe to this bicultural, binational stuff," he said. "That's a fantasy. We are in the middle of something quite different. We are entre siempre." Forever in-between.

That afternoon professor Ricardo Aguilar took me to his home in Juárez. "You see this?" he said, motioning to a bookshelf full of literature about the borderland by Mexican writers. "No one in Mexico City acknowledges this exists. We're a literary wasteland to them, yet this is one of the most productive and intellectually active regions of the country." He started to rattle off the names of local authors just as the phone rang. It was Juan Holguín Rodríguez, one of the writers he had just mentioned, calling to invite Aguilar to a book launching that weekend. The educated world rooted in Juárez and El Paso has, over the years, become a literary free-trade zone. John Rechy's descriptive writings about the El Paso of more than forty years ago revealed the hidden side of an active city. E. L. Bode's poignant slices of life and short stories by Chester Seltzer (aka Amado Muro) on life in northern Chihuahua and South El Paso further color the written panorama.

I spent the following day with Earl Rymkus, the pen name of a janitor on the fourth floor of the University of Texas at El Paso's Fine Arts Building. His office accoutrements consisted of a floor waxer and stacks of toilet paper. Until he settled in El Paso around 1960, Rymkus, a Milwaukee native, had drifted through the West, working odd jobs at minimum wage. He read Jack London, B. Traven, T. E. Lawrence, and Schopenhauer. The extent of his formal training was an unfinished correspondence course from the Famous Writers School. "I bought a Corona portable, put all my papers in a car, and drove to the border," he recalled. Since then he's written innumerable short stories and poems about the borderland, and he's published in scattered short-lived trucker magazines, obscure literary journals, and his own *Starving Artist Times,* which lasted two years in the mid-1980s. He circulates his manuscripts freely.

Rymkus, now retired, said, "I'm attracted to romantic, out-of-the-way things. Neglected things. The underside. This border area, it just got in my blood. The landscape, the attitude, and the language, the different sense of time. There's a lot of poverty and pain and sorrow, but there's also an openness and willingness to accept you as you are." His poetry collection, *The Rio Grande Blues,* heralds the vagabond, the wino, the border rat. Its voice is wonderfully raw, indelicate, and undisciplined.

Bobby Byrd, poet and publisher of Cinco Puntos Press, laughed when I told him what a vibrant literary world I had found in El Paso and Juárez. His publishing house, a vigorous El Paso press that serves its readers well, reinforced this notion: "People passing through say that all the time. We've stopped trying to figure out what we're doing right." Cinco Puntos Press and also San Diego State University Press view writing from inside the frontier as mainstream literature. It is not the other; it is us. Both houses routinely bring out border writing and treat it with the same editorial care that a major publisher would give to a manuscript by Jay McInerny or Cynthia Ozick. From San Diego comes a collection of detective stories, *Line of Fire,* as well as poetry, short stories, essays, and plays. The SDSU Press works closely with the publishing house at the Autonomous University of Baja California, across the line. Cinco Puntos has assembled a strong list of adult and children's borderland books, from Rudolfo Anaya's *Elegy on the Death of César Chávez* to bilingual storyteller Joe Hayes's collection *The Day It Snowed Tortillas.* To further bolster a literary identity along North America's waistband, Las Cruces, New Mexico, hosts an annual Border Book Festival celebrating writers and readers in the literary temperate zone.

When the International Boundary and Water Commission, a binational bureaucracy, buried a time capsule in 1989 to celebrate its centenary, it included documents going back to the border's origins but not one short story, essay, or song about the border. When the curious eventually open that capsule, will they think that no border literature existed?

What would a literary time capsule include? That was the question I hoped to answer when assembling material for this collection. "What is an anthology" asks the writer Ilan Stavans, "if not a miniature, itinerant library?" To stock this itinerant library, I solicited suggestions from writers, publishers, and scholars on both sides of the line and posted notices in as many borderland universities, libraries, and newspapers as I could locate. You hold the results: some of the very best writing about the frontier from the twentieth century (with a detour or two into the surrounding centuries).

Bureaucrats and politicians define the borderland as the ten U.S. and Mexican states reconciled to life as eternal neighbors. The region embraces major cities such as Monterrey and Albuquerque, San Antonio and Chihuahua, yet the more geographically inclusive your borderland, the more diluted it becomes. I'm a strict constructionist when it comes to defining border literature. For me, the work has to touch on a land two thousand miles long and only twenty miles wide. The border itself has to play a role in the story line, either real or figurative. It can be a trampoline or a barrier, provoke enlightenment or depression. I was looking for the literary sparks that flash from America's third rail.

With this in mind, I confess to being bewitched by Orson Welles's outstanding 1958 noir classic of corruption and betrayal, *Touch of Evil.* Disgusted with a Mexican border town, U.S. police captain Hank Quinlan (Welles himself) mutters to his sergeant, "Let's get back to civilization." The movie, a psychological thriller, brutally encapsulates the most dreadful clichés about border towns and the people who inhabit them. It recalls an observation from Octavio Paz: "Americans have not looked for a Mexico in Mexico; they have looked for their obsessions, enthusiasms, phobias, hopes, interests—and these are what they have found."

And it is just these explorations, the wide poetic points of view, that give border writing its scope and texture, its bulging metaphor and its literary integrity. Whether the writing is poised precariously near the edge or safely in the center, its anchor falls squarely in the borderland. It is North America's Middle Passage, and these writers are its witnesses.

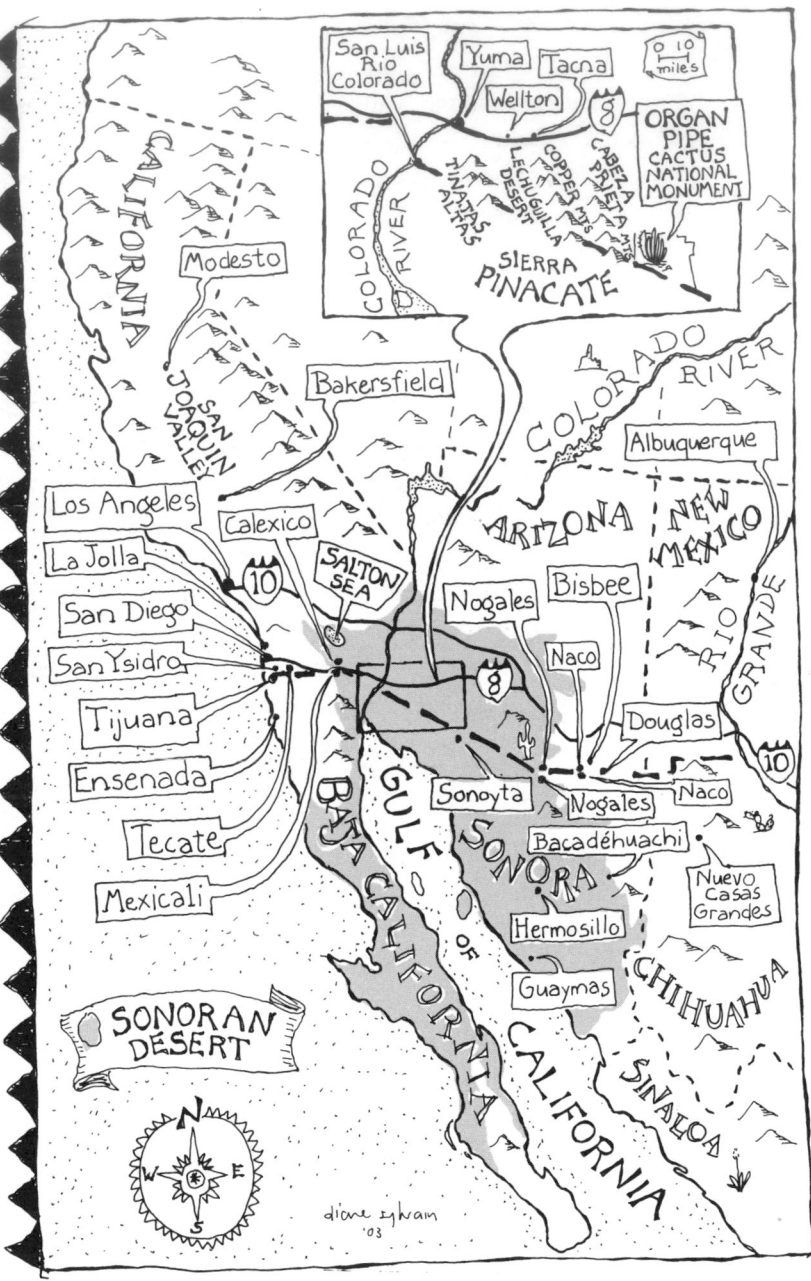

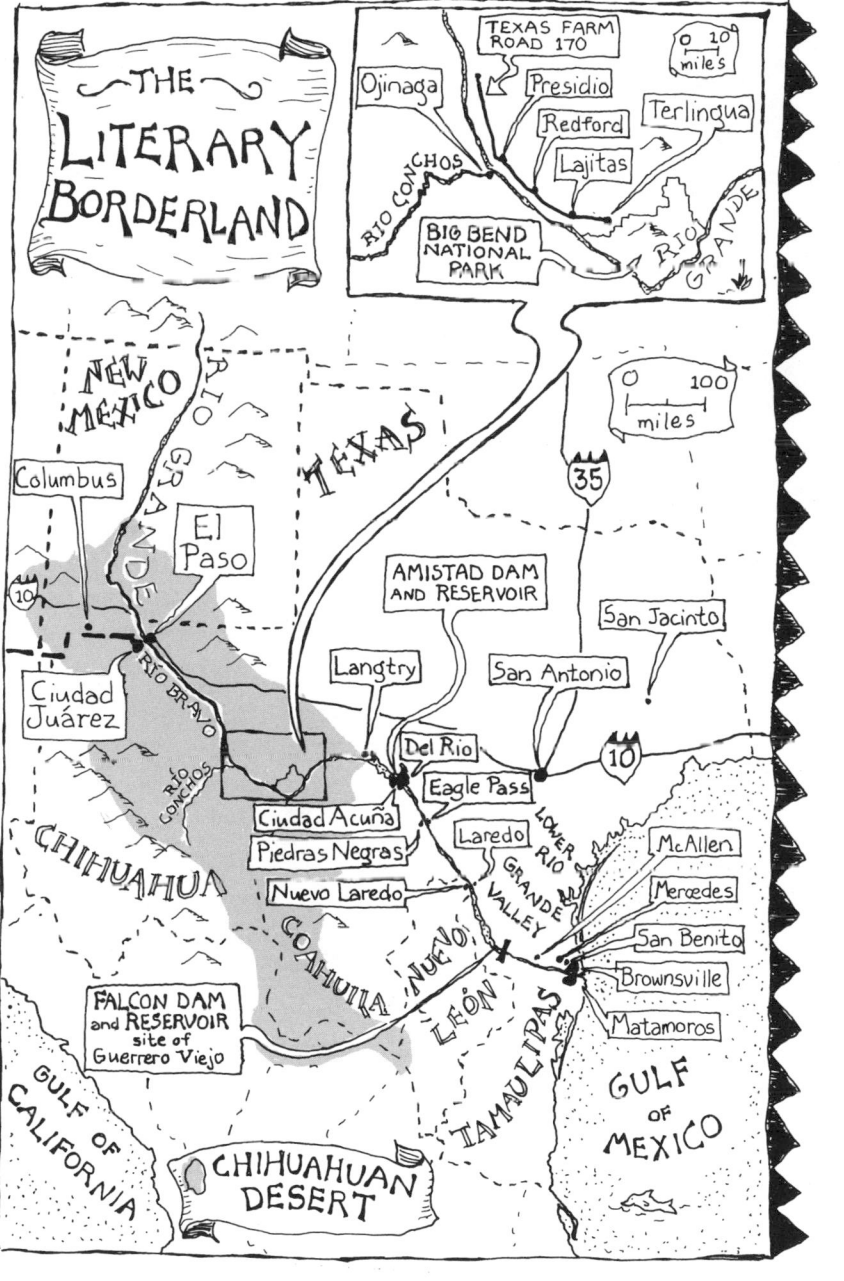

THE
LITERARY
BORDERLAND

TEXAS FARM ROAD 170

0 10 miles

Ojinaga
Presidio
Redford
Terlingua
Lajitas
RIO CONCHOS
BIG BEND NATIONAL PARK
RIO GRANDE

NEW MEXICO
RIO GRANDE
TEXAS
0 100 miles
35

Columbus
El Paso
AMISTAD DAM AND RESERVOIR
San Jacinto
10
Ciudad Juárez
RIO BRAVO
Langtry
San Antonio
RIO CONCHOS
Del Rio
10
CHIHUAHUA
Ciudad Acuña
Eagle Pass
Piedras Negras
Laredo
Nuevo Laredo
McAllen
LOWER RIO GRANDE VALLEY
Mercedes
COAHUILA
NUEVO LEÓN
San Benito
Brownsville
FALCON DAM and RESERVOIR site of Guerrero Viejo
Matamoros
GULF OF CALIFORNIA
TAMAULIPAS
GULF OF MEXICO
CHIHUAHUAN DESERT

Cities and Their Writers

At Large
Eduardo Galeano
Woody Guthrie
María Herrera-Sobek
Gilbert Shelton and
Dave Sheridan

**Agua Prieta, Sonora/
Douglas, Arizona**
Gilberto Maldonado
Herrera
Victor Villaseñor

**Albuquerque, New
Mexico**
Demetria Martínez

**Amistad Dam, Amistad
Reservoir**
Brianda Domecq

Bakersfield, California
Phil Ochs

Bisbee, Arizona
Miguel Méndez

Brownsville, Texas
Américo Paredes
Edward R. F. Sheehan
Hart Stilwell

**Casas Grandes,
Chihuahua**
Earl Shorris

**Ciudad Acuña,
Coahuila/Del Rio,
Texas**
Brianda Domecq
George Rabasa

**Ciudad Juárez,
Chihuahua/El Paso,
Texas**
Oscar Zeta Acosta
Ricardo Aguilar-
Melantzón
Mariano Azuela
José Antonio Burciaga
Cora Hayward
Crawford
Carlos Fuentes
Alicia Gaspar de Alba

Ray Gonzalez
Martín Luis Guzmán
Los Hermanos
Bañuelos
Arturo Islas
Gloria López-Stafford
Oscar J. Martínez
Pat Mora
Marty Robbins
Benjamin Alire Sáenz
Ricardo Sánchez
William Carlos
Williams

Columbus, New Mexico
Earl Shorris

**Del Rio, Texas/Ciudad
Acuña, Coahuila**
Brianda Domecq
George Rabasa

**Douglas, Arizona/Agua
Prieta, Sonora**
Gilberto Maldonado
Herrera
Victor Villaseñor

Eagle Pass, Texas
José Vasconcelos

**El Paso, Texas/Ciudad
Juárez, Chihuahua**
Oscar Zeta Acosta
Ricardo Aguilar-
Melantzón
Mariano Azuela
José Antonio Burciaga
Cora Hayward
Crawford
Carlos Fuentes
Alicia Gaspar de Alba
Ray Gonzalez
Martín Luis Guzmán
Los Hermanos
Bañuelos
Arturo Islas
Gloria López-Safford
Oscar J. Martínez
Pat Mora
Marty Robbins

Benjamin Alire Sáenz
Ricardo Sánchez
William Carlos
Williams

**Ensenada, Baja
California**
Maya Angelou

Guanajuato, Guanajuato
Jorge Ibargüengoitia

Guerrero Viejo, Texas
Elena Poniatowska

Lajitas, Texas
Sam Shepard

**Laredo, Texas/Nuevo
Laredo, Tamaulipas**
Norma Elia Cantú
Stephen Crane
Graham Greene
Vladimir Mayakovsky

Los Angeles, California
Ry Cooder, John Hiatt,
and James Dickinson
Graciela Limón
Rubén Martínez
Luis J. Rodríguez
Richard Rodriguez

McAllen, Texas
Genaro González

Mercedes, Texas
Rolando Hinojosa

Mexicali, Baja California
Allen Ginsberg
Paco Ignacio Taibo II
Gabriel Trujillo Muñoz

Mexico City
Guillermo Gómez-Peña
Bárbara Jacobs
Myriam Moscona
Luis Spota
Agustín Yáñez

Modesto, California
Eugene Nelson

New York City
Janet Arelis Quezada

Part 1

These pieces tax all five senses. Fiction, essay and poetry, they seduce the casual reader inside the borderland.

Through desert and riverland, the border injures its own and brings forth saints. Here, the border rewards both pain and virtue.

from *Mi Tierra*

Ray Gonzalez

We understand what we need and throw our lives into the Sonora and Chihuahua deserts, boundaries for the dust where the family lived and died, where we grew up, the ghosts of *conquistadores* marching and dictating our view of life and death in the desert, the conquest making us wonder what happened to the pueblo people. Where are the skeletons of the Spanish soldiers buried? Where did they dissolve into the earth? In what year did our first *mestizo* great-grandparents cross the Rio Grande?

It is the story that survives dust storms and little rain. Tales of life, death, and wonder in a desert of deceptive beauty—the place where the earth accepted its fate at the hands of the pueblo people who fought to save their civilization, and of the Spanish explorers who came to cut open the earth for its riches and to burn the pueblos down. The Spanish did not know it would never be enough. Their journey north would influence the location of El Paso del Norte, the desolate settlement around the constantly changing course of the river. Rio Grande—its many names deceiving those who tried to cross it and take what they wanted—Rio Grande, Río de las Palmas, Río de San Buenaventura del Norte, Río de Nuestra Señora, Río de la Concepción.

It is a simple truth—we no longer cross the Rio Grande in vain as the conquistadores did. When we cross the muddy river, it is for family reasons. We are branded illegals no matter which side of the border we come from. There are too many old desires to be satisfied under the New Mexico and west Texas sun. The ancient bones of these yearnings roll in the wind, never dissolve, but drift over the desert in the endless search for the vast, hot terrain of the adobe home. "Tierra del Sol"—our refusal to die in the desert as so many died before we were born in El Paso del Norte.

Who will believe us when we give up a few of our secrets? Who will rise to acknowledge that we are telling the truth? Who will come out of their crumbling adobe houses to greet the wandering man in the dirty robes, the stranger who comes praying and calling across the *arroyos* and miles of mesquite, the man who carries something in his folded hands?

We want to understand what we dream, but we continue to dream without understanding, exposing our hearts to the dust where we sleep. Despite the hot ground, the earth turns to give us a chance. It is a difficult vision having something to do with the recurring dream of the rattlesnake, the creature of the desert that speaks in silence and waits for the whole story to be told before darting or slithering toward the next boulder. It disappears, before crawling into someone else's haunted dreams.

We cross the river without the snake because we want to turn into stone monuments, to be discovered by the first explorers who find the path to old adobe walls, artifacts standing for centuries in the sun, refusing to topple in the heat. The people of the desert *believe* in the adobe walls and touch them once a day. The coolness of the hard mud takes turns with the shimmering heat of the roof in protecting anyone who hides within. People stand by these walls, waiting for the stranger to come to their pueblo so they can offer him gifts to carry in his cupped hands.

As the stranger approaches the pueblos, they ask the wind to explain what the families are doing in their houses. It is a quiet gathering, a wounding of old solitude and isolation you carry in your chest if you have been born and raised in the desert; a crossroads touching of various kinds, dark eyes and wisdom clashing under the clouds. Thousands of pueblo people are born hundreds of miles apart, broken treaties with each other now forgotten, new chants grabbing their tongues to protect them against the approaching stranger.

Suddenly you recognize him as the saint maker—the silent one who goes from pueblo to pueblo carving wooden statues of saints, teaching the skeptical how to make *retablos,* tablets containing the colorful etchings and lifelike images of the saints who hide in the desert hills and who warn those who approach as the saint maker brings his crafts to the next pueblo. In his pack, he even carries *bultos*—doll-like figures he carved to remind us that our dead family members will never disappear. They are carved into these dolls and hidden among the holy statues—an act some frown upon as going against the desert god, but the carvings of our dead grandparents survive among the blessed because the saint maker is one of the first and oldest men to welcome you into the desert, one of the first you dream about when you realize, as a child, that you are growing up in a land where too many things have happened, that too many secrets lie buried in the sand.

As he enters the pueblo, the saint maker is welcomed because he participates in your story. He lets the people form a circle around his possessions, your mother and grandmother looking through the bultos, hoping to recognize a face and body that means they no longer have to grieve. The saint maker allows them to unveil the loaf of bread they carry with care to place in his bowl, and they warn him never to look down at the falling crumbs because they will fall through his outstretched hands.

Ana María lived in a Tijuana dump. She was more than the author's heart bargained for.

Negra

Luis Alberto Urrea

Negra was a tiny barefoot girl who had curly black hair and large, star-tling white teeth. She was so skinny that she was firm as wood; when you picked her up, you could feel her angular pelvis and the chicken-wing bones in her back. She was very dark, hence the name "Negra." In Span-ish, it means "black girl." Her real name was Ana María.

I am not sure when I first met her. She just seemed to be there one day, moved into a shack with her mother and sister. Her father was gone; it was never completely clear where, though the obvious destination was clearly visible, about three miles to the north, being patrolled by helicop-ters. Like most people in the dump, she was from elsewhere—freshly arrived from Michoacán—part of an immigrant drive north that died out at the border, either from exhaustion, fear, or a sudden draining of vision and will.

It happens a hundred times a day—if you think the "illegal alien" problem is bad in San Diego, you should see what it's doing to Tijuana. The streets and *barrios* are swelled with nervous strangers from Sinaloa, Oaxaca, Chiapas, Yucatán, Quintana Roo. Then there are the actual ille-gals—Salvadorans fleeing death squads, Guatemalans fleeing the soaring poverty and crime of their homeland, Hondurans and Nicaraguans fleeing God knows what. Tijuana is like a dam, and it's beginning to groan before a tidal wave of human flesh.

Whenever we'd pull in, I'd look for her. Sometimes I'd hear my name being called very faintly, and I'd look up, and this kid would be hurtling through the trash, bare feet throwing up clouds of ash. Always the same dull dress, a kind of brown-gray. She'd leap into the air and fly into my arms like a bird. She usually smelled of smoke. She would be with me for the rest of the day, helping me give out food to the women, whispering secrets in my ear: her sister had a boyfriend, her mother had been in a fight, a boy from down the hill had walked her home. . . .

Negra was the one who taught me to pick trash. We'd take our poles and wade into the mounds. She wanted tin cans to sell for scrap, and any unbroken bottles were small treasures. Mari, Negra's older sister, was pregnant after a mysterious tryst with a dump-boy, and the occasional load of defective or water-damaged Pampers was a dangerously valuable find. We'd hide them under other trash on Negra's cart and hustle back to her shed. Of all the things one could take to the dump-dwellers, Pampers made the situation the most volatile. Imagine raising an infant with no diapers, no water, no baby powder, no baby wipes, no ointment for diaper rash, no formula, no money. We learned the hard way that the best way to start massive fistfights was to show up with a few boxes of Pampers: there is nothing so desperate as a mother fighting—literally—for her baby's ass.

They lived in a one-room shack, and in those days, there was no light. The two girls shared a bed, and their mother slept in another bed. Negra's brother lived with them, too, though he was never there. He attended school every day.

One day, near Christmas, I found Negra sulking with a cap on her head. Her mother had shaved her head. Her scalp had been invaded by a strange white flakiness, and great patches of it would peel off, taking hair with them. None of our salves worked, so her mother took a razor to her head, to "let the sun at it." I thought Negra would die of shame.

Negra wanted one thing in the world—a doll. "A big one," she said, "like a real baby."

Her mother told me, "She's never had one."

I had no money at the time. None. When not in Tijuana, I worked as a part-time tutor in a community college for roughly four hundred dollars a month. One of the students at the college overheard me talking about this poor girl with no Christmas, and surprised me a few days later with a thirty-dollar doll with real hair and blinking eyes. When Negra opened the package, she cried.

They made a little shrine for the doll in their house. Negra kept it up on a shelf, where she could look at it. She never took it out of the box. She didn't want the dust and ash of the dump to wreck her baby, so when she played with it, she'd have it in the box, still wrapped in plastic.

Negra had another problem: to go to school, she needed shoes.

All students in Mexican schools must wear uniforms. The idea behind this is noble: if everyone dresses exactly alike, then the middle-class kids will be no "better" than the poor kids. Everyone will be equal and have an equal chance.

In theory it works beautifully. Of course, the richer kids can wear new uniforms, new shirts and shoes. They can wear a new uniform every day of the week if they please. The poor kids must wear one uniform every day until it falls off; often they go home and wash their pants and shirts every night. And if they're really poor, they can't afford shoes. In Mexico, the bare foot is not a symbol of comfort—it is often a symbol of shame.

Negra had missed the opening of school, and she wanted to learn how to read and write. Her mother came to me and told me about it. She was surreptitious, because Negra was proud.

I invited Negra to come with me to downtown Tijuana. She piled into the van eagerly. We drove into town and shopped in the shoe stores along Avenida Revolución. It was an incongruous sight—little ash-gray Negra, barefoot in the shiny glass-and-chrome shoe store, watched over by yuppie Mexican women in Jordache jeans and duty-free Parisian perfumes. The saleswoman was gracious in the extreme, taking the measure of Negra's black feet and brushing the ashes off gently when she brought out the shoes. We bought Negra black shoes, and with some money to buy a uniform, she was able to attend school.

One day, on her way back home from classes, a gang of *barrio* kids caught her, beat her up, and stole the shoes.

She had to wait two weeks until she saw me again; I immediately bought her a new pair, but when she got back to school, they told her she had failed and been expelled. She had missed too many classes.

It was a warm day in spring: we had pulled in with a huge load of clothing and food. My mother and I had collected 150 half-gallon plastic jugs, and we'd been up at dawn in her backyard, filling them with the garden hose. I hadn't seen Negra for two weeks. I wanted to get a box of food to her family before the crush started. I took cans of corn, string beans, fruit; a sack of pinto beans; a kilo of rice; several jugs of water, bags of doughnuts, bread, bananas, oranges, onions, avocados, and plums.

There were men gathered around Negra's shack, grinning at me, then looking at their feet. I glanced in the door; an undulating shadow revealed itself to be a couple having sex in the dirt. Negra's shack had become a whorehouse. Negra was gone.

When the bi-national Falcon Dam was built in the 1950s to harness the raging Rio Grande/Río Bravo, it formed a reservoir that submerged the Mexican village of Guerrero. Nature and man have since robbed the river of its power, rendering it neither grande nor bravo. One result: the reservoir has dropped so low that the decades-long flooded Guerrero has, tentatively, reappeared. One of Mexico's leading essayists gives her impressions.

from *Guerrero Viejo*

Elena Poniatowska

A stone, a dry leaf, a door, a roofless house, the howl of a dog in the morning solitude. It's the howl, weaker each time, that guides us. We enter an empty house, an entire house with a marvelously proportioned body. In the center of the room absurdly stands an iron bedframe without a mattress and, tied to one leg, the yellow pup. We break the rope, we embrace him. His young heart beats. His body is warm. We embrace an abandoned Guerrero Viejo that takes refuge in our arms: a great stone embrace.

Guerrero Viejo is a stone in the sun, a hard, implacable sun. The rocks in a row at the edge of the road like the earth's teeth. Stone, the men's heads, and stone, their bones, scattered there. Stone, their memory of themselves, of their lives that, for the uninitiated, leave no more of a trace than the rings in the water when a stone is dropped. Stone the memory, stone the hunger, stone the destiny, and stone the end. The gravestones covered in *chaparro prieto, huizaches* and *abrojos, chilinguillo* and *biznaga* that blooms yellow only once a year in the cemetery, all have been abandoned to the mercy of the water. The gravestones are covered with classic sonnets that bring to mind the deceased and refer us to Quevedo, Góngora, Sor Juana Inés de la Cruz. Sea shells, white snails clinging to the *biznagas* and the prickly pears, to the trunks of the few yucca and cacti, or fossilizing on the limey ground under the sun, keep the dead company. Surely the Rio Grande brought them there and left them as a warning that the sea is the end of everything. . . .

The people of Guerrero lost everything, more than 25 thousand hectares of land, their fields of corn, onion, watermelon, and squash, their livestock, which they sold to the highest bidder, their fish that went in search of water down river, leaving the fisherman sitting sadly on the banks upstream, their ancient houses, more than two hundred years old, their ample and well-designed streets, their traditions, their childhood, their balconies, their door keys. They lost the sound of their footsteps, their laughter, their way of being a river. Like the river, the people of Guerrero were dampened and during certain seasons of the year they were happier than during others. Fresher waters ran through their river bed, young waters recently born. And at other times their mature waters grew, running tumultuously, swelling the back of the river that became silvery in the sun and dazzled them with its iridescent reflection. It is said that the more water a river carries, the more water it attracts to its bed. It comes from different streams, the Arroyo del Tigre, the El Chiquito, the San Pedro, the Agua Blanca, the Diablo, the Huizache, it comes from far off tributaries, it comes from the sea.

The Río Bravo or the Rio Grande begins in the Eastern Sierra Madre and empties into the Gulf of Mexico, near Matamoros. The river really flows, it is willful and unpredictable. Like the rain that falls from the sky, it gives life and brings death. The tumultuous water ends life that has been cultivated with such difficulty; it takes houses, uproots the terrace farms on its borders, drowns the corn and the squash. It is a blessing and a curse at the same time. It punishes the riverside populations of Mier, Camargo, Reynosa, Dolores. It rules the destiny of the northerners who live alongside it. It marks their existence with a seal of water, a seal of fire, a tattoo that cannot be erased from the body. It is ever changing. Infuriated, it sometimes brings much water and throws it in torrents at the villages settled on its banks. Suddenly a lightning bolt pierces the sky which shatters into a thousand pieces and the fury of the water sweeps everything away. Sometimes the Rio Grande writhes and dries up, empty, disappears completely and both men and animals await a miracle, pressed beneath the weight of an infernal heat, a sun that reaches 110°F. The droughts are interrupted by violent storms that can wash off and erode the earth in a single day. The great stone banks of the river surrendered the noble material used to pave the streets of Guerrero Viejo. . . .

Perhaps the stones of Guerrero Viejo are so imposing, so tremendously strong because everything that happened on the border (and still happens) was transitory, vanishing, temporary. As a result the houses could be blown away by the wind. The word "duration" didn't exist on the northern border, no one came ready to stay; everyone, men and women, whole families arrived with one sole purpose: to risk their lives in order to cross to the other side. Those who were unsuccessful settled their failures on the Mexican side of the river and lived poorly, without seeing the horizon, and there is nothing worse in life than to live without seeing the horizon.

In the midst of all those flights, those river crossings, that anxiety, and that quest, Guerrero Viejo dropped an anchor and stayed. Its fortitude makes it so special because on a strip of land where everything moves to "the other side," the stones settle and even their shadows turn to stone....

A stone, a dry leaf, a door, the weeping dead who, in the solitude of the morning, spill their tears of stone. Guerrero Viejo has not collapsed in spite of the fact that so many stones have fallen and the water has worn them down. It has been unable to conquer them. Inside the empty homes, the stone sings. The emptiness makes the different sounds more perceptible, the noise of the wood that at 200 years of age still settles, swells and dries out, complaining, the creaking that the wind draws out of the cornices, the window jambs, the arches, the sandy stone. The symbol of Guerrero Viejo is the church. In dry times the church loftily straightens itself, with all its scars left by the water, and in times of water, the grand roofless nave is a stone boat against which the water thrashes. Gusts of wind blow and the music becomes even more powerful. It is the water from the river that can be heard even in times of drought. No song is more beautiful than the song of the stone, the song of those ancient and seignorial mansions that stand erect at the edge of the water. The imminence of their disappearance, the corrosive wearing away to which they have been subjected is also proof of their eternity. They remain stone on top of stone, like those proud proprietresses who, above all else, believe in their lineage because they have discovered a form of survival. The houses of Guerrero Viejo, proudly humble, sing.

Papago Indians changed their name to Tohono O'odham in the early 1980s, but their exasperation goes back more than a century.

from *The Desert Smells Like Rain*

Gary Paul Nabhan

Isidro Saraficio is sitting in a dry irrigation ditch, under the shade of a Mexican elderberry tree, gazing out over a wheatfield wavering in the noonday heat. It's a fine strand of wheat for a desert field grown with just the rain that ran down the arroyos this winter. Isidro diverts floodwaters from a holding pond to the field through hand-dug ditches, letting gravity rather than machines do the work. Now that the grain is ripe, his friends have come to the *ranchería* to help with the harvest. After working since dawn, they lie resting, some snoring or farting in their sleep, while digesting the lunch of beans, *carne asada,* chile, tortillas, and beer. The cool shade of the elderberry soothes them for a few minutes more before they return to the wheat patch, armed with sickles, to hand-harvest the grain.

The quiet of noon is suddenly ruptured. Like a giant raptor, a Border Patrol plane breaks into sight and roars down across the land a few hundred feet over the field, causing quail and doves to flush out of the wheat. The patrolling plane zips westward, straight above the fence line and firebreak that stretches as a scar all the way to the far horizon. Sitting up as if awakening from a bad dream, Isidro's friends realize that the nightmare sound they heard is part of his everyday world. The field lies within a mile of the U.S./Mexico border.

Isidro planted the wheat not only for *pinole* and popovers, but also as a political protest. He was born here on the ranch in Sonora, Mexico, when the elderberry above him first came into bloom thirty-four years ago. Yet his family has never had a deed to this place, which they have probably farmed for hundreds of years. Isidro has planted wheat on land that another man "legally" owns. The field has been worked to show that the homestead has not been deserted. Isidro "borrowed" a tractor from a U.S. high school and illegally drove it across the border to plow the field while it was still sufficiently wet to plant. Now, six months later, his Arizona friends come through the fence as "reverse wetbacks" without visas or permits, neither reporting to customs nor paying any respects to the international line. In short, Isidro is raising hell as well as wheat. He is raising his sickle to question the existence of a boundary that his people have never acknowledged.

Isidro is a Papago Indian, sharing this borderland dilemma with 10,000–15,000 of his people who refer to themselves as the Tohono O'odham. When seventeenth-century Catholic missionaries made their first *entradas* into the Sonoran Desert, they found Papago settlements in many of the places they remain today. As northern Mexico and the U.S. Southwest became Spanish colonies, the Papago adopted many Hispanic customs and technologies. To most outsiders, a place such as Isidro's looks less American Indian than Mexican. In 1853, a political decision made thousands of miles away divided the Papago country between the United States and Mexico. Under the Gadsden Purchase, more than 5,000 square miles of Papago homeland became part of the United States. Although the majority of Papago were now nominally under the jurisdiction of Washington, they continued to associate more with the Indians and mixed-descent mestizos south of the border than with other U.S. citizens. As late as 1900, there were still enclaves of Papago miles north of the international border who thought of themselves as Mexican.

Yet, as more economic opportunities became available for Papago workers in the United States, population shifts occurred. Families that had remained in their desert *rancherías* on both sides of the border now migrated to U.S. towns and artificial agricultural oasis which the Anglos had created with dams and wells. Today, three-quarters of the Papago people live on three reservations established for them, and fewer than a tenth of them remain in Mexico. Isidro's family was one of the minority that chose to stay in Sonora.

Isidro's father did send the boy across the border to a Catholic boarding school to learn to read and write, but the family remained at the ranch in Plenty Coyotes village, just south of the U.S. Papago Indian Reservation on the border. Then Isidro's mother died and he came home from school to live alone with his father for eight years, helping the old man with farming, ranching, and blacksmithing. When the elderly Saraficio died several years ago, Isidro and a brother inherited the family homestead.

Isidro quickly realized that although the inheritance was strong in his heart, it was weak in the courts of Mexico. The people of Plenty Coyotes are part of those called "two-village Papago," for they spend part of the year in their fields, and part at a well village miles away. When the official

Mexican surveyors came through the borderland deserts years ago, they found what they presumed to be abandoned fields, and reported them as "open land." While the Papago families who had worked these lands for centuries were just a few miles away, the land was deeded to new owners, one a wealthy rancher who spends most of his time in U.S. cities. This landlord, Juan Stone, now owns 172,000 acres of land that traditionally belongs to the Papago.

Isidro began to inquire among the authorities about how an absentee landowner could retain so much land under the land reform laws. While he was still under thirty, the Sonoran Papago elected him as their representative in order to challenge the Mexican government's neglect of Papago interests. After more than a dozen journeys to Mexico City to plead the Papago case, Isidro bitterly realized that the bureaucracy does not budge easily. The Papago in Sonora could not be given government assistance in land and water resources improvement unless they legally owned the land. And when Isidro argued that they had prior claim to the land, some officials questioned whether any Papago lived in Mexico historically —hadn't they filtered down from "the other side"?

Infuriated, Isidro left his position as representative of the Papago in Mexico to study the historic sources which documented the early O'odham distribution in the Sonoran Desert. Working in the Catholic mission archives in Arizona, Isidro set out to prove his people's rights to the Sonoran lands that were part of their heritage. Yet most of the social and political scientists who usually assist Indians in these cases were either ignorant or noncommittal. One sheepishly admitted that "Juan Stone's wealthy friends in the Southwest do a lot to support our humanities programs here."

Isidro's effort finally began to be appreciated by the Papago politicians in Arizona. They were intrigued by his attempts to document the aboriginal territory of the Papago, but were not quite sure where his inquiries could lead. Finally, they began to listen to him, not as politicians listen to political radicals, but as tribal elders have always listened to those moved by a vision. Isidro was relatively young, but they felt that he spoke for hundreds of generations of O'odham.

Are not all Papago one people, wherever they live, bonded together by a common culture, language, history, and a sacred sense of community? Hasn't a simple line on a map disrupted this sense of community? Hasn't the international boundary kept Papago families from visiting traditional sites of Papago religion? Isn't the Papago tribe *less than whole* if it continues to let an arbitrary political decision divide its legacy, and dispossess part of its people? The Papago met in May 1979 and passed several resolutions which Isidro and others had drafted.

At the Sells Papago Capital Center, the Tribal Council declared that the Treaty of Guadalupe Hidalgo and the Gadsden Purchase which divided Papago country were signed without consultation or the consent of the Papago people. They agreed that to counter this historic tragedy, they would consider enrolling the Mexican Papago in the Arizona tribe so that they could share all benefits, including the $26 million land claims award granted to the tribe by the U.S. government.

The Council also requested of the Mexican government that the aboriginal lands in Mexico be set aside and reserved exclusively for the Papago, or that they be ceded or transferred to the U.S. in trust for the Papago. Isidro and his collaborators had hoped that this resolution would embarrass the Mexican government into confiscating the deeds from Stone and others in order to set up a reservation south of the border. Yet they kept open a more pragmatic possibility: if Mexico did not act soon, they would approach the absentee landlords and buy the deeds back with Arizona tribal funds, at whatever price. They would the turn over the deeds to Papago who had retained their Mexican citizenship. But the Mexican government responded at last. It helped obtain small land reserves around two Sonoran villages that the Papago could use exclusively.

Finally, the Tribal Council addressed the problem of the borderline touching the reservation, more than 60 miles of jurisdictional headache. They demanded of both national governments that Papago be given free access across the international boundary, so that their people would never be accused of being "illegal aliens" again. They also made clear that both governments had been negligent in maintaining the fence and protecting residents along the border.

Isidro was well aware of the smugglers that frequently crossed the border near his homestead. Drug runners and "coyotes" who piloted wetbacks across the border had realized that U.S. agents patrolled the Papago reservation less vigilantly than any other area along the boundary. The runners had not only cut through the boundary fence; they had cut dozens of field and range fences on Papago lands, allowing cattle to roam and destroy crops. The drug runners sometimes shot at anyone in sight—

not just official-looking gringos, but unassuming Indians too. Isidro had been offered $10,000 a month or 5,000 head of cattle if he would let a crime ring use his homestead as a front.

"I could have been a rich man several times over," he told me once. "But is that a life for a family man? How could I do that to my kids?"

In a meeting with U.S. Customs and other authorities, the Papago once expressed the danger to land and life that the border's proximity created for them. Who was ultimately to be responsible for patrolling it and for protecting residents from damage? One by one, the government agencies replied in their best bureaucratic jargon that they each had partial jurisdiction, but that it was the duty of the "particulars" living along the border to maintain the fences and to keep "aliens" from illegally crossing onto their lands.

Isidro stood up and roared, "THEN IF IT IS UP TO US, WE WILL TEAR YOUR BORDER FENCE DOWN!"

After the resolutions passed, Isidro began to concentrate on the land rather than its legalities. To keep the right to land in Mexico, you must work it. Land abandoned for more than two seasons can be claimed by squatters or *ejido* cooperatives, who can then stay on it as long as they use and improve it. While Isidro had been working in Arizona with resolutions and documents, he had been worried that his homestead might be confiscated, if not by Juan Stone, then by opportunistic *colonistas.* He has thus gone down every weekend, to plant fields and gardens when there was rain, to fix up the buildings and grounds when there wasn't.

The fruition of his wheat planting and the passing of the resolutions coincided. In "*gracias a Dios,*" he began planning for a feast in honor of San Isidro, the agricultural guardian and his patron saint. In early June I stopped by Isidro's place in Sells, but he was not there. Isidro had retired from his research and political activities in order to spend more time farming in Sonora.

The next time I saw Isidro, the talk was of *pinole,* not politics. We spoke too of the best time to plant beans and corn. "To me, the most beautiful thing is the coming of the first summer thunderstorms. I stay outside and watch the sky. I know it is time for things to grow again."

from *Pilgrims in Atzlán*

Miguel Méndez

TRANSLATED BY David William Foster

The fact of the matter was that old man Loreto had a head full of cobwebs. Grand ideals and dignity were the threads that time kept half intact, woven halfway, unraveled. Although if you looked at it from the other side, he'd probably inherited his behavior from the very ancient dignity of his race, a pure-blooded Yaqui with the regal appearance of a statue struck from the very roots of granite.

In recent years he crisscrossed the streets of the growing border city like one of the many unfortunates no one pays any heed to, those individuals who bear their hunger and abandon as if their only purpose were to bear witness to how everybody else was fortunate enough, beyond the simple fact that it is easy to get lost in a whirl of people of so many differing conditions and occupations as different as they were strange.

Loreto was a strange guy. How many times had he seen his reflection in the panes of glass of those buildings, where so many things are for sale, without recognizing himself, until after a few seconds it would strike him that that blackened and wrinkled face was his own? He, who at times persisted in the idea of being the sprightly youth, the terrible warrior, would smile upon seeing himself changed into such an ugly old man, remembering the story of the country fellow who found a mirror and when he picked it up, exclaimed: "Shit, they had good reason to abandon you. You look horrible!" Old man Loreto was already close to eighty, of an age when a man has already buried a world of people and goes on living, or better, dreaming that he's on an unknown planet and confined to oblivion like a foreigner without a country, ashamed of taking up someone else's space.

The old man refused to give up the concept of honor which was in direct conflict with his chronic hunger, and his subsistence became more problematical each day. He gave up washing cars to continue in another line of the same business, that of guarding cars at night while their owners raised hell in one of the many whorehouses or gambled or ran after drugs, which, just like in a drugstore, were always available in every variety. He picked up some loose change that he barely managed to get by on, while the moment approached in which time gnaws at the carrion with the tiny mouths of worms. When exhaustion and his aches and pains kept him in, he would spend his few coins on cans of soup and juice because all he had left were two teeth, although it's true that on occasion he would try out a piece of sponge cake. There he was in a hut that looked like a cave, which he had built he didn't know how or with what. When his provisions ran out, he would drag his humanity forth, burdened under the tools of his trade. Poor trade, the mere pretext for not begging for a living.

The ancient Yaqui could barely haul himself around as he worked with the iron will of a post. He worked hard and his gestures were determined, despite how dry his shell was, tanned like a mummy's hide. He squinted his eyes, blackened by a lot of sun and wind, as though crossing an abyss sunk in a very remote time. . . . Often when he walked through those streets, it was as though he pretended to move. He felt himself suspended in space, as though already caught in the cold annals of yellowing pages like a delicate, dessicated butterfly. What wouldn't many princes with idiot faces have given, their stupidity dangling from their aristocratic smiles, for the solemn regality of the destitute Yaqui. By contrast, other individuals of the same dimension who surrounded him basked in his glory like parasites, paying homage with grotesque clownings. . . .

Often the old Yaqui would entertain himself going over his memories, lost among the heavy traffic swirling around him. He was amused by the parade of gringos buying souvenirs. Some of them would come out of stores wearing sarapes and charro hats, while others sought out burros to have their pictures taken astride their backs. Several walked around as family groups with a joking and naughty tone, the young women showing off beautiful bodies with short dresses. Everything swirled around him, dark faces, shouts, laughter, voices speaking Spanish mixed with words in English, the squeal of tires responding to traffic lights ordering sudden stops, and the maddening song of car horns. . . .

In that very strange frontier town, in appearances so happy but deep down so tragic, of all those who floated without moorings the Indian Loreto was pained to see so many wetbacks teeming around with their faces of hunger and waiting to cross over into Gringoland. Like every peasant who reaches the city, they were timid in their behavior. They revealed so much desolation and appeared to be so hunger-stricken that they looked like a defeated army under Zapata, sentenced to look for food for their families in exile. Despite the terrible drama of their lives, they possessed the noble attitude of those who have caressed the earth like a mother. They had won the Revolution, only to be paid with hunger and fraud. During the periods of electoral farces, they were carted about in cattle trucks as though they were cows. . . .

The day was already into its second half when the Yaqui Loreto received payment from some foreigners whose eyes were a sea of goodness. They gave him two dollars and their thanks with so much respect that you could see from a mile that they were generous of heart. He felt his soul caressed by a gentle breeze. He walked along balancing himself like a penguin until he reached Don Chanito's stand, where he treated himself to a taco which cost him fifteen American cents. When the "chief" handed him his change, he dropped a coin, and it rolled away. La Malquerida picked it up and kindly handed it back to him. The Indian looked at her sweetly by way of reward. The eyes of the poor whore filled with tears. La Malquerida was sitting alone on a corner. You could tell by the bags under her eyes that she had been on a real drinking binge. The truth is that the night before she had created one of her terrible scandals. Valente, the Vaseline Man, had come up to her with his irresistible act. He feigned tenderness and spoke to her about commitment, about getting her out of that life of hell, buying her a house, and building a happy future and leaving the past behind. He got her halfway confused and for a second the embers started to glow in her again. But when she realized Vaseline Man was up to his usual perverse tricks as a pimp and that all he wanted to do was to make her work for him, she broke a bottle and gashed his face, leaving him with a harelip. Valente did not go to the authorities, because he was a criminal himself dealing in drugs. His lip was left hanging by a thread, and had tried to tape it back into place. He had to resign himself to being harelipped for the rest of his life, and his only choice was to grow a mustache like the Kaiser's and, even then, he was left looking like a dog who's always in some scrape or another. Once the incident was over, the cantina owner, who pimped for the women, began harassing them—get the clients to drink, get yourself a client more often, you here, you there, hitting them and insulting them. He looked angrily at Malquerida out of the corner of his eye in his usual abusive way. In addition to being in charge of that bad business because it went with his character, he was more of a coward than a cornered hare.

Loreto carried his food over to where he usually sat, a cement wall facing the street in a small vacant lot. His food consisted of a loaf of French bread larger than his hand. It was about a foot long with the ends narrowing out into little tits. He looked quizzically at the ends of the loaf of bread, which was split down the middle. He saw three pieces of roast beef and five small slices of avocado, *ahuacatl,* he murmured, feeling the ancient voices of Nahuatl stir in his blood. On top of the dark green slices of avocado there where three bright slices of tomato stuck to the bread-crumbs, pieces of fresh-cut onion, and a medium size chile, a jalapeño, stuck in the middle of the bread. He tasted the food with his eyes half-closed, remembering his home, the guerillas in Bacatete and the rattlers adorning the legs of the Yaqui *pascola* dancers beating up a steady din. He only ate half. He dozed for a few minutes, just enough for his subconscious to raise its periscope. His friend who came from the same town crossed through his mind as always when his heart felt heavy.

from *Floating Kingdom*

George Rabasa

Seguila lived on an island. His house was perched about two-thirds of the way up the slope that faced the north side of the canyon. The river flowed below his house and also behind it in a narrow channel between the island and the south face of the gorge. The two forks merged below his island where the river rounded the bend, debouching from the confines of the canyon into a wider bed. During times of drought, the south fork dried into a sand bar. But when the rains came, it could not be said that Seguilandia was on either side of the natural border.

Seguila liked to claim that he was his own territory. Not of the south or of the north, not of the Rio Grande or the Rio Bravo, but floating ambiguously in the river, rising like a castle between the two countries, somehow independent of both, La République Libre de Seguilandia—a curious nation made up at first of him and Aurelia and their three daughters, and later including his son-in-law Adrián and grandson Honguito. After his wife died, the borders to Seguilandia closed tighter as Seguila became even more jealous and protective of his family.

In the early days of his marriage, Seguila built a primitive shack on the ledge where the house now stands on land nobody had claimed. He didn't ask permission. Later, he built the simple house of cinder blocks and corrugated metal roofing and waited for someone to come and tell him to move. When no one showed up, he expanded his property. He built a second story. He raised a shed to one side and used it to store things that might be useful later. That's how the yonque, his own personal junkyard, got started. First with old tires that still had tread on them, then with popular objects like hubcaps, eventually hundreds of them nailed through the center and displayed on poles, then with rearview mirrors and headlights that Adrián brought. Parked away from the sun under a corrugated tin shelter next to the growing heap of rusting car parts was the most valuable of all the finds, a 1976 black Ford Galaxy that some narco on the run had tried to drive across the sandflats along a shallow part of the river. The car had been thoroughly picked apart by the time Seguila and Adrián rescued it, but they set it on blocks anyway, and kept it clean and shiny. They were always on the lookout for parts to rebuild it. Adrián had made good progress: the big Ford had shiny rearview mirrors, a Mercedes-Benz hood ornament, even a cellular phone antenna that Adrián thought was the perfect elegant touch when the big car was viewed from the rear. There would be time enough to steal a phone once they got the car running.

Through the years, they had collected three wheels and two tires, so that only the front right wheel and the rear left one rested on stacked bricks. Seguila had also bought a nearly new set of pistons, an alternator, and a transmission from Mimi's Friendly Auto Mart, one of the big de-shuesaderos on Frontier Street. The parts fit so neatly into the stripped-down engine that they were clearly the originals. Eyes were open for a carburetor, a gas pump, a steering wheel, among other mechanical neces-sities. Faith that the black Galaxy would run again bonded Adrián, Lucio, and Honguito, the males in the Seguila household. One day the whole family would pile into it, the women in nice dresses with their hair done up and the men looking sharp, and they'd cruise the streets of the city, honking and revving up the mighty engine and waving in triumph at all the people who would look upon them with admiration and envy.

Off to one side of the house, inside their wire mesh pen, chickens pecked at the ground for a few grains of corn, their heads bobbing up and down in jerky nods, protesting the scarcity of food with low, irritated clucks. Seguila had built a porch that he'd strung with colored lights visible from the river below. His boom box sent the plaintive mariachi strains echoing through the canyons. He was partial to the women singers —La Tariacuri, Amalia Mendoza, Lola Beltrán, and Aurelia Villa, whose first name was the same as his wife's and whose last name was that of the great general. "Ahi viene Pancho Villa con sus dos viejas a la orilla." Around this part of the country, accordions and thumping string bass and rickety percussion made music that sounded like German polkas, which Seguila thought had no feeling at all.

There was no easy way to get to Seguila's house. From the main ledge that led to the house proper, it was about two hundred feet down a steep path to the river's edge. To get to the southern shore, it was necessary to climb another hundred feet up the cliff and then scramble all the way down a steep drop along only a hint of a trail that wove its way among the rocks. Without a guide, it could be slow, painful going up either slope. Lechuguilla needles and cholla barbs clung to clothes and attached them-selves to the skin. A scratch could cause the flesh to bloat up in minutes.

During the summer, a wide variety of mean-spirited bugs thrived in the thickets; pale golden scorpions as long as a man's finger hid under rocks and dried-out dung patties, river gnats and ticks and spiders nestled among the brambles. Seguila could see visitors coming from half an hour away. In the dark of a moonless night, he could hear them stumble through the brush, sending rocks crashing down the slope. To protect the main gateway into the clearing, Seguila planted dozens of ocotillo bushes close together to form a brambled fence around the outer perimeter of Seguilaland.

Seguila and Aurelia added on to the house, one room at a time, over the course of the first few years of their marriage. From the start, Lucio had resolved to be wild and independent. They would live apart from others, enjoying the basic necessities, raising a few chickens, surviving by their wits. They paid kids who were strong and agile like goats to bring up the cinder blocks that became the house's main structure, one at a time for weeks on end.

In the meantime, Seguila and his wife slept under an improvised shed made of tar paper and an earthen foundation set deep against a rock ledge. Their bed was a massive tubular brass frame with ornate figures of birds and angels at the posts and headboard; it had once belonged to Aurelia's grandparents. Seguila's favorite possession was a La-Z-Boy recliner. For cooking, Aurelia has set up a small propane burner under a covered lean-to. Once they had brought up enough of the crumbly cinder blocks, they started building the house.

Even before they'd finished the first room, Seguila put his sign at the bottom of the cliff: República de Seguilandia. It was his version of a Do Not Disturb notice. They were young and they enjoyed each other at all hours, night or day, any time the mood came. A seemingly innocent glance or an accidental touch would send them into the grandparents' big brass bed.

In the morning they would go down and walk along the river. Seguila watched the water, studied the currents, marveling how in its stillness the river seemed to flow back upstream, all brown and muddy and yet somehow, in those days, pure and clean. He collected river water in plastic buckets and waited for the mud to settle and the sun to warm it. He would cup a handful and pour it over Aurelia's head like baptism.

She'd be wearing a thin white cotton shift that clung to her body when wet. Seguila would turn his back and be on the lookout for intruders while she soaped herself with the bright pink Jardines de California soap that he bought for her whenever he was in the city. Once she had washed, he would stand in front of her with a rebozo while she pulled off her shift and slipped into a simple cotton dress with yellow butterflies on a blue field and large white buttons that went all the way up to her neck. She would sit on a rock at the river's edge, drying her long, shiny black hair in the sun while he stripped down to his shorts and walked into the water.

Sometimes, when he felt sure nobody was watching, he would feel his way along the muddy bottom, searching out the shallow pathways that would allow someone to wade the river to the other side. Occasionally he would make it across without sinking into any unexpected deep spots and wave at Aurelia from the other side. Then he would march back and forth several times, learning the lay of the river bottom, memorizing the subtle landmarks along both banks that later he recognized at night when taking travelers across. A bush that looked like the head of a man with a big nose. Three rocks that formed a straight line. The gentle way a bank sloped up.

A border patrol helicopter would fly between the canyon walls toward Seguila, and he would wave and hold up the bar of pink soap to show them he was only bathing, not really trying to get to the other side. Certainly not in broad daylight. After a while, the pilots recognized him and Aurelia as the couple that lived up on the cliff, and they would wave back at them.

At night the riverbanks came alive with immigrants making their way to the other side. They burrowed in clusters within the ravine and then, following their guides, waded across silently, like pilgrims going to church, signaling in whistles and finger snaps and low hoots. Sometimes there were migra patrols waiting on the other side to get as many of the indocumentados as they could, put them on a bus, take them to jail, and then drive them back across the main bridge the next morning. But there were never enough border guards to catch all of them.

Seguila seemed to know precisely where to land on the other side on cool dark nights with no moon so that his group of travelers was safe. He always called them that, viajeros, not mojados or pollos or ilegales. It was a question of their dignity. Even though they were wading across the river with their new clothes piled on top of their heads, sometimes carrying their children on their shoulders and looking like fugitives, you had to show them respect. It helped them believe that things would turn out fine once they were on the other side.

Adrian—patrician, wealthy, and sympathetic—has recently arrived at the eastern end of the border, where Downsville meets Matablancos.

from *Innocent Darkness*

Edward R. F. Sheehan

Now waves of OTMs [Other Than Mexicans] seemed to overwhelm the valley. Day by day, new droves of Central Americans swam the Rio Grande and invaded Downsville. Alarmed, the government of the north dispatched more men, more rusty trucks, some old helicopters, to reinforce the Border Patrol, but against the flood the show of force seemed futile. When the Patrol arrested a hundred aliens, five hundred followed; the agents caught a few, but the government could barely confine them as its shelters and prisons overflowed. Aliens slept in gutters, in alleys by the white Gothic cathedral, behind the money changers near Gateway Bridge, and when they woke begged for money to feed their children.

Along Central Boulevard stood several abandoned motels, sagging in yellow weeds, without electricity, sanitation, or running water. Aliens moved into them, patching the shattered windows with flattened cardboard boxes and cans of soda pop, cooking gruel of rice and beans over stoves they fashioned from flattened cans, crowding fifteen, twenty adults and children into single rooms, cohabiting with flies, rats, and sickly coughs, defecating into leaky buckets or in the weeds outside, where more aliens with infant children camped without food beneath umbrellas of cardboard against the rain.

Yet when Adrian invaded the motels with Rodrigo, as his friend sought childless aliens to arrest, his keenest sensation was not so much the filth and stench as the sound of slamming doors. Whenever they entered a corridor, it was empty. Aliens scattered in the instant before they came, throwing down their frugal meals, abandoning their stoves of flattened cans, picking up their children and fleeing into fetid rooms, slamming doors and diving out of jagged windows. Once, he glimpsed a child's bare dashing feet before a door slammed. At night, the sound of slamming doors mingled with his dreams of jellyfish, those white transparent blobs, networks of brown tubes with heads that seemed like cabbage stems, floating in and out of rooms, becoming caught in the jambs of doors, oozing free and floating as more doors slammed.

Awake, Adrian thought, Enough of Rodrigo; I can see him at night. He abandoned the Border Patrol, drove his fake junky car to Amigoland, and bought baby food, buckets, mops, medicines, disinfectants, and rat poison. At the motels, he barely knew where to begin. He entered deserted corridors, and as doors slammed he removed jars of baby food and rat poison from cartons and piled them beside the stoves of flattened cans. For his buckets, he had no water. He went out and bought bottled water, then returned to the corridors and began scrubbing them with his disinfectants and a mop. No good; the filth was so profuse it needed first to be swept away. He went out and bought a dozen brooms. When he returned and swept, heads emerged from doorways one by one, and as the minutes passed, hands took up the other brooms and mops, sweeping and mopping in silence with him. For a week or two, his exertions helped. He swept up heaps of dead rats, and throughout the encampments in the yellow weeds he distributed rice, chocolate, and Pepto-Bismol in such volume that he soothed hunger and the diarrhea of sick infants. Yet the squatters crowded the motels and encampments in such growing numbers, the rats and disease were so willful, he could not keep up. Municipal inspectors arrived one day, bulldozers the next, the sagging motels were knocked down, the weedy encampments depopulated by the police, and the aliens dispersed to the gutters of the city to sleep, defecate, and beg.

Soon afterward he discovered another alien refuge. By the bank of the river, in high grass within sight of Amigoland, not far from where he had wrestled with the child, stood abandoned wooden barracks. Decades ago the U.S. Army had been quartered there to patrol the river and chase bandits back to Mexico, but the buildings had been deserted for so long that the roofs were falling in and the walls gaped with holes. Vegetation groped through ghosts of windows. A rusty fence and barbed wire obstructed the surrounding meadow, though in such disrepair that Adrian drove through them: a rusty sign offered the property for sale. Across the river from the barracks, just beyond the shore of Matablancos, beckoned the Zona Zur, a warren of ramshackle adobe bars and brothels and, faintly visible in the flat distance, the pale turrets of what seemed to be a huge prison.

Bands of Nicaraguan and Salvadoran youths camped in the barracks, unmolested for the moment by the Border Patrol because the Patrol had no place to jail them. Adrian rarely read newspapers, but from the babble of television it seemed to him that Central America was disintegrating;

Sandinistas and counterrevolutionaries were casting down their arms in Nicaragua, soldiers and guerrillas were abandoning the battle in El Salvador, and fleeing north. Once across the Rio Grande, they forgot their quarrels in a common struggle to survive. Adrian might have ignored them (didn't guerrillas live off the land?) were they not sheltering women and children.

He wondered, Should I bring them food? He loaded his car with sacks of rice and beans, baby food and bottled water, but at the barracks he was not graciously received. The guerrillas, suspecting a spy for *la Migra*, emerged from the barracks with clubs and knives and told him to disappear.

"At least take the food," he pleaded.

"We can't pay you!" they shouted.

"I'm not here for money."

"Mexican police! raped our women! stole all we had!"

"I hear children crying. Feed them."

"Poisoned food!"

"Good food! I won't leave till you take the food!"

They took it. As he drove off, he thought, They need more than food. He hated his ignorance of how to help them, and again he was bewildered by whatever impulsive steps he took next. At Motel 5 1/2 he picked up a telephone directory and raced through the yellow pages. . . .

He began by buying mattresses, but they would not fit into his car, and lacking patience to lash them to the roof, he wondered, Should I buy a truck? He returned to the junkyard, to that great cemetery of smooth tires, overturned cement mixers, and the fat Mexican in sunglasses. "Chinga, what kind truck you want?"

"A pickup, I think? With lots of room?"

"Clean truck or junky truck?"

"A junky truck that runs."

"Got one, over there. Chinga, she bran'-new, but gimme a day, she look like shit."

"How much?"

"Your drug business it goin' good?"

"It goin' bad."

"Fifteen thousand cash."

As Adrian hauled mattresses, sheets, blankets, bottles of water, and boxes of medicine to the barracks, he gradually gained the guerrillas' confidence. When he brought lumber, hammers, nails, saws, and a power lawn mower, they joined him in his purpose to rebuild the barracks, saw that he knew nothing of carpentry, and taught him how as they took over that task themselves. He replaced kerosene lamps with an electric generator. The guerrillas were a tough lot; as the dozens of men, women, and small children seeking refuge in the barracks grew to scores, the place became an enclave in a mist of violence.

Though they had no guns, the guerrillas patrolled their patch of riverbank at night, beating off thieves and rapists with wooden clubs and saving women and children from evil. Off duty, Rodrigo and a few of his peers in the Border Patrol showed up in jeans and T-shirts and helped with the labor. Rodrigo said, "These OTMs gotta live somewhere. We'll grab them outside the fence." The municipal authorities were less elastic. Adrian asked them to provide the barracks with electricity and water. "Get rid of the rats," they said.

"We got rid of the rats."

"We're coming in with bulldozers."

"You can't!"

"You don't own that property."

Adrian returned to Motel 5 1/2, packed his books and paintings in his truck, and moved into the barracks. At dawn, he ran to the stable near Los Fresnos pump, then rode Prince downriver to a new pasture and a new home in a stall by the barracks that he began to build with his own hands. He thought, Technically it's a crime to shelter the undocumented, and I love that! Should I own this property? He rode to the outer fence and read the rusty sign: THIS PROPERTY FOR SALE OR LEASE APPROX 10 ACRES 542-3876.

When It Comes to Class: Viola Barragán

Rolando Hinojosa

Pius V Reyes was buried in the mexicano cemetery, a mile or two down the road from Bascom, one unseasonably cold October day. It was a simple affair, and the rain that day certainly didn't help attendance. The mourners bunched up here and there trying to defend themselves against the elements, and the steady drizzle never did let up. As soon as the last shovelful hit the casket, the crowd wandered off in search of their cars rather hurriedly. In the Valley, and it's no different in the rest of the world either, death and cold weather usually gang up to ruin someone else's good time; since it happens so often, it's just too much to be coincidental.

The recently buried Pius V, despite his name, was a convert to Presbyterianism. A serious sort even as a youngster and growing up in Flora as he did, he was more serious as time went on, and by the time he was forty, he was as solemn as a goose. Some people are just born that way, that's all; they're singled out, you might say: You, there, you're going to turn out this way. You, over there, you're going to be this other way. And you, yeah, you—and on it goes. As always, man proposes, but the earth encloses.

"And how about, man develops, but the earth envelops?"

That's good, too, but no more interruptions, please. As I was saying: Pius V died at the Holiday Inn over on Route One, right by where there used to be a small colony of black folks; but that was a long time ago.

Pius V was not at the Holiday Inn 'cause he worked there, no; he was there as a guest. Pius V worked as a bookkeeper for Avila Bros. (wholesale & retail, we deliver). Pius V, when he heard Gabriel's blast calling him to join that great number, just happened to be resting a bit on top of Viola Barragán, a woman who some twenty years ago was firmer than tungsten, and who now, right now, is just about as solid as she ever was; one of life's minor miracles, you might say. Pius V bought the farm in medias res, thus joining the silent majority as naked as the day he was born.

Rafe Buenrostro says that he, and he was just a kid then, that he went to the man's funeral; from there, he said, his father took him to meet some Buenrostros who farmed near Bascom. Rafe and his father, by the way, were the last to leave the cemetery that day. (The Buenrostros came to the Valley with the first Querétaro colonists in 1749 with Escandón leading the first group there. According to the late don Victor Peláez, some Buenrostros are poor, some have a little salted away, and others just fall through the cracks.) Well, sir, as the people were heading for their cars, a woman was getting out of hers and walked to the fresh mound of flowers there. She was dressed in a fine, form-fitting, full length suede leather coat; the hat too was suede, but it was fur covered and had a veil attached. She opened a good-sized patent leather purse, took out a small handkerchief which she then begin to untie, and when she did, she came up with a gold wedding band. She looked at it briefly then she buried it in the mound; her gloves were muddied up, but she didn't seem to mind that or the rain and what it was doing to her clothes. And, she didn't break down in tears or anything. A trouper.

Anyway, according to Rafe Buenrostro, Viola had become a widow at age eighteen, just a year or two away from the second of two World Wars we've had so far this century. She played the piano fast, loud, and poorly; it was also said that she wrote and sang her own songs.

Her first husband was from Agualeguas in our neighboring southern state of Nuevo León; he'd crossed the Río Grande as an exile and opened up shop as a medical surgeon in Klail, and that's where he died about a year into the marriage with Viola. It was his own fault for taking that prescription made by an apprentice pharmacist.

Before the year was out, Viola hooked up with don Javier Leguizamón; he owns those lands over to Edgerton there; those were old mexicano lands taken over by Anglo Texans first and by the Leguizamóns after that. Viola was with don Javier up to her twentieth, maybe her twenty-first birthday; it happened that she was replaced by Gela Maldonado, but that's another story. Viola was jettisoned all right, but she was a good student: her eyes opened up, and she learned to see through people; obviously a valuable talent.

"And what about the time that you and . . ."

Please! After the don Javier liaison, Viola married again; this time to a German national stationed at the Consulate in the Mexican Gulf City of Tampico, Tamaulipas. The man had crossed the Rio on a two-three week vacation, and when he returned to Tampico, there was Viola hanging on to his right arm and to his every word, you might say.

From Tampico, the newlyweds sailed for India; Viola's husband had been promoted and his new post was that of first secretary to the German Minister there. World War II came along ruining a lot of plans and a lot of futures for a lot of people, as all of us know. But there was Viola, a mexicana from Ruffing, Texas, only daughter of don Telésforo Barragán and doña Felícitas Surís de Barragán, in India and married to a German national. The couple was interned at an English concentration camp just outside of Calcutta for a while. She was there alongside her husband until they were sent to the birth place of concentration camps: South Africa. And there they were until Oberst-General Jodl signed some peace agreements in a primary school in some obscure French town thus stopping that part of WWII.

Several years after the war, she finally made it back to the Valley to discover that Telésforo and Felícitas had moved to Edgerton. Not one to lose time, Viola pointed her nose and her car toward Edgerton and found them none the worse for wear: she bought herself a two story house, moved her parents in, and then took very good care of the surviving relatives; these had helped the old folks during hard times, and Viola was just paying back. After this, she settled down or so it seemed.

The Valley mexicanos couldn't quite get a handle on what was going on inside Viola's head, and about the only thing they could agree on was that Viola had been gone close to ten years, and that she hadn't forgotten her Spanish during all that time. Chances are that Viola didn't even bother to learn German at all; to tell the rigid truth, some actions do speak louder than words.

Time marched on as it always does, and the Devil, that insomniac, delivered yet one more surprise to Viola: Pius V Reyes.

Pius V, seriousness and discretion, sporting a well-starched, long sleeved striped shirt, had married Blanca Rivera; with no children to raise, Blanca took to religion, and so she and Brother Limón ganged up on Pius V to convert him to Presbyterianism. Pius V said it didn't matter much to him one way or another, and this way the Ruffing, Texas mexicano Presbyterian Church gained another adherent.

So, there was Viola settled in Edgerton, and Pius V had never even heard of her. What happened was that one bright Valley day, Viola with plenty of money and time on her hands, was making her usual run up and down the Valley from Edgerton to Jonesville-on-the-Rio when a red traffic light in Bascom brought them together. Viola was staring dead ahead waiting for the light to change when Pius V crossed her line of fire. She saw that curious face floating by and said, "I'm claiming that one as my property, and I'm doing it 'cause I want to, I don't need the money for food this time."

And so, the Devil saw to it that Viola's car developed a flat right there in the middle of Bascom's main street; Pius V volunteered to help, and that's how the two met.

But the Devil's unions don't last long as a rule; the affair lasted about a year until that fateful day at the motel.

When Pius V keeled over at the Holiday Inn, Viola—Fearless Viola— pushed herself out of the way, sat at the foot of the bed, dressed as carefully as she always did, fixed her hair, touched up her face, glanced around the room, and made for the door and then for Edgerton. Pius V was found later on by a maid who'd come to turn down the bed; she ran to the front desk, and etc. etc.

So he was buried in the mexicano cemetery near Bascom; his loving wife and other relatives prayed to the Lord to save Pius V's soul, and they recommended that He take good care of Pius V, seculae seculorum, amen. The mexicano Presbyterians from The Good Shepherd Church over on Ninth were commended for all arrangements (floral and wailers) from start to finish.

"And Viola?"

Viola's doing just fine, thank you. She's fifty if she's a day, and she's got plenty of money and looks it, too. The burying of the wedding band was a touch of class; as Viola says, "No merit in having class, really; but it's Hell if you don't."

Lucky Strike

Gabriel Trujillo Muñoz

TRANSLATED BY Michelle Joffroy

I

The Ford convertible with California license plates pulls in next to the one shining gas pump at the Calexico Gas Station. A young man in metal-framed glasses and a suede hat steps out of the car. The station attendant, a young Mexican, approaches him.

"Full tank, mister?"

The stranger, not responding, motions toward the south.

"Is that Mexicali?"

The attendant eyes him cautiously.

"No more, no less."

The stranger grins, but his smile is nothing more than a grimace that distorts his face.

"Fill it up and clean the windows."

The attendant hastens to obey the request.

The stranger looks once more toward Mexicali. Sure, he thinks, a dust bowl with lots of cantinas. Just like they told me. He adjusts his hat. The attendant, restrained, slides up next to him.

"For a minute I thought you were a damn gringo. Sorry."

The stranger takes a dollar out of his pocket and tips him with it. Making a half-turn, he gets back in his car.

"Everybody makes that mistake," he says as he leaves.

He pulls out, leaving only the dust to rise in his wake.

II

"You're not from the north either, right?" asks the hotel clerk. "I can tell just by the clothes you're wearing."

The stranger doesn't respond. He finishes counting his money and lays it on the desk: the payment for a first class room.

"I hear that in this town nobody is from here."

"You've got a point there, my dear sir. I, for example, am from a forgotten town in Nayarit. What with the cristero revolution and that whole disaster I just felt like getting out. First I went to Los Angeles and now I'm in these parts, that is to say, smack in the middle of hell. You'll notice soon enough, as soon as summer hits. . . .

But the stranger puts away the rest of his money, takes his knapsack and, without signing the registry, heads for his room leaving the clerk and his words to themselves.

III

"You must be from Jalisco," the young woman says hurriedly as she dresses. "You don't know how to be gentle with a lady. You think you can do anything, don't you? First you haul me out of the bar without so much as two words. Then you act like a damn savage with me. What do you think I am? Just wait until my friend Jaime hears about this. Then you'll know what decent is. Then you'll know. You'll even be asking my permi—

The blow is dry, effective, cold.

The woman topples over, he picks her up by the wrists and drops her on the bed. Meanwhile he pulls down her panties and kisses her.

IV

"Do you know him?" Manuel, the barman, asks one of the girls who's just asked for a tequila.

"God help me! He's the one who beat Lupe and kept her locked in his room all day. When Jaime found out there was nearly a brawl but then he calmed down, Jaime backed right down, the coward. Who knows why."

"Try to get something out of him, Concha. Find out who he is, what he does. You're good at that."

"Find out for yourself: I for one am not getting near him. Before you know it I'll be the one with the black eye."

"Boss's order, Concha. That guy interests him."

Concha polishes off her tequila in one gulp and asks for another.

"Find yourself some other idiot. Why does it have to be me?"

"Concha," says Manuel, delicately taking her arm and leaning his face toward hers, "because the boss, and this is the last time I'll say it, said so. Understood?"

Concha gives in to his touch, takes the glass of tequila the barman offers and backs away moving toward the stranger who drinks, alone, at his table. Manuel goes back to cleaning and arranging the glasses. In the background a trio sings:

De la Sierra Morena
Vienen bajando
Un par de ojitos negros
Cielito lindo
De contrabando.

[From the Sierra Morena
Moving down toward the lowland,
A pair of little black eyes
Sweet heaven,
The sweet black eyes of contraband.]

V

A waiter lights his Havana. The Boss blows out its smoke. His attitude, his gestures, his entire being projects security, power, unlimited confidence in himself.

"Do we know each other?" he asks the man sitting, two platters of seafood between them, across the table from him.

"I don't recall."

"Good. I like it when the people I deal with have bad memories."

The stranger eyes the framed photographs that line the walls of the restaurant: Rudolph Valentino, Errol Flynn, Douglas Fairbanks, Mary Pickford, Mae West, a multitude of actors, actresses and singers. All of them smiling and charming, all as pleased as the Boss who this very moment takes the Havana from his mouth and comments:

"I'd like you to do me a small favor, friend."

"I don't do favors. I charge. I do my job and I get lost. In that order."

The Boss finishes up his whiskey on the rocks.

"Have you got any references from previous jobs?"

The stranger pulls out a Lucky Strike but doesn't let the waiter light it.

"None. But you do, I suppose."

The Boss shifts, uncomfortably, in his seat.

"Well . . . I've heard a few things. Just rumors, mind you, that you outdid yourself in Los Angeles . . . a strike . . ."

"I do what I can."

"It's a similar situation here, Mr . . . ?"

"It's a similar situation everywhere you go."

The Boss nods.

"With regard to your fee," he adds, "we should be able to agree on a fair price. Jaime, one of my boys, will give you the details. Do you know him?"

"I've had the pleasure."

"He's impatient, but reliable. He's never let me down."

The Boss turns his attention to the seafood. The stranger moves his gaze back to the photographs: only then does he notice that some of them include the old man he's with now, sitting there slicing his shrimp. There he is in the photographs, his arms around Hollywood's stars, smiling like some benevolent and generous magnate.

VI

Jesús leaves the cantina at midnight. Two of his buddies are with him. They aren't drunk but every few minutes they burst out singing the *Canción mixteca*. They decide to stop for a couple of tacos at a dim roadside stand. The girl behind the counter recognizes them.

"What's going on with the Colorado thing?" she asks.

Jesús smiles; in this town everyone knows he's the agitator, the one who not only demands the gringos' land but who's brazen enough to take them over.

"It's just about over. Give it a few more weeks."

"We'll be having a meeting tomorrow," adds his friend, "and we'll be sending a petition to the president. You'll see how things end up going our way."

The oldest one in the bunch just shakes his head.

"No matter what, there'll be blows. Don't you think otherwise. Or do you really believe they're going to give over the land just like that? It's not like they're idiots."

Jesús shrugs his shoulders. He eats his tacos in silence. His friends do the same. When they're finished the girl doesn't charge them. The three men thank her and move on at a slower pace, tired now. The girl turns her back and buries their plates in a tub of soapy water. That instant the shots ring out.

VII

The Boss strokes the German shepherd lying at his feet. There's a knock at his office door.

"Come in."

Jaime steps in and greets him politely.

"You sent for me, sir?"

The Boss nods.

"Our friend did the little job I gave him. The gringos will be pleased."

Jaime doesn't show much enthusiasm about the news. The Boss notices.

"So now he's all yours. You can do whatever you want with him."

Jaime grins fiercely.

"I'll invite him out for a drive. I'll bring Lupe and Concha along to make a foursome and . . ."

The Boss raises his hands, visibly annoyed.

"Please. Spare me the details."

VIII

Nighttime. The Boss sits at his desk in solitude. He is concentrating on his book, bound in black with a red swastika on the cover: *Mein Kampf,* by Adolph Hitler. Suddenly he lifts his head and removes his glasses. He thinks he hears footsteps in the hall. Standing up, he takes a Luger from his desk drawer.

"Is that you, Jaime?"

"Who else would it be?" answers a voice at his back as the lights in the mansion go out.

Hours later a neighbor will swear he heard nothing unusual that night.

"Gunshots? No, none."

IX

Early in the morning the Ford convertible pulls up to the gas station. The stranger steps out and asks for a fill up and a tire check. He buys a pack of Lucky Strikes and looks southward. The same Mexican attendant waits on him.

"Did you like Mexicali?" he asks once he's finished checking the tires. The stranger takes out a twenty and hands it to the attendant.

"Keep the change."

"Well, at least you were lucky," adds the attendant. "It's the same with everyone. People come here just to find their fortune. And when they've done that they go on to better places to enjoy it. Right?"

The stranger cleans his glasses with a handkerchief. He looks southward once more.

"It's the same everywhere you go."

El Otro Lado

Rubén Martínez

El otro lado,
the other side,
that's where I'm from,
el otro lado,
that's where you're from,
the other side.

Over there! Where it's free,
por allá, ¡sin impuestos!
You know, las calles de
Good Housekeeping oro,
rascacielo-hielo dreams.
Wall Street!
The Street Of Walls!
Wall of Neon!
Wall of Mall!
Wall tall!
Ya lo sabes, ahí te espera
todo bien chico . . .
¿Qué what?
Violence?
Never! Not on the streets
of Nuestra Señora la Reina de Los Angeles de Porciúncula!

¡Ay! Pero cómo te deseo,
aquí, desde este lado,
come, cruzá la línea cruda,
vení, vení, come, come,
how I want you on this side!
Let me suck your otherness!
Now, outside of history!
Are you? Are you
outside or inside, playing

the neo-conquistador
and I el suberviso,
a plaything for them?

Deseo-desire deseo-desire deseo-desire
y este deseo acaso real
que se mezcla con quién putas
sabe que verdad
political economic cultural
deseo desire deseo desire deseo
tu saliva extranjera
on this side, but here I
go over there, al otro lado
past your arms to the other
sea and your land
is my water, salty now
with my absence in your
mouth . . .

Baby, where are you now?
¿En Valparaíso?
In Washington DC?
¿En Bogotá?
In Norfolk?
¿En Panamá?
In New Orleans?
¿En Guatemala?
In Santa Fe?
¿En el D.F., guey?
In Las Vegas?
¿En Zacatecas?
In East L.A.?
¿En Chihuahua?
In San Clemente?
¿En Tecate?
In San Diego?
¿Tijuana?

In San Diego?
¿En Tijuana?
In San Diego?
¿En Tijuana?
In San Diego?

Now. At last. Here.
Far from the mortars,
the hungry cities, the false treaties.
Aquí. Al otro lado.

We will finally have each other.
In spectacular contorsion.
¡Deseo! Open me, close me,
here, on this side,
in the exhibition cage
before us and them,
on "Nightline" and "24 Horas."

But tomorrow, it's back
to el otro lado.
Me serving you your breakfast,
your jumbo margarita,
wiping the guacamole off your trousers.

¿Me oyes?
Over there, por allá,
hear me?
Here, me!
This me, this me,
desde este lado,
on this side, este yo
y no el yo del otro,
not your me.
But this me, the one
that wears all the colors
of the continent!

Operadora? Operator?
¿My oyes? Hear me?
No, no te oigo.
Click.

Los Angeles, 1989

Part 2

A sense of motion permeates these pieces, movement provoked by emotions, reflection, and speculation.

from *Rain of Gold*

Victor Villaseñor

"Okay," said Epitacio as he and Juan came walking down the busy street of Douglas, Arizona, "I feel lucky! Let's have a drink and double our paychecks!"

Juan and Epitacio had been working at the Copper Queen Mining Company for over a month and they'd just been paid.

"All right, whatever you say," said Juan, feeling good about his brother-in-law who'd returned across the border to get them.

But Epitacio got drunk and lost both of their paychecks, then he refused to go home with Juan. The next day Epitacio didn't show up for work. Rumor had it that he'd taken off, gone back to Mexico.

Juan wasn't able to support his family by working only one shift at the Copper Queen, so he decided to change his name to Juan Cruz and get a second job on the night shift. After all, he was going on thirteen. He figured that he could hold down both shifts.

But, getting into line that night, one guy recognized Juan. His name was Tomas. He was seventeen years old and he had been in the poolhall the night Epitacio lost both of their paychecks.

Quickly, Juan winked at Tomas, signaling for him to keep still and not let on that he knew him. And it went easier than Juan had expected. Hell, the big, thick-necked *gringo* boss couldn't tell him apart from all the other Mexicans.

"Hey, Juan," said Tomas, once they were inside the smelter. Molten ore moved all about them in great kettles. "You want to make some extra money?"

"Sure," shouted Juan above the noise of the smelter. "Why the hell you think I'm working a second shift? Because I love the smell of wet armpits?"

"Well, then, meet me at midnight on our taco break," winked the handsome young man. "And I'll show you a fine trick."

"Sure thing!" yelled Juan. So they met at midnight and ate together and Tomas explained to Juan the plan. First, they'd put a sack of copper ore alongside the outside fence so they could steal it later; then the next day, they'd sell it in town to an American engineer.

"How much we gonna make?" asked Juan.

Tomas had to smile. He liked his young friend's greed. "Oh, maybe six dollars each," he said.

"Six dollars!" shouted Juan. He only made a dollar for an eight hour shift as it was. "That's a fortune!" But then he thought again and he became suspicious. "Wait," he said, "just how do you know about this *gringo* engineer, anyway?" Juan was only twelve, but he had forty years' worth of experience.

"Buddy," said the tall, good-looking young man, rolling his eyes to the heavens with great style, "I got my means." And he laughed a good, full, manly laugh, and Juan believed him.

They did it, and it worked beautifully. The next day they sold the ore to the American engineer in town for six dollars each. But, the following night, as they came up alongside the fence to do the same thing again, the lights came on and they were surrounded by sixteen armed men. The American engineer that they'd sold the ore to had set them up. He also worked for the Copper Queen. They were immediately taken to town, tried, found guilty and taken to Tombstone, Arizona.

"But I'm only twelve years old!" screamed Juan. "And my family will starve without me!"

"Sssshhh!" said Tomas. "You tell them that and they'll send you to a boys' place, and I won't be able to protect you! I got a plan. You just keep quiet and stick by me!"

So Juan stuck by his friend, saying he was eighteen, and that night in Tombstone, he saw what his friend's plan was. When the other prisoners saw them, and they came on them like wolves to rape the sheep, Tomas turned his ass up at them so they wouldn't beat him.

"Not me! You son-of-a-bitches!" bellowed Juan with all his might. "I'm from Los Altos de Jalisco! I'll castrate the first *puto cabrón* who touches me!"

That night, shooting broke out in front of the jailhouse, and a terrible explosion blew out the back wall. A Mexican on horseback yelled "Vámonos, Aguilar!" Prisoners ran every which way as a dozen horsemen continued shooting. They had their brother on a horse, and they took off. Everyone else was left standing there, naked as plucked turkeys under the cold, night sky.

Instantly Juan took off on foot after the horsemen through the *arroyo* behind the jail. He ran uphill all night. And daybreak found him at the foot of a great mountain. But in the distance, there came a dozen armed horsemen, cracking leather. He took off as fast as he could through the cactus. It was his birthday, August eighteenth, 1916. He was thirteen years old, but the only presents the *gringos* brought him were well-placed bullets singing by his ears. Finally, they caught him, beat him, tied him to a horse and dragged him back to town.

By the time his mother, two sisters, his nephew and two nieces finally found out what had happened to him, Juan was in the Arizona State Penitentiary at Florence, Arizona.

His mother cried and cried. Luisa screamed and cursed and banged her head. Emilia couldn't stop coughing, and his nephew and nieces wept hysterically.

Then, the rich Mexican from Sonora, who'd driven Juan's family to the penitentiary to visit him, asked to speak to Juan alone.

"Juan," said the tall and thin old man once they were alone, "your mother is a wonderful lady. She's nursed me back to health with herbs and massage. I love her dearly, and I regard you as my own son."

Juan almost laughed at the stooped-over old man. Why, the son-of-a-bitch was an even smoother talker than the big bastard who'd converted Tomas into a woman.

"You see, Juan, I have a very high-spirited son like you. And I love him and I'd do anything for him. But you see, *mi hijito* killed a Texas Ranger." The dignified old man began to cry, leaning on his gold-headed cane. "I've been told that it was an honest battle, but the *americanos* don't see it that way and they're going to execute him."

Juan's heart came to his eyes. "I sympathize with you, señor," he said.

"I'm glad to hear that," said the old man, "because, well, I have a proposition to make you. I'll give your mother, God bless her soul, two hundred dollars in American money if you confess to the crime my son committed."

Juan couldn't believe his ears. He felt like spitting in the old man's face. Hell, he only had six years to serve for stealing the six dollars worth of ore. But for murder, shit, man, son-of-a-gringo-bitch, he'd be executed or be in for life.

"Calm down," said the old man, "please, and listen to my whole proposition. After all, they already have you locked up, so how much more can happen to you?"

Juan calmed down and looked into the eyes of the old man who, it was said, owned more cattle in the State of Sonora than the rails had ties.

"Your mother, look at her," he continued, "see how desperate she is. This is a terrible time for us mejicanos." He went on and on, and Juan didn't curse him and send him packing—as the *gringos* said—but, instead, he listened and looked at his mother and sisters and nephew and nieces over there by the far wall. Finally, Juan pulled down into his gut with all the power of his balls, his *tanates,* and spoke.

"Make it five hundred in gold!"

And so the deal was made, and a new trial was set for the murderer of the famous, Mexican-killing Texas Ranger of Douglas, Arizona. Juan Salvador Villaseñor—known as Juan Cruz—was found guilty and was sentenced to life imprisonment.

Mericans

Sandra Cisneros

We're waiting for the awful grandmother who is inside dropping pesos into *la ofrenda* box before the altar to La Divina Providencia. Lighting votive candles and genuflecting. Blessing herself and kissing her thumb. Running a crystal rosary between her fingers. Mumbling, mumbling, mumbling.

There are so many prayers and promises and thanks-be-to-God to be given in the name of the husband and the sons and the only daughter who never attended mass. It doesn't matter. Like La Virgen de Guadalupe, the awful grandmother intercedes on their behalf. For the grandfather who hasn't believed in anything since the first PRI elections. For my father, El Periquín, so skinny he needs his sleep. For Auntie Light-skin, who only a few hours before was breakfasting on brain and goat tacos after dancing all night in the pink zone. For Uncle Fat-face, the blackest of the black sheep—*Always remember your Uncle Fat-face in your prayers.* And Uncle Baby—*You go for me, Mamá—God listens to you.*

The awful grandmother has been gone a long time. She disappeared behind the heavy leather outer curtain and the dusty velvet inner. We must stay near the church entrance. We must not wander over to the balloon and punch-ball vendors. We cannot spend our allowance on fried cookies or Familia Burrón comic books or those clear cone-shaped suckers that make everything look like a rainbow when you look through them. We cannot run off and have our picture taken on the wooden ponies. We must not climb the steps up the hill behind the church and chase each other through the cemetery. We have promised to stay right where the awful grandmother left us until she returns.

There are those walking to church on their knees. Some with fat rags tied around their legs and others with pillows, one to kneel on, and one to flop ahead. There are women with black shawls crossing and uncrossing themselves. There are armies of penitents carrying banners and flowered arches while musicians play tinny trumpets and tinny drums.

La Virgen de Guadalupe is waiting inside behind a plate of thick glass.

There's also a gold crucifix bent crooked as a mesquite tree when someone once through a bomb. La Virgen de Guadalupe on the main altar because she's a big miracle, the crooked crucifix on a side altar because that's a little miracle.

But we're outside in the sun. My big brother Junior hunkered against the wall with his eyes shut. My little brother Keeks running around in circles.

Maybe and most probably my little brother is imagining he's a flying feather dancer, like the ones we saw swinging high up from a pole on the Virgin's birthday. I want to be a flying feather dancer too, but when he circles past me he shouts, "I'm a B-Fifty-two bomber, you're a German," and shoots me with an invisible machine gun. I'd rather play flying feather dancers, but if I tell my brother this, he might not play with me at all.

"*Girl.* We can't play with a *girl.*" *Girl.* It's my brothers' favorite insult now instead of "sissy." "You *girl,*" they yell at each other. "You throw that ball like a *girl.*"

I've already made up my mind to be a German when Keeks swoops past again, this time yelling, "I'm Flash Gordon, You're Ming the Merciless and the Mud People." I don't mind being Ming the Merciless, but I don't like being the Mud People. Something wants to come out of the corners of my eyes, but I don't let it. Crying is what *girls* do.

I leave Keeks running around in circles—"I'm the Lone Ranger, you're Tonto." I leave Junior squatting on his ankles and go look for the awful grandmother.

Why do churches smell like the inside of an ear? Like incense and the dark and candles in blue glass? And why does holy water smell of tears? The awful grandmother makes me kneel and fold my hands. The ceiling high and everyone's prayers bumping up there like balloons.

If I stare at the eyes of the saints long enough, they move and wink at me, which makes me a sort of saint too. When I get tired of winking saints, I count the awful grandmother's mustache hairs while she prays for Uncle Old, sick from the worm, and Auntie Cuca, suffering from a life of troubles that left her face crooked and the other half sad.

There must be a long, long list of relatives who haven't gone to church. The awful grandmother knits the names of the dead and the living into one long prayer fringed with the grandchildren born in that barbaric country with its barbarian ways.

I put my weight on one knee, then the other, and when they both grow fat as a mattress of pins, I slap them each awake. *Micaela, you may wait outside with Alfredito and Enrique.* The awful grandmother says it all in Spanish, which I understand when I'm paying attention. "What?" I say, though it's neither proper nor polite. "What?" which the awful grandmother hears as "¿Güat?" But she only gives me a look and shoves me toward the door.

After the all the dust and dark, the light from the plaza makes me squinch my eyes like if I just came out of the movies. My brother Keeks is drawing squiggly lines on the concrete with a wedge of glass and the heel of his shoe. My brother Junior squatting against the entrance, talking to a lady and man.

They're not from here. Ladies don't come to church dressed in pants. And everybody knows men aren't supposed to wear shorts.

"¿Quieres chicle?" the lady asks in a Spanish too big for her mouth.

"Gracias." The lady gives him a whole handful of gum for free, little cellophane cubes of Chiclets, cinnamon and aqua and the white ones that don't taste like anything but are good for pretend buck teeth.

"Por favor," says the lady. "¿Un foto?" pointing to her camera.

"Si."

She's so busy taking Junior's picture, she doesn't notice me and Keeks.

"Hey, Michele, Keeks. You guys want gum?"

"But you speak English?"

"Yeah," my brother says, "we're Mericans."

We're Mericans, we're Mericans, and inside the awful grandmother prays.

from *Rainbow's End*

Genaro González

"Papá's old friend, El Bruto, was naturalized last week," Imelda told her husband over breakfast. "He's a U.S. citizen now, eligible for old age assistance. That's the third one this month."

Gilberto scooped up a tortilla from the griddle the moment it puffed up. "I've told you. Almost everyone past sixty in this barrio's made his peace. Your father's the only rebel left."

"Forget the rebel part. We sure could use that monthly government check. Prices these days are up in the clouds." She hushed on hearing don Heraclio in the hall telling his grandson a joke. Armandito entered the kitchen laughing, but his mother evaporated his humor with a stern look.

The old man followed, his thin legs swimming in the wool trousers that knew all seasons. What his erratic hearing sometimes missed, the soft, brown eyes rarely overlooked, and taking his place at the table he sensed a conspiracy in Imelda's smile. He turned more guarded than usual and began grooming his mustache with his fingertips. He had honed the white fringe to a minimal essence that seemed to have unhinged from under his nose and now hung above his upper lip. The hair along his temples had gone past gray, to the amber of aged tequila.

Imelda tried to soothe his suspicions with a forced cheerfulness. "And what'll it be this morning, papá?"

"You mean I have a choice? Like a condemned man?"

She overlooked the sarcasm. "Of course."

"In that case I'll have armadillo sausage with bull's testicles."

Gilberto gestured her to humor him. "What a pity, papá. Armadillo's out of season at Bernal's, and there's a shortage of bull's . . . uh . . . eggs. They're just not laying this year. How about huevos rancheros?"

"I hate huevos rancheros."

"But you have them every morning."

"There you have it, then. I'm fed up."

She watched him stir the steam from his coffee while he read a

Mexican newspaper. She repeated the news to Gilberto: "El Bruto passed his citizenship test." She tried for spontaneity, but it was too early for a convincing performance.

"Hell, if he could do it, my father-in-law here should pass like a chili seed through an intestine." But either don Heraclio had lapsed into one of his deaf spells or was playing possum, so this time Gilberto told Imelda the news. Finally don Heraclio glanced up from his paper.

"What's this business of trading old gossip back and forth?"

"I was telling Imelda that your friend . . ."

"Yes, yes." He dismissed the news as ancient history. "They shot Kennedy."

At that moment Marina came in and tore whatever net her parents were trying to snare the old man in. "Not another one! Esteban, turn on the news!"

Esteban rushed into the crowded kitchen. "What's wrong?"

"Your parents." Don Heraclio showed him the newspaper. "The people are up in arms in Guerrero, and here your folks are honoring . . ."

"What 'people', suegro? What 'up in arms?' "

"Here, read! Open your eyes a bit."

"Working men don't have time for political crossword puzzles."

"But they do have time to sit and watch soap operas or gossip about an old-timer turning americano."

Imelda answered without thinking, "At least that old-timer's bringing in some money with his old age assistance." She immediately wanted to bite her tongue.

Don Heraclio carefully folded his paper. "No need to throw stones. I'm sharpening my field hoe first thing tomorrow morning."

"Heavens, no, papá! Why, as soon as the carrot season starts I'll join Gilberto at the packing shed." She pressed her plump side with a grimace. "I'd sooner rupture my inflamed gall bladder than have you suffer a nosebleed in the sun."

Gilberto hid his admiration. Actually she had planned to join him next week but had postponed her decision, fearing it might ease their pressure on the citizenship question. This time Gilberto sided with her, but his objection was less sentimental: "All you do is get in the way of other workers." He reminded the old man of his last attempt as a field hand three years ago. Besides chopping more plants than weeds, he had tried to organize a strike for higher wages.

"I would have pulled it off, too," said don Heraclio, "but the mucha-chos without papers couldn't afford trouble."

"Naturally!" said Gilberto. "The grower was the mayor's brother! Is nothing sacred, señor? Don't you have an ounce of respect?"

"Respect for my gray hairs is what I should have gotten from that crew boss. Instead he almost left me stranded."

Gilberto anchored his argument to mundane concerns. "See? There's no need to suffer heat or humiliations. Not at your age, not with a monthly check waiting for the picking."

"Now you're saying it's for my own good . . ."

"For the good of the family!" Gilberto said crossly. "My miserable wages barely keep our noses above water."

"I had no problem raising a family on a tenth of your salary."

"Stop living in the nineteenth century. Now that wouldn't even cover burial insurance." He lowered his voice before his children. "These days even beans cost you a nut."

Don Heraclio raised his cup. "I'd rather have a huevo hanging than end up castrated."

"Nobody's out to castrate you, señor. But face the facts. You've lived here over forty years. Your children and grandchildren were born here. Your wife was born and buried here. You're practically an americano already."

Don Heraclio buried himself behind his newspaper once more.

They thought he had conceded the argument when he added softly, "In some ways leaving Mexico was the best move I ever made. In others it was my biggest mistake. Now I'm stuck in a swamp, unable to turn back or move ahead."

Esteban censored a flippant remark on the tip of his tongue. Even Imelda, calloused by their daily skirmishes, had trouble swallowing her morsel of food. Don Heraclio stood, sopped up a coffee ring with his newspaper and said hoarsely, "If anyone needs me, I'll be at Bernal's."

A small, elderly flock had queued by the bus bench in front of Bernal's supermarket. Most were waiting for the shuttle to the free breakfast program at the Christian War Veterans Center. Others, like don Heraclio's neighbor, don Clemente, came to chat and hear Heraclio harangue the rest for accepting alms. Don Clemente's relatives had placed him in five dif-ferent rest homes, and each time he had slipped back to the barrio in his bedroom slippers. "Like an old cat," he said. "If I don't come back one day, just go scrape me off the highway." His excuse for returning was the same one he gave for refusing to eat at the free meals program: the gringo diet gave him diarrhea.

Doña Gertrudis, a regular at the Veterans Center, caught sight of don Heraclio and passed the word. "Here comes that old Quixote. Too bad the bus is late."

Don Clemente offered him a cigarette, but he shook his head and pointed to his friend's khaki shirt, peppered with pinholes from live ashes. He scanned the faces around him. "Someone's missing."

"Josefina," said doña Nestora, then calmed their fears. "Sprained her leg shooing a dog from her garden." Doña Nestora was compact and intense, and a facial tic added to her energetic image. The tremors mimicked rapid head shakes, and people speaking to her had the uneasy impression she was not believing one word. Don Heraclio often wondered whether it persisted in her sleep, since she insisted she would stay active until her dying day. "The day I stop shaking, don't bother winding me up again."

He would have liked her except for one fault: her living room had turned into a small museum of Kennedy memorabilia. Between icons of obscure saints that even Father Coronado failed to recognize and religious calendars going back decades, she had crammed Kennedy plates and portrait plaques that switched faces at different angles. "She's not content with church fairy tales," he once said. "Now she worships millionaires."

The dislike was mutual. Whenever he said, "They shot Kennedy," she winced and crossed herself.

The group carried on several conversations at once until an ex-smuggler from the tequilero days caught their attention. "I'm thinking of turning gringo before the government changes its mind."

Someone chuckled. "Just don't give them your old alias."

"They're almost giving away the test answers to old mexicanos like us," said someone else.

Don Clemente frowned. "I heard you have to spit on the Mexican flag."

"I myself did no such thing!" said doña Nestora.

The argument splintered into several chatterings. From somewhere in the crowd, someone seeking a little excitement asked, "Heraclio, when are you turning yankee?"

Don Heraclio rested a hand over his groin. "On the day this gets stiff and swollen"—he continued down one leg—"from rigor mortis."

Señorita Gertrudis, the barrio's vintage virgin, looked away in case the other old men had ideas. Someone else said, "Quit being such a diehard, Heraclio. With a pension you could guzzle a few brews now and then."

He looked at them as if they were whores on promenade. "You're like those Anglo mummies in make-up and girdles . . ."

"It's not just women," said doña Nestora.

"Men too," he agreed. "One foot in the grave and they still pester bar maids for polkas. Remember Edelmiro Zuñiga? He barely broke in his new name—Eddy—when his warranty expired. A month after becoming a señor citizen. Didn't even cash his first check."

"All the more reason to enjoy life a little."

"That measly allowance just brings out the worst in you. Enough for your vices and maybe an aspirin afterwards."

"Maybe that's true for some," said the widow Clotilde. "But a lot of us live hand to mouth. That check is our only salvation. We don't have a family to care for us like you do."

Don Demetrio Chávez, the oldest, voiced their resentment. "You criticize everything, my friend. The americanos are only trying to help."

"Help screw us, you mean. Where were the decent wages when we were their farmworkers and maids? You, Clotilde, slaving for that politician's family for fifteen years. Did they lift a finger after you got t.b. and couldn't iron their shirts?"

She lowered her voice, but the memory had not lost its bitterness. "They almost threw me out in the street, as if I had the plague."

He nodded as if he had heard similar stories. "And now they throw us peanuts and expect us to kiss their hands."

"So what's your solution?" asked don Demetrio.

"It's too late for solutions. But we can take a stand, toss back their slop, like we organized our strikes in Mexico." For a moment the hoarse nostalgia in his voice made him imagine he was rousing the rabble. "We showed them in Nuevo León! Shut down their company stores . . ."

"Stop being an anachronist," don Demetrio said wearily.

"Anarchists? Never! We were organizers!"

"A-na-chro-nist, Heraclio. In your fantasies Jacinto Treviño still terrorizes Texas Rangers. Those times are dead."

"Not until we are."

Don Demetrio snorted and lifted his friend's arm. "And how much longer for that? Look at your own carcass."

Then let's die with our dignity, as Mexicans."

"Mexico never gave me anything except plenty of reasons to leave."

A bowlegged woman bent by the years added, "Nowadays all you hear in this barrio is that rock-and-roll noise. It's even worse in Mexico."

"Face it, Heraclio, the whole world is turning gringo."

He had no time to reply; someone shouted, "The bus!" and the more nimble ones jammed in line first.

He waited until they started inching slowly in single file, then said, "There goes the hyena pack." From within the silent crowd an empty stomach growled its agreement. "Hear that, Clemente? That tit barely keeps them alive."

After the driver shut the door someone answered back: "I hope the Devil catches you confessed, Heraclio! You might be the first planted this season!"

He threw them a farewell taunt over the diesel's roar. "You're going to get freckles from all those hamburgers!" . . .

Mr. Olivares, the courthouse examiner, wore a pastel guayabera to hide his ample, civil servant's backside. He escorted them through a maze of corridors and elevators until they entered a large room with fluorescent lights and no windows. Its spartan furnishings caused echoes to collide. When he bent to check the bottom file of a cabinet, the target proved too tempting for don Heraclio's barbs: "That's how Japan lost the war."

"What about Japan's defeat, Señor Cavazos?" he asked with the monotone of a man with his mind on other matters. Without waiting for a reply, he added, "Some time back this old Japanese soldier surrendered almost forty years after the war ended. Imagine, everyone's made peace and he's still out in the jungle." He retrieved a folder and read it carefully. "You lived in Nuevo León before coming here?" Imelda and Gilberto held their breath until he added, "I have relatives in Nuevo León. Never bothered to meet them, though. I'm afraid they'll ask me to help them get citizenship here." He turned and smiled. "We have enough people here to take care of."

He opened another file cabinet. "The exam, then." He sat and sighed audibly the moment his contours assumed their former inertia. "Let's see . . . I think one question should be enough."

Imelda immediately saw the risk. "Just one?"

Mr. Olivares turned to the couple with a faint wink. Don Heralcio, who had not dropped his guard once, caught it too. Then, unable to look the old man in the eyes, Mr. Olivares glued his attention to the sheet in front of him. "Now tell me, señor . . . who discovered America?"

Don Heraclio looked at Imelda and Gilberto, who were grinning from ear to ear, then at his examiner. No one returned his gaze, and in the midst of the mockery he assessed everything: he had committed to memory states whose odd names mirrored their gerrymandered borders, had shuffled and reshuffled scores of dates, in the end had come prepared to answer trivia too obscure even for most gringos, and it had all come to this—the farce of answering something his grandson could have told them.

Imelda's rasp ricocheted off the walls. "His hearing goes at times."

Mr. Olivares, his hand still shielding his eyes, pencil suspended a fraction of an inch from the answer sheet, raised his voice: "Who discovered America, señor?"

Don Heraclio gave them a final, disappointed gaze, then answered truthfully: "Los indios."

In that moment of collective horror the answer flew wildly around the room like an exotic, expensive bird loose from its cage. Mr. Olivares dug the pencil point in his right ear and returned it to the same infinitesimal distance from the answer sheet. "Beg your pardon. I don't believe I heard you right."

"LOS INDIOS!" his echo thundered. "The Indians discovered America!"

Mr. Olivares hesitated a split second then slashed a bold check on the sheet. "Correct, señor!"

Gilberto and Imelda stood and hugged each other as Mr. Olivares navigated around the desk to shake hands. Congratulations were offered as enthusiastically as bureaucratic protocol allowed. No one paid much attention to don Heraclio, who was now only a warm technicality.

Alone within the celebration, he chastised himself for always falling for the same ruse. "Americanos and their rules," he told himself aloud. "They won't even give you the pleasure of losing."

This Memory Begins with Flight

Luis J. Rodríguez

Cry, child, for those without tears have a grief which never ends.—Mexican Saying

This memory begins with flight. A 1950s bondo-spackled Dodge surged through a driving rain, veering around the potholes and upturned tracks of the abandoned Red Line trains on Alameda Street. Mama was in the front seat. My father was at the wheel. My brother Rano and I sat on one end of the back seat; my sisters Pata and Cuca on the other. There was a space between the boys and the girls to keep us apart.

"Amá, mira a Rano," a voice said for the tenth time from the back of the car. "He's hitting me again."

We fought all the time. My brother, especially, had it in for La Pata— thinking of Frankenstein, he called her "Anastein." Her real name was Ana, but most of the time we went by the animal names Dad gave us at birth. I am Grillo, which means cricket. Rano stands for "rana," the frog. La Pata is the duck and Cuca is short for cucaracha: cockroach.

The car seats came apart in strands. I looked out at the passing cars which seemed like ghosts with headlights rushing past the streaks of water on the glass. I was nine years old. As the rain fell, my mother cursed in Spanish intermixed with pleas to saints and "la Santísima Madre de Dios." She argued with my father. Dad didn't curse or raise his voice. He just stated the way things were.

"I'll never go back to Mexico," he said. "I'd rather starve here. You want to stay with me, it has to be in Los Angeles. Otherwise, go."

This incited my mother to greater fits.

We were on the way to the Union train station in downtown L.A.

We had our few belongings stuffed into the trunk and underneath our feet. I gently held on to one of the comic books Mama bought to keep us entertained. I had on my Sunday best clothes with chewed gum stuck in a coat pocket. It could have been Easter, but it was a weeping November. I don't remember for sure why we were leaving. I just knew it was a special day. There was no fear or concern on my part. We were always moving. I looked at the newness of the comic book and felt some exhilaration of its feel in my hand. Mama had never bought us comic books before. It had to be a special day.

For months we had been pushed from one house to another, just Mama and us children. Mom and Dad had split up prior to this. We stayed at the homes of women my mom called comadres, with streams of children of their own. Some nights we slept in a car or in the living room of people we didn't know. There were no shelters for homeless families. My mother tried to get us settled somewhere but all the indications pointed to our going back to the land of her birth, to her red earth, her Mexico.

The family consisted of my father Alfonso, my mom María Estela, my older brother, José René, and my younger sisters, Ana Virginia and Gloria Estela. I recall my father with his wavy hair and clean shaven face, his correct, upright and stubborn demeanor, in contrast to my mother who was heavy-set with Native features and thick straight hair, often laughing heartily, her eyes narrowed to slits, and sometimes crying from a deep tomb-like place with a sound like swallowing mud.

As we got closer to the Union station, Los Angeles loomed low and large. A city of odd construction, a good place to get lost in. I, however, would learn to hide in imaginative worlds—in books; in TV shows, where I picked up much of my English; in solitary play with mangled army men and crumpled toy trucks. I was so withdrawn it must have looked scary.

This is what I know: When I was two years old, our family left Ciudad Juárez, Chihuahua, for Los Angeles. My father was an educated man, unusual for our border town, a hungry city filled to the hills with cardboard hovels of former peasants, Indians and dusk-faced children. In those days, an educated man had to be careful about certain things—questioning authority, for example. Although the principal of a local high school, my father failed to succumb to the local chieftains who were linked to the national party which ruled Mexico, as one famous Latin American writer would later say, with a "perfect dictatorship."

When Dad first became principal, there were no funds due to the massive bureaucratic maze he had to get through to get them. The woman he lived with then was an artist who helped raise money for the school by staging exhibitions. My father used his own money to pay for supplies and at one point had the iron fence around the school torn down and sold for scrap.

One year, Dad received an offer for a six-month study program for foreign teachers in Bloomington, Indiana. He liked it so much, he renewed it three times. By then, my father had married his secretary, my mother, after the artist left him. They had their first child, José René.

By the time my father returned, his enemies had mapped out a means to remove him—being a high school principal is a powerful position in a place like Ciudad Juárez. My father faced a pile of criminal charges, including the alleged stealing of school funds. Police arrived at the small room in the vecindad where Mama and Dad lived and escorted him to the city jail.

For months my father fought the charges. While he was locked up, they fed him scraps of food in a rusted steel can. They denied him visitors — Mama had to climb a section of prison wall and pick up 2-year-old José René so he could see his father. Finally, after a lengthy trial, my father was found innocent—but he no longer had his position as principal.

Dad became determined to escape to the United States. My mother, on the other hand, never wanted to leave Mexico; she did it to be with Dad.

Mama was one of two daughters in a family run by a heavy-drinking, wife-beating railroad worker and musician. My mother was the only one in her family to complete high school. Her brothers, Kiko and Rodolfo, often crossed the border to find work and came back with stories of love and brawls on the other side.

Their grandmother was a Tarahumara Indian who once walked down from the mountainous area in the state of Chihuahua where her people lived in seclusion for centuries. The Spanish never conquered them. But their grandmother never returned to her people. She eventually gave birth to my grandmother, Ana Acosta.

Ana's first husband was a railroad worker during the Mexican Revolution; he lost his life when a tunnel exploded during a raid. They brought his remains in a shoebox. Ana was left alone with one son, while pregnant with a daughter. Lucita, the daughter, eventually died of convulsions at the age of four, and Manolo, the son, was later blinded after a bout with a deadly form of chicken pox which struck and killed many children in the area.

Later Ana married my grandfather, Mónico Jiménez, who like her first husband worked the railroad. At one point, Mónico quit the rails to play trumpet and sing for bands in various night clubs. Once he ended up in Los Angeles, but with another woman. In fact, Mónico had many other women. My grandmother often had to cross over to the railroad yards, crowded with prostitutes and where Mónico spent many nights singing, to bring him home.

When my parents married, Mama was 27; Dad almost 40. She had never known any other man. He already had four or five children from three or four other women. She was an emotionally-charged border woman, full of fire, full of pain, full of giving love. He was a stoic, unfeeling, unmoved intellectual who did as he pleased as much as she did all she could do to please him. This dichotomous couple, the sun and the moon, this curandera and biologist, dreamer and realist, fire woman and water man, molded me; these two sides created a life-long conflict in my breast.

By the time Dad had to leave Ciudad Juárez, my mother had borne three of his children, including myself, all in El Paso, on the American side (Gloria was born later in East L.A.'s General Hospital). This was done to help ease the transition from alien status to legal residency. There are stories of women who wait up to the ninth month and run across the border to have their babies, sometimes squatting and dropping them on the pavement as they hug the closest lamppost.

Our first exposure in America stays with me like a foul odor. It seemed a strange world, most of it spiteful to us, spitting and stepping on us, coughing us up, us immigrants, as if we were phlegm stuck in the collective throat of this country. My father was mostly out of work. When he did have a job it was in construction, in factories such as Sinclair Paints or Standard Brands Dog Food, or pushing door-bells selling insurance, Bibles or pots and pans. My mother found work cleaning homes or in the garment industry. She knew the corner markets were ripping her off but she could only speak with her hands and in choppy English.

Once my mother gathered up the children and we walked to Will Rogers Park. There were people everywhere. Mama looked around for a place we could rest. She spotted an empty spot on a park bench. But as soon as she sat down an American woman, with three kids of her own, came by.

"Hey, get out of there—that's our seat."

My mother understood her but didn't know how to answer back in English. So she tried in Spanish.

"Look spic, you can't sit there!" the American woman yelled. "You don't belong here! Understand? This is not your country!"

Mama quietly got our things and walked away, but I knew frustration and anger bristled within her because she was unable to talk, and when she did, no one would listen.

We are inside the vast cavern of the station. Pews of swirled wood are filled with people. We sit with our bags near us, and string tied from the bags to our wrists so nobody can take them without taking us too. My father turns to us, says a faint goodbye, then begins to walk away. No hugs. He doesn't even look at us.

"Poncho."

The name echoes through the waiting area.

"Poncho."

He turns. Stares at my mother. The wet of tears covers her face. Mama then says she can't go. She will stay with him. In L.A. I don't think she's happy about this. But what can a single mother of four children do in Mexico? A woman, sick all the time, with factory work for skills in a land where work is mainly with the soil. What good is it except to starve.

"Está bien," Dad says as he nears my mother. "We will make it, mujer. I know it. But we have to be patient. We have to believe."

Mama turns to us and announces we are not leaving.

from *Canícula: Snapshots of a Girlhood en la Frontera*

Norma Elia Cantú

Mami isn't even nineteen when she's photographed as a china poblana at the plaza in front of Santo Niño de Atocha Church, with a whole setup— fake horse and all. She holds her skirt and points her foot as instructed; on the wide-brimmed charro hat the embroidery screams ¡Viva México! She who wasn't even born in Mexico, who went there as a ten-year-old knowing only to read and write in English because the nuns at Sacred Heart in San Antonio wouldn't tolerate Spanish. Settled in the tiny hamlet of Rodríguez with the sunbaked packed dirt yard, and the two-room adobe; Rodríguez, where school was a few rough-hewn wood benches and a young teacher brimming with socialist ideas—after all it was during the Cárdenas presidency—taught the songs of a nationalism rooted in revolution. She saw her gentleman father drown in self-pity and drink, a gentleman who wrote poems and owned a Model T, a gentleman who took his daughters on picnics to Breckenridge Park and to the beach in Corpus Christi every summer, a gentleman who inherited everything on the Mexican side of the border when his mother died, the maternal family's store in Monclova, Coahuila, and the paternal properties, the ranch in Tamaulipas. He lost everything on both sides because of a curse his own family laid on him—pure jealousy, pura envidia, as the aunts tell it. He sang a favorite song, evenings on the porch in San Antonio, strumming the same guitar he had played when courting Bueli in Monterrey. Bueli's uncles didn't allow her to have anything to do with the foráneo, after all he was from Tejas and who knows who his people were. Of course, Bueli's grandmother couldn't do much—she knew she wouldn't be around to protect the young orphan whose mother had died in childbirth and whose father was always off, a telegrapher for the railroad. In a household of absent men what could she do? And of course Bueli had been flattered and had fallen in love with the handsome romantic Tejano. And she and her grandmother had arranged the "elopement" so that they would be married at her co-madre Adela's house both by el civil and by a priest, too. But soon after they were in San Antonio the revolution had come and things were hard. Her uncle had been killed and perhaps her father too. She never knew for sure. Never saw her grandmother again, and many years later visited comadre Adela and her daughters, her childhood friends in Monterrey, couldn't even put flowers on her mother's grave—no one knew where it was. But for her dead children—four she lost when they were barely walking, buried in San Antonio and Corpus Christi, she prays on the day of the angelitos, lights a candle, and makes a mark on the waxy taper and says a prayer for each of their angel souls. Lights another white candle on the day of the dead for her parents and all her adult dead. Teaches me to pray for all the holy souls, las santas ánimas, each night as we set aside a glass of water for the lost souls, las ánimas perdidas. . . .

An awkward teen, shy and reticent, I face the camera, wearing a sleeveless, morning-glory-blue cotton blouse. My eighth-grade school picture—not many others exist from that time when I suffered the pains of growing up—literally leg cramps that kept me up all night and which Mami would rub with "volcánico," a foul-smelling ointment for horses, and the more subtle but just as painful growing pains, for which there was no salve, of being thirteen and the victim of so many changes. During lunch time, I'm reading in the cafeteria. Nearby, Sarah, the daughter of the Jewish family Mami worked for before she married, is talking to Susan and Janice in a voice loud and clear so I can hear, "All I know is unplucked brows and hairy legs and underarms make a girl look like a boy." The tears streaming down my hot face I run to the bathroom where some of the chucas are smoking. I blurt it out, what they said; they've been after me to pluck my brows, shave my legs. We talk about them as if they were from another planet. "No les hagas caso a esas pendejas," says Rita, who came back last year from El Norte, wearing makeup and talking dirty. Her thick braid held with a red rubber band is all I see as I sniffle and control my tears. I feel torn; these same "pendejas" are sometimes my friends and we work on school projects together; I go to their ritzy houses in the Heights amazed that their parents aren't around, that they drive cars, that they go across to Nuevo Laredo, that they drink and smoke. I'm torn but I believe Rita; they don't know what they're talking about—Mami doesn't shave or pluck her eyebrows either, neither did her comadres until much later. Many Chicana classmates behave like gringas, but my friends, most of us who ride the Saunders bus, we don't yet shave, much less pluck our eyebrows, or wear makeup—our parents forbid it. The bell rings and as I walk back to English class to our Friday quiz, head held high like the protagonist in the book I'm reading, *Head High, Ellen Brodie,* I whisper to

Rosario, the only other Chicana in the accelerated class, "I bet we can beat them." I can tell she smiles even though I can't see her face; her ears with the Mexican gold loops redden, and she silently nods "Let's." And we both know who I mean, and we do. But it is Susan's paper that Mrs. McDonnell reads from on Monday morning as an example of good work.

Two years later, it's the same group. And it's jeweled pumps and penny loafers. I beg and beg Mami for a pair of black leather flats with red, green, yellow, shiny rhinestones just like Lydia's. When I finally get them, Papi wants us to take them back—they're shoes for a puta, not a decent girl. But Mami's on my side, after all we spent her hard-earned money on the shoes, so I keep the shoes but wear them rarely. To church and school I wear my old scuffed oxblood red loafers and bobby sox. I'm wearing the rhinestone flats defiantly in my quinceañera photo as I sit in our front yard with friends and family all around.

Laredo, Texas

Vladimir Mayakovsky

TRANSLATED BY Marian Schwartz

"Moscow. Is that in Poland?" they asked me at the American consulate in Mexico.

"No," I answered. "The USSR."

No impression whatsoever.

I got my visa.

Later I found out that if an American does nothing but sharpen needle points, he knows his business better than anyone in the world, but he might not have a clue about needle eyes. Needle eyes aren't his specialty, and he's under no obligation to know about them.

Laredo is the border of the North American United States.

I spend a long time explaining the purposes and reasons for my entry in my half-French and half-English, both very broken (nothing but shards).

The American listens in silence, thinks it over, doesn't understand, and finally addresses me in Russian:

"Are you a Yid?"

I was taken aback.

The American did not undertake any further conversation due to a shortage of additional vocabulary.

He agonized another ten minutes and then blurted out:

"Great Russian?"

"Great Russian, Great Russian," I rejoiced, reassured that the American was not inclined to violence. Strictly bureaucratic interest. The American pondered this and after another ten minutes spoke:

"Go see the commission."

One gentleman, who up until this moment had been a civilian passenger, put on a uniform jacket and turned out to be an immigrations officer.

The officer stuffed me and my things into an automobile. We drove up and walked in to a building where a jacketless and vestless man was sitting under a starry flag.

Behind the man were more rooms with bars. They put me and my things in one of them.

I tried to leave, but they drove me back with a cautionary waving of arms.

Not far off, my New York train blew its whistle.

I sat there for four hours.

They came and inquired what language I planned to explain myself in.

Out of shyness (it's embarrassing not to know a single language) I said French.

They led me into a room.

Four scary old men and a French interpreter.

I can make simple French conversation about tea and rolls, but I didn't get any of what the Frenchman told me and could only snatch fitfully at his last word, trying to penetrate the hidden meaning intuitively.

Meanwhile, the Frenchman guessed I hadn't understood. The Americans waved their arms around and led me back to my cell.

I sat there another two hours and found the Frenchman's last word in the dictionary. It turned out to be "oath."

I could not swear an oath in French, so I waited for them to find a Russian.

Two hours later the Frenchman arrived all excited and reassured me: "They found a Russian, the owner of the furniture store."

"I have to swear an oath," I stammered shyly, to open the conversation.

The Russian interpreter casually waved his hand: "You'll tell the truth if you don't want to lie, and if you do want to lie, you won't tell the truth anyway."

A well-reasoned point of view.

I started answering hundreds of questionnaire questions: my mother's maiden name, my grandfather's parentage, the address of my high school, etc. Things I'd totally forgotten!

The interpreter turned out to be an influential man, and once I started speaking Russian, he took a liking to me, naturally.

In short: they let me into the country for six months as a tourist on a five hundred dollar bond.

Half an hour later the entire Russian colony had converged to take a look at me, vying to bowl me over with their hospitality.

The owner of a small shoe store, seated on a low stool for measuring feet, showed me different shoe styles, brought me ice water, and rejoiced:

"The first Russian in three years! Three years ago a priest came through with his daughters. At first he cursed us, but later (I'd arranged for his two daughters to go dancing at the café chantant) he said: "I like you, even if you are a Yid, you must have a conscience if you'd do that for an old man."

The linen merchant intercepted me, sold me two shirts at cost for two dollars apiece (one dollar for the shirt, one for the friendship), and then, touched, led me all the way across town to his house and made me drink warm whiskey from his only glass, which he also used for brushing his teeth—it smelled foul and was covered with spots.

This was my first encounter with the American dry law—Prohibition. Then I went back to the interpreter's furniture store. His brother took the price tag off the best green plush couch in the store and sat down opposite me on a leather one with a tag that said "$99.95" (a trick of the trade, so it doesn't say "$100").

At that point a quartet of doleful Jews walked in—two girls and two boys.

"The Spaniards," the brother advised reproachfully. "From Vinnitsa and Odessa. They spent two years in Cuba waiting for visas. Finally they put themselves in the hands of an Argentine, who took $250 to bring them in."

The Argentine had looked respectable and had a passport that said he had four traveling children. Argentines don't need visas. The Argentine had brought four or six hundred children into the United States—and got caught on the six hundred and fourth.

The Argentine's in good shape, though. People have been depositing hundreds of thousands of dollars in the bank for him—which means he's important.

And he bailed out the brothers—not that it did any good. They were going to be convicted and deported anyway.

This Argentine is a major businessman—and honest, too. There are also lots of small fry here. They take people across from Mexican Laredo to American Laredo for a hundred dollars apiece. The clients pay the hundred, get halfway there, and are drowned.

Plenty of people have emigrated directly to the next world.

This is my last Mexican story.

A brother's story about a brother, the furniture man, the first American. The brother lived in Kishinev. When he turned fourteen, he heard a rumor that the most beautiful women were in Spain. That very night the brother ran away because he had to have the most beautiful women. But he didn't reach Madrid until he was seventeen. There weren't any more beautiful women than anywhere else, and they paid even less attention to the brother than the pharmacists' wives in Kishinev had. The brother was insulted and rightly decided that he needed money to get Spanish eyes to shine in his direction. The brother went to America with two other vagabonds but with only one pair of shoes among them. He boarded a ship— not the right one but the one he could get on. Upon arrival, America suddenly turned out to be England, and the brother mistakenly disembarked at London. In London, the three barefoot men collected cigarette butts. The three hungry men would make new cigarettes out of the tobacco from the butts, and then one (each in turn) would put the shoes on and ply his trade up and down the embankment. Within a few months, the tobacco business had expanded beyond the scope of butt cigarettes. It had expanded to an understanding of where America and prosperity were located—to the point of shoes and a third-class ticket for everyone for some place called Brazil. On board ship they won a tidy sum at cards. In Brazil, through enterprise and gambling, they increased the sum to thousands of dollars.

Then the brother took everything he had and went to the races, putting his money down on the tote. His ungrateful mare brought up the rear, little concerned about the brother she had made a pauper in thirty-seven seconds flat. A year later the brother jumped to Argentina and bought a bicycle, having acquired a lifelong contempt for nature.

When he became adept at the bicycle, the indefatigable son of Kishinev took up bicycle racing.

To come in first, the racer had to make a small detour onto the sidewalk, which did gain him a minute, but he also pitched some inattentive old lady into the gutter.

The upshot was that he had to surrender his great big first prize to one slightly rumpled granny.

Grief-stricken, the brother went to Mexico, where he quickly penetrated the artless law of colonial trade—the 300 percent markup: 100 percent for naiveté, 100 percent for costs, and 100 percent filched on the installment plan.

After he made a tidy little bundle, he moved over to the American side, where all profit is protected.

Here the brother doesn't get bogged down in any one business. He buys a soapmaking factory for six thousand and sells it for nine. He acquires a store and resells it when he sniffs bankruptcy a month off. Now he's one of the most respected figures in town. Chairman of dozens of charities, when Pavlova came to town he spent three hundred dollars on one dinner.

"There he is," my admiring storyteller pointed him out on the street. The brother was whizzing by in a new auto, testing it out; he had sold his own car for seven and rushed out to buy this one for twelve.

My companion was standing servilely on the sidewalk and smiling so hard you could see his gold crowns, his eyes locked on the car.

"That's the young haberdasher," I was told. "He and his brother have only been here four years, but they've already been to Chicago twice for merchandise. The brother's a real washout, Greek, I think, always writing poetry. They appointed him teacher in the next town, but nothing's going to come of him anyway."

Overjoyed at my being a Russian, my fantastically cordial new friend led me through the streets of Laredo.

He ran ahead to open doors for me, fed me a very long meal, winced at a single offer from me to pay, and took me to the cinema, all the while gazing only at me and rejoicing if I laughed. And all this without the slightest notion of who I was, just because of one word: Muscovite.

from *The Rain God*

Arturo Islas

Tía Cuca was lighter-skinned than her sister Chona. Nevertheless, like Mama Chona, she was unmistakably Mexican with enough Indian blood to give her those aristocratic cheekbones the two sisters liked the younger generation to believe were those of highborn Spanish ladies who just happened to find themselves in the provinces of Mexico. Their Spanish was a cultivated imitation of the Castilian Spanish they believed reigned supreme over all dialects, and they despaired that anyone in Miguel Chico's generation, because they were attending "American" schools, would ever master it. They were right.

Mama Chona and Tía Cuca were taught by nuns in Mexico before the 1910 revolution. If they did not approve of the language in which Miguel Chico and JoEl were learning to read and write, they did approve of the discipline under which they were instructed. "Listen to your teachers at school," Mama Chona told them in Spanish, "and learn to speak English the way they do. I speak it with an accent, so you must not imitate me. I will teach you how to speak Spanish properly for the family occasions."

Tía Cuca was more romantic about language. "Italian is the language of music," she said to the children in her lovely contralto voice. "French is the language of manners, English is the language of business, and Spanish—don't forget, children—is the language of love and romance." The only poetry she thought worth reading was that written in Spanish, "because it sings!"

Because of them Miguel Chico and his cousins learned to communicate in both languages fluently, a privilege denied the next generation, who began learning to read and write after Tía Cuca was dead and Mama Chona nearly senile. That generation understood Spanish but spoke it in ways that would have scandalized Mama Chona and her sister. "A truly educated person," Mama Chona told them, "speaks more than one language fluently."

The snobbery Mama Chona and Tía Cuca displayed in every way possible against the Indian and in favor of the Spanish in the Angels' blood was a constant puzzlement to most of the grandchildren. In subtle, persistent ways, family members were taught that only the Spanish side of their heritage was worth honoring and preserving; the Indian in them was pagan, servile, instinctive rather than intellectual, and was to be suppressed, its existence denied. Aunt Eduviges, Aunt Jesús María, and even Miguel Grande had learned this lesson well, taking to heart their mother's prejudices; Felix and Mema would have no part of it.

Miguel Chico's father practiced this kind of bigotry when he referred to the Mexican women who helped Juanita with the housework as "wetbacks." One of those "wetbacks" helped take care of Mama Chona in her last years with the devotion and humor of those saints who dedicate themselves to poverty.

"Is the Indian here yet?" Mama Chona would ask from the heights of her sickbed, even after she had forgotten most of her own children's names. "Tell her to do the dishes." The "Indian"—the last in a long line of distinguished women from across the border to be closely associated with the family—would say without sarcasm and with a wink at the children, "I've been here for several months, Señora Angel, and the dishes are already dry. Can I get you anything?" Having forgotten her question, Mama Chona would comment grouchily on the terrible accent of the illiterate masses.

Had she been alive in that period of Mama Chona's long act of dying, Tía Cuca would have joined her in criticizing the accent. She would not, however, have commented on any of the Indians' personal lives, no matter how often her sister asked her opinion of this or that girl who happened to be cleaning the house that year. Tía Cuca judged no one in matters of the heart.

Tía Cuca and Felix loved each other and were drawn together with the instinct of great sexual sinners. Like fat, contented cats, they enjoyed sharing a meal alone or in Mama Chona's company. Their frequent, unprovoked laughter would cause Mama Chona to ask, "What are you two up to now?" Since they were "up to" nothing, Tía Cuca, unable to resist teasing her puritanical sister, would answer, "You wouldn't understand, Chona; you've never understood anything about love." She meant "lust" and Chona knew it. Her defense was to ignore Cuca's comments except to indicate with a slight twitch of her nostrils that she had just caught the traces of a bad smell in the air. Tía Cuca and Felix laughed all the more.

Because his father was her favorite and because he was the youngest grandchild, JoEl spent more time in his childhood with Tía Cuca than did any of his older cousins or siblings, who had already served their periods of paying her their respects. He was frequently at Mama Chona's and thus it often fell to him to accompany her on the long bus ride to the house in the desert where Tía Cuca lived with a man named Davis. JoEl did not like these weekly visits, which were tediously the same, and he felt nothing for the old lady—an antipathy reinforced by his father's devotion to her.

JoEl and Mama Chona took the bus at ten in the morning when the weather was good, stayed for lunch, and returned by three to take their naps. For these visits, Mama Chona wore her formal black dress, put on black gloves, and carried her black umbrella. Puzzled, JoEl asked why she needed the umbrella, since rain fell only six or seven times a year in torrents that lasted but a few minutes. "I don't want the sun to burn my skin," she said. "It's dark enough already." JoEl looked closely at her very dark, leathery skin but asked no more questions. It was all a mystery, like her wearing even on the hottest days the black woolen dress that reached almost to the ground.

The mystery was enhanced by the atmosphere of sin that surrounded Tía Cuca's relationship with Mr. Davis. The old man, very white, tall, and skinny, reminded JoEl of a plucked pigeon, though he had a nice voice and a kind manner. Tía Cuca and Mr. Davis had lived together for as long as any of them, even his oldest cousins, could remember, and they remained together until they both died several weeks apart some time after JoEl's father was killed. Everyone knew they were lovers, but because Tía Cuca's explanations were deliberately evasive, no one knew if they had ever married. She always called him "Meester Davis," and he called her "Dolly." . . .

JoEl remembered mostly the way she smelled. All little old ladies, even Mama Chona, seemed to have that rancid odor, like dried-up sticks. He did not like touching his great-aunt or his grandmother. When he had to give Tía Cuca a hug at their arrival and departure, he closed his eyes and held his breath. But she always embraced him long enough for him to have to breathe again and inhale her sour acacia mustiness. Then she gave him a nickel and told him to hide it somewhere. In that way, when he needed money, he would remember it and be wonderfully surprised. He never hid them. What good would nickels do him in the future? Such gifts were a great sacrifice for her, but he did not think of that. He bought his chiclets and chewed them.

His grandmother and her sister were the oldest human beings he knew, except for his mother's uncle Celso, who cut JoEl's hair every three weeks and smelled of lavender and Vitalis. Mama Chona and Tía Cuca must have been seventy and sixty-five respectively when he was born, though age was another mystery and no one ever said exactly how old they were at any given time, not even at their deaths. Rumor from his mother's side of the family calculated that Mama Chona was ninety eight years old when she died, an estimation exaggerated to provoke Jesús María and Eduviges who had stopped counting after their forty-fifth birthdays. JoEl loved it when the grownups argued about their ages. As far as he was concerned, however, Mama Chona's life had ended when she could no longer remember the names of her children, much less those of their children.

On their visits, Mama Chona always warned him not to notice Tía Cuca's lame leg. But he loved to watch her use the black cane with the pewter handle, and later the crutches, with grandeur, as if they were extensions of herself. The two old ladies would soon settle down to talk, and their conversation, unimportant and for its own sake, after a while bored JoEl. When he grew restless he could on warm days play in the small yard within sight of the living room. On cold and windy days he was permitted to look at some of the picture books Tía Cuca had brought from Mexico. He enjoyed those books and was able to recognize some of the words Mama Chona had taught him in Spanish. Sometimes he would say them, and the two old ladies commented on his brillance with bird-like sounds and exclamations, returning then to their conversation as if there had been no interruption. . . .

Although they were always poor, the old ladies retained their aristocratic assumptions and remained señoras of the most pretentious sort. Their hands were never in dishwater, and cleaning house was work for the Indians, even if the old ladies could not afford to have them do it. Consequently, their homes were dusty, and his aunt Juanita or his father would do the weeks' collection of dishes. The only time JoEl saw Mama Chona lose her composure was when his uncle Miguel Grande scolded her for letting the cockroaches lick her plates clean on the sideboard. After his uncle left, Mama Chona held the plates one by one under the faucet in such a way that her fingers did not get wet, and she cried before, during, and after the loathsome task. JoEl's aunt Juanita, a meticulous housekeeper like his own mother, never could put up with his grandmother's ways.

Juanita seemed more tolerant of Tía Cuca's laziness, partly because she was lame and partly because the idea of cleaning up her place seemed hopeless, even to Juanita who would have gotten rid of the dust in the desert if she could. Until the day she died, no matter who threatened or cajoled her, Tía Cuca refused to do menial work. Her hands were small and exquisite and with great pride she said, "We may not have enough to eat, but when I go out, I put on my gloves and my hat. I am a civilized human being." She was secretly proud of having lighter skin than Mama Chona, and she made certain that the sun never touched her face and hands, the only parts of her any of them ever saw.

I Will Send For You or I Will Come Home Rich

Richard Rodriguez

You stand around. You smoke. You spit. You are wearing your two shirts, two pants, two underpants. Jesús says if they chase you, throw that bag down. Your plastic bag is your mama, all you have left: the yellow cheese she wrapped has formed a translucent rind; the laminated scapular of the Sacred Heart nestles, flame in its cleft. Put it in your pocket. Inside. Put it in your underneath pants' pocket. The last hour of Mexico is twilight, the shuffling of feet. Jesús says they are able to see in the dark. They have X-rays and helicopters and searchlights. Jesús says wait, just wait, till he says. Though most of the men have started to move. You feel the hand of Jesús clamp your shoulder, fingers cold as ice. *Venga, corre.* You run. All the rest happens without words. Your feet are tearing dry grass, your heart is lashed like a mare. You trip, you fall. You are now in the United States of America. You are a boy from a Mexican village. You have come into the country on your knees with your head down. You are a man.

Papa, what was it like?

I am his second son, his favorite child, his confidant. After we have polished the DeSoto, we sit in the car and talk. I am sixteen years old. I fiddle with the knobs of the radio. He is fifty.

He will never say. He was an orphan there. He had no mother, he remembered none. He lived in a village by the ocean. He wanted books and he had none.

You are lucky, boy.

In the nineteenth century, American contractors reached down into Mexico for cheap labor. Men were needed to build America: to lay track, to mine, to dredge, to harvest. It was a man's journey. And, as a year's contract was extended, as economic dependence was established, sons followed their fathers north. When American jobs turned scarce—during the Depression, as today—Mexicans were rounded up and thrown back over the border. But for generations it has been the rite of passage for the poor Mexican male.

I will send for you or I will come home rich.

In the '50s, Mexican men were contracted to work in America as *braceros,* farm workers. I saw them downtown in Sacramento. I saw men my age drunk in Plaza Park on Sundays, on their backs on the grass. I was a boy at 16, but I was an American. At 16, I wrote a gossip column, "The Watchful Eye," for my school paper.

Or they would come into town on Monday nights for the wrestling matches or on Tuesdays for boxing. They worked over in Yolo County. They were men without women. They were Mexicans without Mexico.

On Saturdays, they came into town to the Western Union office where they sent money—money turned into humming wire and then turned back into money—all the way down into Mexico. They were husbands, fathers, sons. They kept themselves poor for Mexico.

Much that I would come to think, the best I would think about male Mexico, came as much from those chaste, lonely men as from my own father who made false teeth and who—after 30 years in America—owned a yellow stucco house on the east side of town.

The male is responsible. The male is serious. A man remembers.

Fidel, the janitor at church, lived over the garage at the rectory. Fidel spoke Spanish and was Mexican. He had a wife down there, people said; some said he had grown children. But too many years had passed and he didn't go back. Fidel had to do for himself. Fidel had a clean piece of linoleum on the floor, he had an iron bed, he had a table and a chair. He had a coffee pot and a frying pan and a knife and a fork and a spoon, I guess. And everything else Fidel sent back to Mexico. Sometimes, on summer nights, I would see his head through the bars of the little window over the garage at the rectory.

The migration of Mexico is not only international, South to North. The epic migration in Mexico, and throughout Latin America, is from the village to the city. And throughout Latin America, the city has ripened, swollen with the century. Lima. Caracas. Mexico City. So the journey to Los Angeles is much more than a journey from Spanish to English. It is the journey from *tu*—the familiar, the erotic, the intimate pronoun—to the repellent *usted* of strangers' eyes.

Most immigrants to America came from villages. The America that Mexicans find today, at the decline of the century, is a closed-circuit city of ramps and dark towers, a city without God.

It is 1986 and I am a journalist. I am asking questions of a Mexican woman in her East L.A. house. She is watchful and pretty, in her 30s, she wears an apron. Her two boys—Roy and Danny—are playing next door. Her husband is a tailor. He is sewing in a bright bedroom at the back of the house. His feet work the humming treadle of an old Singer machine as he croons Mexican love songs by an open window.

For attribution, mama says she is grateful for America. This country has been so good to her family. They have been here ten years and look, already they have this nice house. Outside the door is Mexican Los Angeles; in the distance, the perpetual orbit of traffic. Here old women walk slowly under lace parasols. The Vietnam vet pushes his tinkling ice cream cart past little green lawns. Teenagers in this neighborhood have scorpions tattooed onto their biceps.

The U.S. Border Patrol station at San Ysidro has a PR officer who handles journalists; he says he is glad to have us—"helps in Washington if the public can get a sense of the scope of the problem."

Right now he is occupied with a West German film crew. They were promised a helicopter. Where is the helicopter? Two journalists from a Tokyo daily—with five canvas bags of camera equipment between them—lean against the wall, arms folded. One of them brings up his wrist to look at his watch. A reporter from Chicago catches my sleeve. Did I hear about the other night? What? There was a carload of Yugoslavians caught coming over.

The Japanese reporter who is not looking at his watch is popping Cheez-Its into his mouth. The border patrol secretary has made some kind of mistake. She has me down as a reporter for *American Farmer*. Fat red steer in clover. Apologies. Whiteout. "I . . . agree to abide by any oral directions given to me during the operation by the officer in charge of the unit . . ." Having signed the form, I am soon assigned a patrolman with whom I will spend the night.

We stop for coffee at a donut shop along the freeway. The patrolman tells me about growing up Tex-Mex in Dallas. After city college, he worked with an antipoverty agency. Then he was a probation officer. He got married, needed money, moved to California and took his job with the *migra*.

Once into the dark, I cannot separate myself from the patrolman's intention. We ride through the dark in a Ramcharger, both intent upon finding people who do not want to be found.

We come upon a posse of border patrolmen preparing to ride into the canyon on horseback. I get out of the truck; ask the questions; pet the horses, prickly, moist, moving in my hand in the dark. The officers call me sir. It is as though I am being romanced at some sort of cowboy cotillion. "Here," says one, "have a look." He invites me so close to his chin I can smell cologne as I peer through his night-vision scope.

Mexico is poor. But my mama says there are no love songs like the love songs of Mexico. She hums a song she can't remember. The ice cream there is creamier than here. Someday we will see. The people are kinder—poor, but kinder to each other.

My mother's favorite record is *Mariachis de Mexico y Pepe Villa con Orquesta.* Every Sunday she plays her record ("Rosas de Plata"; "Madrecita Linda") while she makes us our pot-roast dinner.

Men sing in Mexico. Men are strong and silent. But in song the Mexican male is granted license he is otherwise denied. The male can admit longing, pain, desire.

HAIII-EEE—a cry like a comet rises over the song. A cry like mock weeping tickles the refrain of Mexican love songs. The cry is meant to encourage the balladeer—it is the raw edge of his sentiment. HAIIII-EEEE. It is the man's sound. A ticklish arching of semen, a node wrung up a guitar string, until it bursts in a descending cascade of mockery. HAI. HAI. HAI. The cry of a jackal under the moon, the whistle of the phallus, the maniacal song of the skull.

Tell me, Papa.
What?
About Mexico.
I lived with the family of my uncle. I was the orphan in the village. I used to ring the church bells in the morning, many steps up in the dark. When I'd get up to the tower I could see the ocean.
The village, Papa, the houses too. . . .
The ocean. He studies the polished hood of our beautiful blue DeSoto.

Mexico was not the past. People went back and forth. People came up for work. People went back home, to mama or wife or village. The poor had mobility. Men who were too poor to take a bus walked from Sonora to Sacramento.
Relatives invited relatives. Entire Mexican villages got re-created in

three stories of a single house. In the fall, after the harvest in the Valley, families of Mexican adults and their American children would load up their cars and head back to Mexico in caravans, for weeks, for months. The schoolteacher said to my mother what a shame it was the Mexicans did that—took their children out of school.

Like wandering Jews. They carried their home with them, back and forth; they had no true home but the tabernacle of memory.

Each year the American kitchen takes on a new appliance.

The children are fed and grow tall. They go off to school with children from Vietnam, from Kansas, from Hong Kong. They get into fights. They come home and they say dirty words.

The city will win. The city will give the children all the village could not—VCRs, hairstyles, drumbeat. The city sings mean songs, dirty songs. But the city will sing the children a great Protestant hymn.

You can be anything you want to be.

We are parked. The patrolman turns off the lights of the truck—"back in a minute"—a branch scrapes the door as he rolls out of the van to take a piss. The brush crackles beneath his receding steps. It is dark. Who? Who is out there? The faces I have seen in San Diego dishwashers, janitors, gardeners. They come all the time, no big deal. There are other Mexicans who tell me the crossing is dangerous.

The patrolman returns. We drive again. I am thinking of epic migrations in history books—pan shots of orderly columns of Paleolithic peoples, determined as ants, heeding some trumpet of history, traversing miles and miles . . . of paragraph.

The patrolman has turned off the headlights. He can't have to piss again? Suddenly the truck accelerates, pitches off the rutted road, banging, slamming a rock, faster, ignition is off, the truck is soft-pedaled to a stop in the dust; the patrolman is out like a shot. The cab light is on. I sit exposed for a minute. I can't hear anything. Cautiously, I decide to follow —I leave my door open as the patrolman has done. There is a boulder in the field. Is that it? The patrolman is barking in Spanish. His flashlight is trained on the boulder like a laser, he weaves it along the grain as though he is untying a knot. He is: three men and a woman stand up. The men are young—16, 17. The youngest is shivering. He makes a fist. He looks down. The woman is young too. Or she could be the mother? Her legs are very thin. She wears a man's digital wristwatch. They come from somewhere. And somewhere—San Diego, Sacramento—somebody is waiting for them.

The patrolman tells them to take off their coats and their shoes, throw them in a pile. Another truck rolls up.

As a journalist, I am allowed to come close. I can even ask questions. There are no questions.

You can take pictures, the patrolman tells me.

I stare at the faces. They stare at me. To them I am not bearing witness; I am part of the process of being arrested. I hold up my camera. Their eyes swallow the flash, a long tunnel, leading back.

I will send for you or I will come home rich.

The Trouble with English

Gloria López-Stafford

In the Segundo Barrio during the 1940s, people spoke Spanish. They spoke the Spanish they brought with them from their *ranchos,* villages, and cities. They also brought the music of their accents. You could tell by the quality of their speech whether they were country or city people. Spanish in the 1940s in south El Paso was formal and polite. People apologized if they said a word like *estúpido.* I would often wonder why that required an apology. And I would be told that people from rural areas are not open with criticism and do not want to offend with what they consider vulgar language.

When people left the barrio, they began using English more. You still spoke Spanish at home because that was what your family used. Then when you spoke with someone who also spoke both languages, the language evolved to a mixture of English and Spanish that became an art form. Sometimes sentences might be in one language with certain words in the other. Other times whole paragraphs might be in one language and only a few sentences in the other. It was a living language, a musical score that conveyed the optimal sense, meaning, and feeling from both languages that a single language might not achieve. The combination drew criticism from purists and people who did not speak both. They accused the bilingual person of being lazy or undisciplined. But I think it was a love for both languages that made it impossible to be faithful to just one. On the other hand, cussing or profanity were best in English. The words were just words to me. Cussing in Spanish was painful and created emotions that led to guilt. And, it was unacceptable to our parents and priests.

The first time I remember having problems with English was the year before Carmen came to live with us. At least once a week Palm and I would have a talk about why I wasn't learning English. I saw no reason to. I had to experience a need for it, and that is what happened.

"You have to learn English, Gloria," Palm would say.

"I don't want to. I don't have to. I don't need it," I would stubbornly refuse.

"I suppose you didn't need it at the border on Saturday when immigration held you after you were in Juárez with López and you couldn't answer their questions?" he said firmly. "I had to leave the store to go and get them to release you. All because you can't carry on a conversation in English."

I had created problems for Palm and myself, but I didn't want to learn English and that was that.

On this particular morning, I waited for Palm to get tired of the topic and to move on to something else. But he didn't. He continued.

"The note the teacher sent home says that you will not speak English. She says that everyone speaks for you. And she says that you talk all the time, but in Spanish! Its been a month since school started and she says you will not cooperate. She says she is going to have to punish you. She wrote to inform me that she is at the end of her patience with you," Palm said.

"So that is what the *mugre,* dirty, note said. I thought she liked me," I said as I thought of how she and I grinned at each other every day. I didn't understand what she was saying and she didn't know what I was saying. She could have been speaking Chinese just like the Chinos near the Cuauhtemoc market in Juárez. I just didn't want to speak English.

"It sounds ugly. And I look stupid speaking it," I admitted when I saw the look on Palm's face.

"It's because you don't use it enough to get used to it," Palm tried to explain.

"My friends and I don't need to speak it. We have our own way of speaking." I continued the argument until I noticed that Palm was frustrated and quiet. I decided to play. I put my left hand on my hip and shook my right index finger menacingly.

"Wo do bo to do ri ra do fo, da mo, meeester!" I said in gibberish. "Ha, no, meeezter?" I raised my eyebrow and looked at Palm. "That's English!"

"Payasa. You are very stubborn. You need to learn English." Palm started up again. "My son is coming to visit and he speaks English."

The last remark caught my attention. I turned my eyes to the picture of Palm's son, which was displayed in a large oval frame. He resembled Palm. I wondered why he was only my half brother. When I was younger, I thought it was because only the upper part of his body was in the picture. Palm corrected me. He told me his son had a different mother and was the only one of his children that stayed in touch with him. He loved Palm very much and would write to him every week. He was the youngest child and had been in college when my father went to Mexico. Palm's son's light eyes seemed to follow me around the room.

Palm was still talking about a visit from his son when I found my voice and said, "¡Que suave! When he comes, I'll tell him all about me and the neighborhood." Palm just nodded his head and gave me a strange look.

The next week, when I got home from school, I was frightened because I thought someone was in the apartment. But Palm called to me when I pressed my nose against the screen to look inside.

"Entra, mi'ja." Palm's voice was happy. I pulled the screen door open and entered the living room. A man was with my father. He looked like my father, but he wasn't old; he looked familiar. Then, suddenly, my eyes turned to the picture on the wall. I looked at the man and I looked at the picture. They were the same!

"¡Hola! ¿Cómo estás?" I yelled with happiness as I ran to hug the stranger. He returned the hug. I was overjoyed. Palm was telling the truth about his son coming to visit. Here he was . . . all of him!

Palm's son opened his mouth and said something to Palm who was telling him something too. They were speaking Chinese!

"Papá, tell him that I speak Spanish," I told my father.

"Yoya, he knows." Palm spoke slowly because he knew how I would react. "He doesn't speak Spanish. He only speaks English. I told you many times."

I was speechless. What a dirty *trampa,* trick!

"Didn't you tell him I didn't speak English? Did you forget?" I questioned my Palm as the other Palm looked on with the biggest and sweetest smile. How could he not speak Spanish? I started to cry, but the other Palm understood as my father told him in Chinese what the problem was. Palm's son laughed as he picked me up and kissed me as he said something to my father. I looked to Palm for a translation.

"He says you're as precious as he knew you would be. He's sorry that he can't speak Spanish. He has never been able to learn," my father said.

I hugged his son and just watched them as they talked. Occasionally, Palm would tell me what they were saying if he thought it might interest me. I just kept looking into our visitor's beautiful face. My little chest was heavy with the weight of my broken heart. I had so wanted to be able to talk with him. I couldn't believe it. And I knew Palm had warned me.

When the sunset, the color of West Texas sweet potato flesh, began to spread across the barrio, our visitor said he had to leave. We went outside. Palm's son picked me up and kissed me. Palm softly told me what his son was saying to me.

"He says he loves you, Yoya. He hopes that when you meet again, either you'll know English or he'll know Spanish."

I hugged and kissed my favorite visitor back. It would be many years before I would see him again and it would be long after our father's death. But on this evening, my father and I watched him as he walked to Virginia Street where he had parked his car. Palm and I sat on the cement step. As the car pulled off with my half brother, I turned to Palm and said with determination and sadness,

"It's time I learned English, Papi."

"Sí, corazón, yes." He understood.

Los mexicanos que hablan inglés / The Mexicans Who Speak English

A CORRIDO FROM THE TEXAS-MEXICAN CANCIONERO

FOLKSONGS OF THE LOWER BORDER, BY AMÉRICO PAREDES

Anonymous

In Texas it is terrible how things are all mixed up;
no one says "hasta mañana," it's nothing but "goodbye."

And "howdy-dee-do, my friend, and I'll see you tomorrow";
when they want to say "diez reales" they say "dollar and a quarter."

I made love to a Texas-Mexican girl, one of those with a parasol;
I said to her, "Will you go along with me?" and she told me, "Looky
    heah!"

I made love to another fashionable lady, one of those with a *garsolé;*
I said to her, "Will you go along with me?" and she told me, "What you
    say?"

Then I went to the depot to talk to Doña Inés;
I talked to her in Spanish, and she answered me in English.

All of us want to speak the American language,
without understanding our own Spanish tongue.

In Texas it is terrible how things are all mixed up;
no one says "hasta mañana," it's nothing but "goodbye."

. . . .

En Texas es terrible
por la revoltura que háy,
no hay quién diga hasta mañana,
nomás puro *goodbye.*

Y *jau-dididú mai fren,*
en ayl sí yu tumora,
para decir "diez reales"
dicen *dola yene cuora.*

Yo enamoré una tejana,
y de esas de sombrilla,
le dije:—¿Te vas conmigo?—
y me dijo:—*¡Luque jía!*—

Enamoré otra catrina,
de esas de garsolé,
le dije:—¿Te vas conmigo?—
y me dijo:—¿*Huachu sei?*—

Luego me fui pa'l dipo
a hablar con doña Inés,
yo le hablaba en castellano
y me contestó en inglés.

Todos queremos hablar
la lengua americana,
sin poder comprender
la nuestra castellana.

Y en Texas es terrible
por la revoltura que hay,
no hay quién diga "hasta mañana,"
nomás puro *goodbye.*

Part 3

A border implies limitations, a frontier intimates
the land beyond.
These poets write of the frontier.

To Live in the Borderlands Means You . . .

Gloria Anzaldúa

are neither *hispana india negra española*
ni gabacha, eres mestiza, mulata, half-breed
caught in the crossfire between camps
while carrying all five races on your back
not knowing which side to turn to, run from;

To live in the Borderlands means knowing
that the *india* in you, betrayed for 500 years,
is no longer speaking to you,
that *mexicanas* call you *rajetas,*
that denying the Anglo inside you
is as bad as having denied the Indian or Black;

Cuando vives en la frontera
people walk through you, the wind steals your voice,
you're a *burra, buey,* scapegoat,
forerunner of a new race,
half and half—both woman and man, neither—
a new gender;

To live in the Borderlands means to
put *chile* in the borscht,
eat whole wheat *tortillas,*
speak Tex-Mex with a Brooklyn accent;
be stopped by *la migra* at the border checkpoints;

Living in the Borderlands means you fight hard to
resist the gold elixir beckoning from the bottle,
the pull of the gun barrel,
the rope crushing the hollow of your throat;

In the Borderlands
you are the battleground
where enemies are kin to each other;

you are at home, a stranger,
the border disputes have been settled
the volley of shots have shattered the truce
you are wounded, lost in action
dead, fighting back;

To live in the Borderlands means
the mill with the razor white teeth wants to shred off
your olive-red skin, crush out the kernel, your heart
pound you pinch you roll you out
smelling like white bread but dead;

To survive the Borderlands
you must live *sin fronteras*
be a crossroads.

burra. Donkey.
buey. Oxen.
gabacha. A Chicano term for a white woman.
rajetas. Literally, "split," that is, having betrayed your word.
sin fronteras. Without borders.

Río Grande

José Antonio Burciaga

P'Osoge de los Tiguas
change to Río Caudaloso,
superseded by Río Grande
also called El Bravo
by the Meskins
and Reeo Grand
by John Wayne
mean big river
of running water
from bleeding clouds
upon Mama Earth's
soft dry bosoms
that trickles down
to the banks
of dry recuerdos
floating down,
chicharras serenading
lazy summer noons
hot as black rubber tube
down swift currents
on stomach high
or knee deep water
where big boys and little men
drowned long time ago.

Steel lace bleed pain
and barbed wire dances long
U.S. declarations,
"Where you from?
What you got?"

Stalled 55 Chevy
with overheated injun
behind wheel
while viejo

staggers under
heavy news print
of bad news cause hunch
and tin suitcases bulge
with sweet dresses
for Toña la novia,
la hermana y la olvidada,
from the bracero home,
from el otro lado,
from the mirada,
to the escapada,
for few pennies to cross
across the cruz
to work, to dance,
to hear foreign tongues
while back home
two mariachis sing along
to a sweet shoeshine.

The Río is called Bravo
because of the walking Pirañas
that patrol along
the steel laced fence.

Pirañas eat brown meat
certified by department of aliens,
where fishing license
is a Visa or green paper.

Holes in fishing nets piss Pirañas off
and brown fishermen walk on water
when Pirañas sleep or look the other way.

Nos Sentamos

PART 6: EL PASO

Ricardo Sánchez

el paso,
southernmost city
of New Mexico,
westernmost city
of Tejas,
you recline
between nations
and feel tensions
amidst
    peoples distrusting
  each other,
all
the
while
desert visages
dance
upon sage,
sand,
   and smog filled skies,
your mountains
fear
that someday
greenery
might bloom
upon them,
and sometimes
you whitewash murals
that people
might not learn
to laugh and sing,
schizoid city,
your definition of self
cries out

in chaos
every tuesday morning
and then is silent
for the rest of the week,
    your militants
roam
your alley ways,
each one wanting
to become
more than a furtive shadow
burrowing
through the bleakness
of a defeated city . . .
you are loved
for being a landing pad
for many a people
seeking quivira,
and you are hated
for being
an illusion
to those
who seek
meaning in
    the sunsets
o'er your mountains

Journeys

EL PASO/JUÁREZ, 1984

Benjamin Alire Sáenz

Every day she crosses. She
has been here before, has passed these streets
so often she no longer notices the shops
nor their names nor the people. No longer
notices the officials at the bridge who let her
pass as if she were going shopping. They know
her, know where she's going, do not ask questions.
They have stopped smiling at each other.
Each morning she walks from her
Juárez home, crosses the bridge to El Paso.
Downtown, she waits for a bus that takes her
to a house where she irons and cleans and cooks.
She is not afraid to get caught. The Border
Patrol does not stop her as she waits for
the bus after work. They know what she does,
know she has no permit—but how would it look
arresting decent people's maids? How
would it look? And besides, she's a woman
getting old. The Migra prefers to chase young men.
She no longer notices their green
vans. They do not exist for her.
Nor she, for them.
She does not mind the daily journeys,
not far, and "really," she says to herself,
"it is all one city, Juárez and El Paso.
The river is small and tired. A border? Ha!"
She sits, she laughs, she catches her bus to go home.
The woman whose house she cleans
asked her once if she wanted to be an American.
"No," she smiled, "I'm happy." What for,
she thought, what for? My children, they want

to live here. Not me. I belong in my Juárez.
She cooks, she cleans, she takes her bus.
She journeys every day. The journey is easy,
never takes a long time, and always it is sunny.
When it rains, the people who live here
praise God—but she, she curses him
for the spit that soaks her skin.

Naturalization Papers

Myriam Moscona

TRANSLATED BY Cynthia Steele

We daughters of foreign women
were born with minute compasses.
In nobler days
we visited Parisian museums.
We went into the Louvre in search of the Gioconda.
We too grew up amid adversity
and smiled predictable smiles.
If the war blew us out of the Old World,
a gust of wind condemns us to double vision.
We'll remain for perpetuity.
Torn between staying and leaving,
we'd like to give birth to storms,
so our blood will fall on terra firma
till our roots are lost in history.

To Tijuana

Miguel de Anda Jacobsen

TRANSLATED BY Miguel González-Gerth

There's a luminous flood of
colors in your shrill nocturnal thirst,
city of sorcery,
the sensual urn where highest love became sublime.

You turn your simple wildflowers
into taciturn evening moths,
leaving their day's caress to languish
in the glitter touching honey
and dawn.

In amber liquor you emerge,
dotted with citrus-like blisters,
a thousand grapefruits offering juicy morbid flesh.

A Saxon madness plunders your storehouse
while the steady prayer of your nuns begs forgiveness for parochial sins.

A Border Rose

Robert L. Jones

(Tijuana/San Ysidro, returning)

Four cars back from the checkpoint, Sunday
at dusk, and the radio and I are arm-
in-arm belting out "Guadalajara" when
a third voice, static-free and in tune,
joins us: it's the rose man!
We're the best mariachi trio ever!
We're so good the radios around us tune in
on their own, and the tourists, suddenly bi-lingual,
are with us, and the blanket seller, a family's worth
draping his shoulders, and the ceramics vendor,
one shoulder sustaining a flat-backed elephant,
the other a roped-together farrow of piglet-banks,
and the dead-battery man, parking for once
his live shopping-cart garage, with us too.
Even the border guard, who bends to one knee, arms outspread,
and croaks out the last few bars.
I'm about to spring from the car and hug them all
when I realize I'm next.
Instead I buy one white rose.
I pull up and the guard is all smiles,
his first since he took the job.
I tell him I'm a citizen
but my rose is alien and undocumented,
and he loves it, waving us through with both arms.
But ten miles toward home and ten to go,
I wonder how long it's been without water.
I turn on the interior light
and it's, no, not possible.
I pull over. But even flash-lit
it's pink.
Match-lit, moon-lit, streetlamp-lit,
it's still pink, and getting pinker and pinker
until it's red, then a red

so deep and real I'm a paramedic
flattened to the wall of the van,
afraid to touch the heart smoldering before me.
That's your rose.

for Patricia, the Rose Woman

Legal Alien

Pat Mora

Bi-lingual, Bi-cultural,
able to slip from "How's life?"
to "Me'stan volviendo loca,"
able to sit in a paneled office
drafting memos in smooth English,
able to order in fluent Spanish
at a Mexican restaurant,
American but hyphenated,
viewed by Anglos as perhaps exotic,
perhaps inferior, definitely different,
viewed by Mexicans as alien,
(their eyes say, "You may speak
Spanish but you're not like me")
an American to Mexicans
a Mexican to Americans
a handy token
sliding back and forth
between the fringes of both worlds
by smiling
by masking the discomfort
of being prejudged
Bi-laterally.

To My Fatherland

Trinidad V. Sánchez

TRANSLATED BY Trinidad Sánchez Jr.

Fatherland I ask for pardon
to the sky, I extend my arms.
I keep you in my heart
even though it is broken in pieces.

For a false paradise
today, I am an American,
if destiny wanted it this way
inside, I will always be Mexican.

But, Fatherland, we won't cry
a son you will never lose,
when I am born again
I promise, we will see each other again.

Dog Days

Once there was a dog who crossed the border from California into Baja California every day. The dog had a soft coat and manicured toenails. She even wore perfume. Her name was Oh-La-La. One day while crossing the border, the Tijuana dogs gathered around. "Where are you from?" one of them asked Oh-La-La.

"Oh, I'm from La Jolla."

"Very impressive," said the mangy mutts of Tijuana. "And what's your life like?"

"My owners have a big house, but they also have a yard where I can run. I sleep in a little wooden house of my own."

"That's quite something!" the Tijuana dogs said. "What do you eat?"

"Well, in the morning, I get canned dog food, in the afternoon a mix of cheese and meat, and later, leftovers from the family dinner. I also take a pill for my coat."

"You don't say!" proclaimed the Mexican dogs. "Well, tell us—if you live in La Jolla, you have a house of your own with a yard, and you eat meat—why do you come here all the time?"

"Pues," said Oh-La-La as she turned her head sideways. "To bark."

Part 4

For a boundary with obelisks
marking every mile, the U.S.–Mexico line
can be pretty hard to pin down.

Looking north, the writer discovers "Mexamerican culture" in border towns, with its inequities intact.

Two Faces, One Reality

Brianda Domecq

Alone now, the river runs nonchalantly, between the steep sierras, and the mountains and the desert without a single human trail along its banks. With the exception of a few isolated hamlets and some tiny settlements, dreaming beneath the sun in hopes that some day the highway will reach them, everything remains exactly as Robert T. Hill saw it, on his historic 1899 journey. He and his men were already tired; they had rowed ten hours a day for an entire month, anxious about potential dangers, worn out by the daytime heat and the nighttime cold and overwhelmed by the solitude of the canyons. Of little interest to them was the beauty of the region's landscapes; they wanted "civilization," to see a human face, to find themselves before a peaceful herd of sheep and, above all, to leave behind that river with its surprises and threats. They combed the crags and terraces in search of the sign which for decades had told the travelers they were near the town of Langtry: a giant eagle's nest, the biggest in America, in a cave above the southern bank. Finally, rounding a bend, they saw the enormous structure of boughs that hailed a meeting with their own kind.

The nest still exists as an enticement to visitors and ornithologists willing to sit for hours in the shade of the willows on the opposite shore waiting for its occupants to return. A futile wait: the nest has never been used again. It would be more worth their while to turn their binoculars toward the thick and robust willow grove around them where birds of all sizes and colors hide in the shadows. Hummingbirds and yellow finches, red and brown cardinals, flycatchers and woodpeckers raise a clamor in the cool verdure of the forest. On the bank, a trunk sawed down by sharp teeth testifies to a beaver's visit. The fresh footprints of wild boars, deer and wild turkey reveal the reason for so much illegal hunting in the region.

A few kilometers away you'll find the "town" of Langtry beside the highway, which might just as easily be missed if traveling at high speeds. A gas station, a dry goods store advertising cold beer and a tourists' center which preserves the Tavern/Judge's Chambers of Judge Roy Bean where the "Law West of the Pecos" was handed down in past centuries. Roy Bean, travelling whiskey salesman, arrived at these lairs just after the completion of the Southern Pacific Railway, in 1882, and convinced the Texas Rangers, with reason or cunning, to name him the first judge of the county. He handed out justice and booze equally from his perch in the "Jersey Lily" saloon, which was named after the British actress Lillie Langtry, with whom he was hopelessly in love and whose photograph presided over both judicial blunders and outrageous drunkenness. But on the southern shore Roy Bean was best known for having organized the first full-fledged prize-fight over the river. In one of the major islets of the Bravo, which for a long time had remained outside the jurisdiction of both countries, the colorful judge arranged, to international cheers, the encounter between Maher and Fitzsimmons, prohibited by the laws of the United States, Mexico and Texas.

In those days the Bravo, more than accustomed to feuds between humans, flowed along, absorbing the waters of the Pecos River and the Devil's River. It passed between the dry and dusty Villa Acuña on the right and the green and blossoming Del Rio on the left, to begin its descent toward the Villas del Norte in Tamaulipas. But, in 1969, it found itself before a long and tall concrete wall stretching from one side to the other: just like millions of years before in the Juárez Valley, the Bravo was forced to whirl back upon itself until it formed the third largest international dam in the world: the Amistad Dam.

On the sustaining wall of the dam two enormous eagles—one with a serpent in its beak and the other with an olive branch in its talon—face each other, their backs turned upon the brilliant sapphire of the lake resting in that brown and semi-arid landscape. There, presidents Gustavo Díaz Ordáz and Richard Nixon, their backs turned upon Tlatelolco and Vietnam, exchanged handshakes to inaugurate the dam; and there, its back turned upon the Mexican reality, American tourism plows through the waters on both sides of the border in expensive ski, fishing, and sail boats.

Saturdays in Ciudad Acuña and Del Rio reveal different activities; along the north shore it is barely nine o'clock in the morning, while on the other side ten has already struck and a crowd of people waits in line to prettify their cars at the automatic car wash of the Bravo. Just below the international bridge, dusty autos wait upon a rocky clearing while their owners share hot bean burritos, pass out chorizo and potatoes being passed out from a basket; a vendor distributes beer from an ice-filled tub. The river, which has deposited its mud and silt at the bottom of the dam, runs clean and clear; the cars back up until the water reaches the mud-flaps. Children and teen-agers, between play and work, rub, polish and scrub, and douse each other with tubs of water.

Don Andrés oversees while two of his ranch hands make his Ford pickup sparkle. He brought it over from north of the Bravo just two months ago, but it was carefully painted with colorful streaks and other designs of his choice by a Mexican artist. Today especially he wants it to shine because at noon he'll be going to the famous Super Bull in Del Rio where some of the bulls from his own cattle ranch will appear. Equally flashy are his cowboy boots, his new denim jeans, its thick belt with a silver buckle, the white shirt specially tailored in San Antonio to accommodate the dimensions of his beautiful beer belly, and his new grey Stetson with its rattlesnake headband. With one hand he touches up his flowing gray moustache with the other he fondles the greenbacks in his pocket that later will go toward bets and the fifteen dollar entry fee. This gives him the right to a place in the shade where he'll meet his friend, the rich Texan, from whom he has every intention of obtaining some pocket money.

On the other hand, it isn't so easy to make don Pepe's old Chevrolet shine, with its bodywork "hand-done," as they say, and its multitude of scrapes, dents and craters already beginning to rust. Maybe this year he'll paint it. At least the kids will leave it clean. Don Pepe couldn't manage a ticket to the Super Bull, not because he didn't try, but because the cheapest one a seat in the sun, cost eight dollars, with the economic crisis that would be too many pesos just to go see bulls ridden and drink gringo beer at a dollar-fifty a can. Once, years ago, he had gone alone, because it wasn't quite a family atmosphere—too many drunks, too much betting, lots of shouting—and it wasn't even that great a spectacle. There was no music, the beer was flat and nobody could hope to understand the announcer's jokes, except maybe the white guys. Nothing but bull riding. Essentially it was the same as a *charrería,* or horse show, with less grace, more machismo and, without a doubt, bulls three times bigger than any bull in a Mexican ring. He'd rather take the family for a visit to the dam, then out to eat downtown and maybe later to the rodeo being advertised for five o'clock right there in Acuña. Even though there would be no big bulls, skirmishes or horsemen's bets, the live music and the announced appearance of Pedro Infante's sons, just beginning their nationwide tour, would thrill the family.

So it is in the sister cities. The Super Bull in San Felipe del Rio, Texas, is nothing more that a grandiose imitation of the diverse Mexican jaripeo, or rodeo, in Ciudad Acuña de Coahuila. The Anglo colonization has not succeeded, in its 150 years, in erasing the more than 300 years of Hispanic traditions. The new colonizers were colonized in turn, and a "Mexamerican" culture was created. What Hollywood did for the cowboy, the Mexican cinema could never do for the vaquero. The Mexicans saw the transformation, via a revolver, of an image of themselves, romanticized in a North American hero, that had very little to do with the hard life on the range. Ropes, horses, boots, hats, cowhandling skills and machismo are first cousins on either side of the border, though the New Yorkers may view them as John Wayne inventions.

The same is true with food. Over there they call "fajitas" what over here are "*arracheras*": strips of grilled meat in a tortilla. Nachos were born in Piedras Negras, Coahuila, though today they are eaten with more frequency in Washington, D.C. than in Mexico City. You can add "chili" and ground beef to beans and call it "chili-con-carne" but it's still just frijoles.

Perhaps for this reason doña Soledad finds herself so comfortable on the north side and doesn't really miss anything though she is a native of Saltillo. She now has her own house with its roofed "porche" where she sits in her rocking chair in the afternoons and her own front yard which borders a wide tree-lined street. Hers is exactly like every other house on the street, but she has added her own personal touch: plastic, one-gallon water jugs filled with different colored water, blue, red, yellow, green and orange, adorn each side of the walkway leading out to the sidewalk. They say the jugs ward off ants and perhaps that's true, but what she likes best about them are their colors, which remind her of the piñatas and the delicate paper lanterns of her youth. Yes, she's happy; she's pleased with the new life she found in Texas, though her daughter complains and wants to return to Mexico. That's how children are. She had thirteen; the first five died and the rest live and work nearby. In the afternoon her daughters and daughters-in-law come by chat a spell while the grandchildren play in the yard. She doesn't work; she only has to worry about her food, so she sits here, waiting for them to bring her "little check." This is what she likes best. In the end, if she feels like visiting, Mexico is less than a kilometer away.

from *La Frontera*

Alan Weisman

The Camino del Rio, a Möbius strip of a highway, begins on the American side west of Lajitas. Suddenly, vehicles must negotiate fifteen-degree grades and vertiginous passes, while the Rio Grande churns menacingly below. Hoodoos, ghostly wind-cut formations in the white volcanic tuff, hover along the Camino's writhing path. There is no nearby alternative route on the Mexican side, which is simply perpendicular.

Between two of the most stalwart Camino del Rio ridges lies a jarring sight—concrete Indian teepees decorated with an unintelligible fusion of American Indian symbology: buffaloes, New Mexico suns, snakes, thunderbirds. These anomalies were erected in 1964, for Lady Bird Johnson when she rafted downriver to visit Big Bend National Park. Beyond, the Camino relaxes a little. Land and river meet and expand; strings of adobe Mexican villages come into view on the southern horizon beyond broad, river-irrigated fields. On the U.S. side, the terrain is less benevolent. Piles of boulders add character but interfere with notions of extensive cultivation, and attempts at crops like melons have produced varying results over the years.

The Camino becomes simply Texas Farm Road 170. It arrives at a town, a collection of colorless structures spread one-deep along the highway. On its western extreme, a few aged adobes and a former church drop back from the road and extend thinly a half mile to the riverbank. Cavalrymen stationed here during 1916 noted that the red sandstone banks formed a shallow place to ford the Rio Grande, and began to call it Redford. The name stuck and appears on maps today. Where it doesn't appear is in the vocabulary of the primarily Spanish-speaking inhabitants, who use the old name: El Polvo, meaning dust. Dust, Texas.

El Polvo has just 125 inhabitants, but Redford's post office serves at least 500 people. Tall poplar obelisks filled with fat sparrows line the short walk that leads to the mail room, which is located in the front of postmistress Lucía Morales's house. Several generations of Moraleses have lived here, often concurrently. As the family increased, so did the house's adobe appendages, anticipating the concept of modular homes by nearly a century.

Behind a caged window next to wooden PO boxes, Lucía bends her diminutive bulk to the task of packing a shipment of rolls of stamps that came by mistake—people only buy singles here. A glassed-in diorama against one wall contains a three-dimensional Morales family saga, portrayed by painted sycamore figures carved by her great-uncle Benito. Generations of little wooden men and women drive a wooden oxcart across a river, break ground, plant cotton, build ocotillo huts, and fire up tiny diesel engines. On an adjacent wall hangs a complicated, spreading family tree.

Outside, the women who sit and converse under the portico come to attention when a blue Chevy van rattles up and Faustino Pineda gets out. For thirty-eight years, he has brought the morning mail down from Marfa, the county seat. He also brings medicines, food, and dry cleaning, and takes more orders back.

It doesn't take Lucy long to sort the mail, most of which she tosses into a cardboard box. These are for people in the pueblos across the river, who use General Delivery, Redford, as their mailing address. The closest Mexican maildrop for them is Ojinaga, two hours away over discouraging roads. Postal inspectors figured this out a few years ago and wanted to close Lucy's operation. But someone pointed out that stamp sales were repatriating dollars, so they stopped inspecting. The notion of Mexicans sending letters destined for someone in Mexico via the United States seems circuitous and possibly illegal, but practically all the mail in the cardboard box originates in the United States. "Everyone they know is working over here," Lucy explains.

A man in his sixties enters, wearing a flannel shirt, a corduroy coat, and scuffed wingtips. Eleuterio Salazar is a predicador from across the river, a preacher of God who has found, he tells everyone, perfect peace. His mission in life is to describe that peace to all he meets. Lucy hands him the cardboard box. Eleuterio lives by doing double duty, delivering the mail as he passes among the river pueblos on his evangelical wanderings. His card states that he represents the Church of Christ of Amarillo, Texas.

At the edge of town, Eleuterio heads south along a dirt road. Near the river, Redford is virtually Mexico. The houses are long, one-story adobes. At one of these, Eleuterio parks the car he borrows from his immigrant sister and follows a worn path to the Rio Grande. A red-faced, grizzled man in a stocking cap rows over in a chalupa with pieces of board bolted to aluminum tubes for oars. He charges 100 pesos to paddle Eleuterio to

Mexico, where his red Ford pickup awaits. Behind the fringed windshield, a vinyl-covered Bible rests on the sun-cracked dashboard.

For the next four hours, Eleuterio travels in second gear through irrigation ditches and over roads soft with dust. He drives as if by Braille, feeling the way, wondering when the missionaries in Amarillo will send him money for new tires. He visits border towns that don't appear on maps. Palomas. El Salitre. Loma de Juárez. Labor de Abajo. The villages are indistinguishable, blinding reflections of each other in the bright, early winter light. The roads intertwine and turn back on themselves, meandering down gulches and rolling up hillocks. His route's circuitry has no internal logic, except that Eleuterio knows it. After generations, knowledge of local trails becomes part of the genetic imprint in rural Latin America.

Except for his truck, the village streets are empty of vehicles. The pueblos seem nearly deserted, as though people were driven away by the implacable sun. Only women and very old men emerge from the mud brick interiors to meet the postman. The able-bodied are all in the United States.

For each delivery, Eleuterio receives payment, sometimes in the form of a bottle of milk, a kilo of eggs, or fresh asadero cheese. Otherwise, he charges 100 pesos per letter. But sometimes the price goes up to 200 or even 300. As he bumps into Loma de Juárez, he fishes out one of the expensive kind. The green computer card showing through the manila envelope's window is a U.S. Treasury check. The grateful anciano who hands over 300 pesos is one of sixty thousand residents of Mexico who receive monthly U.S. Social Security payments.

"Gracias a Dios y a Tío Sam," he gums fervently.

Other envelopes are fat with cash, sent home by men working the oil fields or citrus orchards. In his sermonettes, Eleuterio preens a bit, reminding that "for nineteen years people have trusted me to deliver their mail because they know I'm a preacher of the Lord and would never steal." When he retires, he doesn't know what they're going to do.

He has more than a hundred families on his route, and, like Faustino Pineda, he also handles other services. Women do piecework sewing and tailoring for customers as far away as Marfa, using the postman for pickups and deliveries. He also takes orders for candy and cosmetics. Sometimes he slips Bible tracts into the packages he brings. "How many customers have you actually converted?" someone asks.

"Eight."

"Only eight?"

"Most people reject me. They just want their letters. I don't get disappointed. My faith is in God, not people." He reaches for the Bible and turns to Juan 14:6. "Yo soy el camino . . ." he reads.*

The way he knows this uncharitable camino, it's possibly true.

In El Salitre, he delivers a Sears catalog to his daughter. Her husband, who works on oil rigs near Odessa, languishes in a Texas jail for being repeatedly apprehended as an illegal. "They should arrest men for being drunks, not for doing honest work," Eleuterio tells her.

From a hilltop, the view of the aquamarine river and adjacent fields refreshes his senses after the glare of the shadeless pueblos. Columns of Villistas, Pancho Villa's followers, once descended this same hill in pursuit of Federalist troops, driving them across the river and into the United States. Today, the only pursuit is of drug traffickers, and rarely at that. Little Switzerland, the island just below that neither country claims, ripples with marijuana.

The road approaches the fields, passing an incongruous mansion of brick and stained wood. The mafioso who owns it lives in the States, but likes having a little cottage on his home tierra. Eleuterio won't deliver mail there. A little farther along is Eleuterio's own adobe house. He has a hectare planted in wheat and corn, a few pear and apple trees, and his church. "Here," he tells his eight converts, "I work both heaven and earth." The wooden chapel has gas lamps and two pews apiece for each of his parishioners. It was built years ago by the Amarillo mission; the missionaries haven't returned since. The following day in Redford, Eleuterio dictates a letter to them, which Lucía Morales translates into English.

"Dear brothers," he says, "can you please send money for shock absorbers?"

*"I am the way . . ."

from *The Lightning of August*

Jorge Ibargüengoitia

TRANSLATED BY Irene del Corral

We were in the train (General Headquarters of the North Expeditionary Forces), planning out strategy, when we were notified that Mr. Robertson, the American consul in Pacotas, had just driven up in a flag-bedecked automobile and that he wanted to talk to us.

"If a single bullet falls on the other side of the river," warned Mr. Robertson, who was so red in the face we thought he was about to explode, "the Government of the United States will declare war on Mexico."

Our plan of attack included preliminary bombing to be carried out in such a way that not *one* shell would drop on American territory—it would be more like a thousand.

"But surely you understand," Trenza argued very reasonably, "that if we're aiming from here to there, a few shells might easily overshoot the target and land on your side of the river."

Instead of replying, the consul whipped out a letter from his State Department which, according to one of our captains who understood English, said that they would indeed declare war on us if a single bullet went astray.

"Your country has always been very selfish!" I exclaimed. I was really burned up.

"We're sick and tired of all your revolutions," he shouted.

I said that this was no way to treat a country that had struggled as hard as Mexico had for Social Justice.

"We think it's very nice that you're struggling for Social Justice, but if you can't keep your revolution on your own side of the river, we'll come in and occupy Pacotas ourselves!"

Those were Mr. Robertson's very words.

Trenza wasn't his usual belligerent self that day. He said, quite pleasantly, "Surely you realize that we're trying to open up the border so we can do business with you."

"Well, then, open up the border and do business with us," the cunning *americano* replied, "but . . ." and he repeated his warning that if a single bullet went astray the United States would declare war on us. Et cetera.

Then he took out a sheet of paper he wanted us to sign. It was a formal commitment to respect the property of American citizens, and all that.

"I'm not signing anything!" I grumbled. I'd sooner have sent Mr. Robertson before a firing squad.

"If you refuse to sign," he answered, "the Armed Forces of the United States of America will match in and occupy Pacotas tomorrow."

Germán Trenza signed; the Jinx signed; I had no choice—I signed too.

"What do we do now?" I asked Trenza as soon as the consul was gone. There was no way we could attack without half the shells falling on the American side.

"Maybe Pacotas will surrender without a fight," he answered.

But the commander of the Pacotas garrison was perfectly well aware of the fix we were in and refused to surrender.

We sent Juan Paredes, that Hero of Mexican Aviation, to make a reconnaissance flight in the Curtiss we'd brought along on our train for this very purpose. The situation was a delicate one and we had to know exactly where the enemy's defenses were located.

He brought back some very bad news. The defense positions were set up in a semicircle, on the far side of the railroad station, very close to the river, and right behind them was . . . General Pershing.

I was about to suggest that we take our business elsewhere when Benítez had another of his brilliant ideas.

We would load a railroad car with dynamite, tow it up to the top of the hill eight kilometers outside the town, and let it go from there. The tracks sloped downward all the way from there to the station, and we figured the car would gather enough speed to run straight into the stationmaster's office and blow all the troops to Kingdom Come, yet cause not one bit of damage to American property.

The plan received our whole-hearted, unanimous approval and, since there was no time to spare, we set to work immediately.

As the vehicle to be used in our delicate mission, we chose a dining car that had seen better days. It took us all night to get the dynamite and prepare the detonators, and the sun was coming up by the time a locomotive was brought and hitched up to the diner. Benítez and I climbed aboard with a motorman and a stoker. When I gave the command to move out, the wheels began to move very slowly, then gradually picked up speed. The uphill climb started near Kilometer 10. I was afraid somebody might start shooting at us (and our hundreds of pounds of dynamite), but there was no one in sight. It was drizzling.

When we reached the top of the hill, we stopped the engine, disconnected the diner, got behind it and pushed it a few meters; at last it started to coast downhill. It was moving quite fast by the time it disappeared around a curve.

We looked at, our watches and waited.

Nothing happened. There was no explosion.

We went back to camp. Germán Trenza and the Jinx were waiting for me.

"What happened?" Trenza asked. "Why didn't it blow up?"

"I have no idea," I admitted.

We sent a cavalry squadron back along the tracks to investigate.

The suspense was awful. We were all anxious to get this whole business over and done with. We wanted to move forward or back—but move! Everything was all set for the "lightning maneuver" we'd planned so carefully, the attack we'd have launched if the Americans hadn't butted in. And now we were stymied, so to speak, and to make matters worse, we didn't know what had become of our rail car and our dynamite.

It was nearly noon when the squadron returned and reported that the car was standing at Kilometer 4.

I immediately hopped onto the locomotive, which had been kept in readiness and still had a full head of steam. Benítez got on too.

"Take us to Kilometer Four and a half," I ordered the motorman.

There it was, just as they'd told us it would be, standing at Kilometer 4. I've never been able to figure out what made it stop there because the tracks still sloped downhill and there were no obstacles or anything.

"It wasn't going fast enough," Benítez decided. "Let's push it some more."

I said no because I didn't want to crash into the stationmaster's office—diner, dynamite, and all.

We hooked up the car again and towed it back to Kilometer 8 and the top of the hill. We stopped. The stoker unhitched the car.

"Okay, let's go! Full speed to Kilometer Six!"

And off we went, scared stiff, pushing the diner as fast as the engine would go (downhill too) with a ton of dynamite right under our noses.

When we passed Kilometer 7, I told the motorman to slow down.

The diner pulled away from us and raced ahead.

We couldn't hear a thing above the noise of the engine, so we couldn't be sure if there'd been an explosion or not. We came to a stop.

"There should be a big bang!" Benítez said.

So we stood there at Kilometer 6, not knowing what to do and unable to see anything because the tracks curved out of sight.

I didn't want to press my luck because I knew that sooner or later we'd run into enemy advance guards; on the other hand, I hated the idea of going back to camp. I'd only have to send out another squadron to investigate and all that. It would mean another whole day wasted.

"Why don't we go just as far as the next curve?" Benitez pleaded.

"Are you sure you didn't hear anything?" I asked the two railroad men, not wanting to get any closer to the enemy than absolutely necessary.

"Not a thing," they replied.

"Well, all right then, let's go. But take it easy!"

So we started moving very slowly and when we came around the curve, we saw the car. It was standing at Kilometer 4´ again!

We all cursed.

We pulled up to the diner and hooked it to our engine very cautiously.

"Let's go back to camp. Maybe we'll think of something else we can do," I said. But Benítez wanted to give it one more try.

"We could let the whole thing go, locomotive and all!

We can walk back," he suggested.

"Oh, no! In the first place, with the locomotive running, there's a chance it might keep going all the way over to the American side, and in the second place, I don't want to waste an engine, because we don't have any to spare," I told him.

He was still convinced his invention would work, but I ordered our return to camp, the diner in tow.

"We have to consult the others," I said, to end all argument.

"Couldn't we push it a little more? Just to Kilometer Three, General."

I must confess that the main reason I wanted to get back to camp was that I was tired of fooling around with the dynamite this way and that. *If they want to push it to Kilometer 3,* I thought to myself, *somebody else can do it.*

So we headed back to camp.

I gave orders for the diner to be left on the most remote siding because I didn't want to be blown to bits in case it should suddenly decide to explode.

At this rate, we'll be here the rest of our lives, I thought. Besides, none of all this would have been necessary if Jinx had done his job. From the very outset we should have sent him somewhere else, to do something less important. He always had such rotten luck.

That afternoon we held a staff meeting.

"I could drop a few bombs," Juan Paredes offered.

"Too bad we don't have any to drop," Germán reminded him.

I thought we should go back to Cuévano and from there march on Mexico City; Odilón Rendón wanted to attack Piedras Negras, just this side of the border from Eagle Pass, Texas.

"If we beat Macedonio Gálvez, the americanos will be willing enough to open up the border to us."

The Jinx had nothing to say; Trenza had bawled him out.

Benítez still had faith in the dynamite.

"We could send it off with the engine running," he persisted.

"You can send it off any way you please," I said abruptly, "but you'll have to do it yourselves."

Rough Portrait

Bárbara Jacobs

TRANSLATED BY David Unger

My father is from the States.

When he came to Mexico to marry my mother—and that's a whole other story—he bought a four-story hotel with at most some twenty rooms usually rented by yoyo champs who only had to cross Reforma Avenue to reach the National Auditorium and perform, or by retired gringos who spent their mornings reading mysteries in the lobby and their nights talking among themselves about the good old days when they all aspired to be famous.

My sister and I loved to visit the hotel on Sundays. We would go up the spiral staircase above the day manager's head; from the top floor, through the opening, we would drop paper cones pulled one after the other from a kind of dispenser on the side of the huge Electropure water container, bought specifically so our guests wouldn't end up with Mexican amoebas breeding in their gringo bellies.

My father loves to sit on an orange garden rocker and read in the patio terrace behind our house. He sways the foot of his crossed leg rhythmically and, when I was a little girl, I entertained myself watching his soft leg hair contrast with the white skin between his pant cuffs and his socks.

As a kid I hardly ever asked him things. I was scared to be alone with him since my English was so poor and got worse when I tried to talk to him or when he spoke to me.

My father barely speaks Spanish.

My sister and I had an English tutor who complemented the daily English classes we took in a French school with Sister Roberta, a teacher from England who struggled with us to learn her language.

There were times I'd ask myself why my parents insisted that my sister and I learn that other language. Whenever they wanted to say things to each other in front of us that they didn't want us to understand, they spoke in English. And when our old and fat and loveable but strange private tutor arrived to teach us in the afternoons, I did my best to learn everything so I could understand as soon as possible what my parents wanted or didn't want me to understand.

I tried so hard that I even reached the point where I'd cry when I heard "The Yellow Rose of Texas" on the Hit Parade, though I hardly understood a word.

My sister and I were attracted by the jackets of my father's books—those he himself placed in two wooden bookcases my mother would have polished one year and varnished two years later—that had naked women with daggers buried deep in their ample breasts.

We discovered the bookcase closest to the fireplace had the most striking jackets. The books in the other case had the author and title on the front, nothing else, and thick hard covers; almost all had something to do with History or Politics and we, by common consent, wouldn't even touch them.

One day my sister asked my father if he wasn't frightened to read mysteries; he answered, smiling, that they weren't mysteries but intrigues. This confused us and led us to hide one book under the mattress and to glance secretly through it by matchlight, as if reading it like that would help us figure out what an intrigue was.

My sister was great at stirring up the nuns with stories about our father. Rumor had it, for example, that he had been in a concentration camp and was an atheist.

The evidence we two gathered to prove this was that he didn't go to mass and wouldn't talk even at the dinner table. These two facts, in our eyes, made him more interesting than our mother.

The only problem my sister and I had with our father had to do with his last name.

In school all the nuns except Sister Roberta pronounced it incorrectly one way while all our schoolmates but Athene Baker and Patricia O'Gorman pronounced it incorrectly another way: the nuns because they were French and our schoolmates for being Mexicans.

My sister and I tacitly struggled with them to pronounce it correctly and all we got for this was for the nuns and our schoolmates to brand us gringas and to claim behind our backs that we weren't Mexicans.

Back then we didn't quite understand what one's nationality could mean nor did we imagine it could have more than its face value.

But we instinctively defended ourselves and we also defended papá about whom we really knew very little.

"He's from the States," we'd say; but papá is no gringo. He doesn't read mysteries; he doesn't chew bubble-gum; he plays bridge and wins silver trophies which my mother places on tables either to the side or facing the living room chairs and which she polishes twice a month with Silvo.

When they went after bandits who robbed border-crossers, the San Diego Police Department barfers (members of the Border Alien Robbery Force) went through some rough and tumble attitude changes.

from *Lines and Shadows*

Joseph Wambaugh

Once when both the varsity and junior varsity were walking on the upper soccer field at dusk they decided to join the throngs of pollos preparing for the night's crossing. They were utterly in character that evening, mingling with the madding crowd, listening to tales by twilight campfires, stories of prior crossings laced with hopes and dreams. Stories of fabulous jobs and great wealth, which in answer to specific questions meant half the pay of a San Diego policeman. In fact, one robbery victim when he learned that Manny Lopez was really a San Diego cop, had said sincerely, "I pray to one day become *rich*. Just like you."

During firelight conversations with other pollos, the Barfers mostly had to listen, since only Manny Lopez, Eddie Cervantes, Carlos Chacon, and possibly Ernie Salgado spoke Spanish well enough to fool anybody. But the others understood, and it was sad to listen to the pollos. It also caused things to happen inside their heads and more than once a Barfer would catch himself wanting to tell an alien of certain realities in the land of silk and money.

Sometimes the guides would warn them of San Diego cops who prowl the canyons at night dressed as pollos, about how bloodthirsty these cops were and how they beat and killed pollos just for trespassing on their land.

"They're madmen," the guide said. "They must take them from an insane asylum and bring them out here."

That evening there were at least three hundred people on the soccer field. There were a dozen guides happily jumping from group to group offering their services. There were vendors selling tacos as all waited for the orange fireball to drop behind the hills.

There were peddlers selling soda pop and coffee. There was a man with a guitar singing mournfully of the land he was about to leave. There were five motherless daughters saying good-bye to their father and they were *all* crying.

Easily the most sensitive and sentimental of the Barfers was Renee Camacho. And because of this and his boy-tenor voice which became a soprano singsong when he attempted to talk like an alien, the others called him *maricón* and said he was in love with his pal Joe Castillo. Renee was usually jolly and fun loving and could give it back as well as any. On this particular night as they waited for the curtain of darkness to fall on Deadman's Canyon, he sat by a fire with some pollos and had never felt sadder about all of it. Their role. His role. The entire drama or melodrama being ritualistically played in those canyons at night.

He wondered if it was the season. Spring had brought the desert flowers—purple and white, red as sunset—surprisingly delicate in the harsh canyons, the colors flickering in dusky silver light. Cadaverous, skin-twitching dogs circled the campfires warily. The ground was scabbed up with dropped food and brought the animals, baring their gums in ecstasy.

"I'll never forget it," Renee Camacho said. "This young man, my age, telling us how it was."

"I love my little pueblo," the alien told Renee Camacho. "I love our country, but I must make a home for my children."

Eddie Cervantes was a chatterbox who liked to ask questions. Not entirely familiar with the peso exchange, Eddie asked the alien how much his weekly earnings would buy in his pueblo.

The answer was: enough tortillas and beans to keep four children from getting sick. He could buy one scrawny chicken, but only on a good week.

Renee Camacho was deeply affected and even confused. It seemed so hopeless. It made him start to think: what if his grandfather had not got caught up with the nonsense of Pancho Villa and migrated north? He looked around at the soccer field, at the women with babies. At the elderly men and women who were unable to resist the lure of America. He looked at the man beside him and was ashamed. The man was frail, with uncut scraggly hair. He smelled putrid like all the others. Nobody had suitcases. They rarely had bundles. Renee realized something startling from talking to them: first, that they were the bravest of Mexico's poor, to come in the first place. Second, very few *wanted* to come north. They dreamed of making enough money to return to their homeland.

Some had two or three dollars and that was all. Some had several hundred. Renee Camacho always said he never met a mean one, and he kept asking himself, how can *anyone* be cruel to these people?

And after that, when he encountered aliens who had been robbed or stabbed or raped and terrorized, he began to feel what *they* felt. And he wasn't the only one. They all started to *feel* the poverty and fear. It made funny pains in the stomach, they discovered. It made them sigh a lot. Finally it made them mad, but the anger was without direction. And this produced *more* funny pains in the stomach. Renee Camacho, for one, was beginning to change in his treatment of bandits.

Even as a group, odd things began to happen to them. For instance, when the Border Patrol helicopter would make a low-flying pass over a group of aliens, sometimes the Barfers too would begin to run in panic.

"What're we doing?" Manny Lopez yelled one evening when they were doing just that, hightailing it just like aliens. "Why're we running?" he asked them in utter bewilderment. "We're armed to the fucking teeth. We're on duty. We're the *good* guys. Why're we running?"

But of course they figured it out without consulting Lee Strasberg or the Screen Actors Guild. It's just not that easy for a performer to jump in and out of character. And then they talked of how aliens felt like that *all* the time.

Manny would tell them: "It's okay to feel sorry for them, but remember that everyone else is scum. Their government's corrupt. Their cops're corrupt. Don't mix things up or you'll end up dead."

Once, when they were in fact near their substation, starting for the canyons by climbing through a two-strand barbed wire fence, they were surprised by a voice behind them saying, "Okay, motherfuckers! Freeze!" The voice belonged to a border patrolman sneaking up.

The strange part is they threw their hands up and answered in *Spanish.* "¡Somos policías! ¡Somos policías!" They were *into* character.

They also had a few laughs on the upper soccer field. Someone made up a name for a little tamale vendor with the chin whiskers of a goat. They called him Chano B. Gomez, Jr. And on a few occasions some of them actually bought tamales and *ate* them, which Manny Lopez said was the most daredevil act he'd yet witnessed out there, and that it made his gunfight look pussyish.

Chano B. Gomez, Jr., had a transistor radio strapped to his belt and carried some maracas and shook them to the Latin beat from a Tijuana radio station: *cha cha, cha cha cha!*

Sometimes he sold *churritos,* fried sticks of bread dough and chili. And of course a couple of those hardball chili-sucking bandit busters also risked parasitic paralysis by buying and eating the *churritos*. Just like pollos.

Chano B. Gomez, Jr., had an eye for the ladies and he'd skip from group to group hustling his tamales and playing his ghetto blaster and shaking his maracas at any little cutie who caught his eye: *cha cha, cha cha cha!*

And many a time his evil eye would be observed by some father/husband/brother who didn't like his action at all. But Chano B. Gomez, Jr., would just wiggle his goat whiskers at them and play his hissing maracas and skip off as surefooted as a goat on those hilltops.

The author, among Mexico's most widely read post–World War Two novelists, captured desperation and prejudice with intimacy and dignity.

from *Murieron a mitad del río*
(They Died in the Middle of the River)

Luis Spota

TRANSLATED BY Beth Henson

"Get over fast, if you don't want to meet your maker." That's what Pancho Orozco's wife had to say.

The ground was suddenly rough under their feet and punctuated with sharp pebbles. As he climbed out José Paván felt the twinge of a cramp run down his thigh, violent as an electric shock. Seated, rubbing his leg, he was reminded of a scene in a movie where a man condemned to death remembers his whole life and everything that has brought him to the electric chair, in the immeasurable space of time it takes for the executioner to connect the current that will cause his death. That's how Paván reconstructed the immediate past of that afternoon, when Orozco's woman watched them set out on their adventure.

"Most of all, don't take anything, just what you have on," she warned them.

"I can't leave my things," said Cocula.

"I'm telling you," added the woman. "You can buy what you want on the other side."

Cocula fell silent and went on eating. Like him, the other three swallowed their food without pleasure. Like him, their eyes were fixed on the other side, on the American bank, with its lush pasture and yellow Texas dirt, the valley that needed their arms the same way they needed its dollars.

The night was neither cold nor warm. Pancho Orozco would be out driving, looking for passengers at the foot of the bridge, to take them to brothels, cantinas, and all the dens of sin in Matamoros. His wife would be watching them leave in a few minutes. Four Mexican boys, who had been their guests for a week, waiting as hundreds had waited before them, from Monterrey, from Mexico City, until it was dark enough to cross the Rio Grande. "Take care," the good woman repeated.

Paván got up, still chewing the last mouthful of supper. The others followed.

"You're going to suffer. It will make men out of you," she foretold, without directing her words to any one of them in particular.

They were alone in the miserable street, lit by a dim bulb. A dog howled and others, unseen, took up the chorus. Matamoros sprawled on its outskirts with cafes, beer stores, cantinas, dance halls. Cars cruised around with their lights dimmed. They arrived at the highway lined with palm trees. A train reposed on the exit ramp. They turned several times to look for Cocula who had found a reason to turn back.

"Now a bit of luck and we're across," he thought. And luck they would need. Pancho Orozco knew what he was talking about when he told them, "Nobody's going to lend you a hand to help you across. Just you yourselves, on your own."

As for the ones who wade the river at night, chasing the dream of Texan dollars, Pancho had seen and heard it all. "There's not a night goes by," he added, "when they don't fish somebody out of the river. The duckmen are always at work."

"What duckmen?"

"The ones who take people across in their boats. Wetbacks like you. They murder them so they can rob them."

"What about the cops?"

Orozco let loose a chuckle. "Beware of the cops as if they were the devil! They go halves with the duckmen, they protect them. Each wetback means ten, fifteen, twenty pesos of earnings and they cross by the dozen. A good business. When they carry real money they kill them, they beat them or shoot them, then they tie them to a rock and let them sink. Lots of them come up on the shore all bloated. And the cops, they're on another planet."

Just the evening before a corpse had been found near the bridge. Some women were bathing when one of them saw something float nearby. Approaching, they found a cadaver, livid meat that had once been a man.

The police came and dragged the sack of decomposed flesh and bones out of the river. A length of wire, still tied to a rotten cord, almost parted the head from the trunk. Someone figured it must have been a month in the water.

The discovery caused only the response that was natural to death floating on the waters.

"One more over the side," said the onlookers, once the ambulance had carried off the remains.

"If the rope hadn't broken, he'd still be down there."

And they left, thinking about everyone who had stayed at the bottom with a rock wired to their necks.

"May it not happen to you," said Pancho Orozco when he told them the story.

The three headed for the river. A car going the other way lit up a stretch of highway with its headlights.

After a while, Luis suggested, "Let's wait for him." They lit cigarettes in a ditch where they could hide. Cars passed by and time slowed down.

"I think he's coming," said Lupe, standing up. He had heard rapid footsteps, crushing the sand that covered the asphalt.

It was Cocula. In his hand he carried a brown cardboard suitcase, the same one he had brought from Mexico.

"Why did you bring that?" Paván grabbed and shook him by one his limp arm.

"Hey." He mounted a weak protest. "They're my things."

"Leave them."

"But they're my *things*. My clothes, my perfume, a mirror."

He had nothing for him but two short words: "Leave them."

When he looked him in the eye, Cocula knew he had no alternative but to obey. He picked up the suitcase and headed back where he came from. "Fucking faggot." It was a wordless insult, uttered between clenched lips.

"Hurry," he called to his back. "We'll wait for you where we were this afternoon."

They began walking again. Feet like roots. He would have liked to have run. Always forward. The other two fell behind, together.

Near the bridge, a dancehall spat bursts of blue light and tobacco smoke into the March night. Suffocating music throbbed inside. Gringos got out of a car with their women.

There was the bridge, the obligatory passageway between the two countries. From the shore, the waters appeared inviting, tranquil, silent. In the middle of the bridge, the Immigration booth gleamed like a shop window. Jewel-like, the beacon burnished the international sky.

"There can't be another border up there."

Now in open country, they waited twenty minutes for Cocula. They had passed the last dwelling a long time ago. Impatiently, Paván trod his cigarette butt with his heel and stood up.

"To the water!" he said with a laugh that meant to be jovial.

He took off his belt, then untucked his shirttails. Lupe and Luis began to undress, following his lead.

"Why the fuck should we drag along a coward," he said to himself.

Paván could not understand that the others weren't like him, that they did things, gave orders and obeyed, without too much thought. That they acted because to take action and finish what you had started was something innate, particular to them. He did not understand other people's fears: Cocula's fear at being left behind, Lupe's fear because Cocula had stayed. As for Luis, no problem, he did what everyone else did. If they rested, he rested.

For the first fifty yards, the water came up to their chests. It was then, close to the sandbank, that they heard Cocula's first cry.

But the river was mute, except for his wretched voice. Together the three of them plowed up the bank and waited for their clothes to dry, airing them now on the foreign side.

"All he needs is a bullhorn."

"But you know what he's like," Lupe excused him.

The cramp had stopped hurting and Paván flexed his leg a few times. He was dressing his damp flesh. Under his skin the blood rebounded, warm and thick.

"If he doesn't cross," he thought between one shoe and the other, "he'll go back to Pancho Orozco's house. Maybe tomorrow or the day after he'll find a way."

Pancho Orozco, the duckmen, the dead men in the river.

Carelessly, Luis lit a cigarette. With one blow, Paván struck it from between his lips. The sparks fell on the sand. "Animal, do you want to get caught?"

"Listen, asshole—"

"You're an idiot. To light a cigarette to the four winds as if the migra were blind!"

Luis got mad. He liked Paván for the way he took charge, but he couldn't stand it when he insisted on showing who's boss and treating him rudely.

"I'm getting sick and tired of you," he threatened.

"If you don't like it," Paván replied calmly, without looking his way, "get out!"

Paván waited irritably for them to finish dressing. The mist rose ever thicker from the river. Now at last they were in Texas, on the impossible other side they'd been talking about, thinking about, ever since they had left Mexico City weeks ago. In Texas, where no one but José Paván knew what they would find, where so much could happen that no one but him would know about.

His temper past, he asked gently, "How's your leg, Luis?"

Resentful, Luis took his time in answering. "It still hurts."

Paván bit back a reproach for having been rude. "I shouldn't have struck his cigarette away." They left the river behind and treaded the soft slope of the bank. The harsh grass beat at the cuffs of their wet pants.

Sonoyta Interlude

Tom Miller

Sonoyta, Sonora, one of the older western border towns, is the meeting place of three major Mexican highways, and the key passageway to Mexico's interior for travelers from the West Coast. One hundred fifty buses pass through daily. In the 1850s, Major William Emory's border survey team reported that the town was "a resort for smugglers, and a den for a number of low, abandoned Americans who have been compelled to flee from justice." Sonoyta's reputation has stayed intact: here more than a hundred years later, Ken Kesey bribed his way into Mexico after his LSD journeys through America.

A big white adobe-walled building sits a few yards inside the border. The building's vacant high-ceiling front room is big enough to have been a dance hall. The rear divides into a series of small rooms, each slightly larger than a broom closet. Some are locked, others have no doors at all. Eduardo Polín, a Mexican customs man in his early thirties, is part-owner of the building.

"Al Capone used to come here," Eduardo said. "He owned this place. His gang would come down during Prohibition and throw parties. But when there was trouble, they'd sneak out through a tunnel which goes underneath the border and ends up on the American side. They could also escape the United States into Mexico through the tunnel if they had to." He pointed with a finger. "I'll show you where the tunnel begins."

Inside, Polín took a long metal rod and started tapping the floor. "The tunnel starts around here," he announced, listening for hollow sounds. "No, maybe it's over here." He tapped some more. "You know," he said, continuing to tap, "there were actually two tunnels—one which went under the border to the American side and another which led across the street." Tap-tap-tap. "They'd use the second one if there was trouble in the bar itself." His eyes brightened. "I think the tunnel under the border starts in this room." Eduardo turned the handle to a door but it wouldn't budge. "Ah, Alfredo has the keys to all the locks here and he is in San Luis today. But the tunnels are here somewhere, of that I am sure." He kept tapping.

Eduardo planned to convert the building into a museum of Al Capone artifacts where tourists could come to see the famous gangster's borderland hideaway. The centerpiece of the museum would be the actual bar which Al Capone had ordered custom-made from France. The bar had been handcrafted from beautiful wood, and people came from as far as El Paso and Tijuana to see it. Eduardo's eyes glazed over and his hands swept through the air as if the bar stood right before him. It was like the tunnels under the border, however; Eduardo had never actually seen the bar. He had only heard stories about it from long-time Sonoytans.

He sensed that his story was losing credibility. "Pancho, the bartender at Vásquez Cantina across from the Post Office, he will tell you all about it. Why not go visit him?" He continued tapping his long metal pole down the hall, cocking his ear for the entrance to the tunnels.

At Vásquez Cantina Pancho nodded his head vigorously: "Yes, it is so—Al Capone used to come and throw parties." He paused. "At least that's what they say." He pointed to a pile of wood in the corner next to the jukebox. "That is part of Al Capone's bar over there." The wood looked like discarded timber, unfit for service as a small card-table, much less a grandiose bar.

"Well, maybe that isn't Al Capone's bar," Pancho admitted. "Leonel, the owner of this cantina, would know. He will tell you all about the white building and Al Capone's bar when he returns from Mexico City next week. For now, perhaps Señora Vásquez, his mother, can help."

Leonel's mother lived in a small apartment at the rear of Vásquez Cantina. An aged woman born and raised in Sonoyta, she smiled broadly at the mention of the white building next to the border. "Years ago they would throw big parties there. People always talked about gangsters coming over from the other side, but I never saw any myself. Everyone called the place La Dorina. Come back in a little while and I'll have someone help you in your search for the bar. I know it is here somewhere."

Returning to the white building, I found Eduardo Polín gone, replaced by his brother and co-owner, Manuel. "In four or five years we will build a motel here," said Manuel, an artist from Mexico City. "We would like to help develop tourism in Sonoyta. But no one comes here because the border gate is closed between midnight and eight in the morning, and the Americans won't make it a twenty-four-hour port until more people come. A círculo vicioso, ¿verdad?

"There is a bar across the line in Arizona that stays open until after midnight. People from Sonoyta go there all the time. They always come home through a hole in the fence west of the crossing." He grinned. "The American authorities know all about it, but they say nothing. It's just local people."

Manuel was less sure than his brother about Al Capone and the elusive tunnels beneath the building. "Al Capone may have come here a few times, ¿quién sabe?" As for the tunnels, Manuel thought they started in the bathroom, the last room down the hall on the right, but we never found any sign that the passageways began there. He furrowed his forehead. "Maybe they've been cemented over."

The legend of Al Capone's tunnels, so vivid and convincing, sank further a few days later when a man present at La Dorina's construction assured me that the only thing below the floor was hard ground. "La Dorina was originally built as a lodge for hunters on expeditions into Sonora," he said. "I played in it as a kid, exploring every nook and cranny. If anything as exciting as a tunnel existed, I would have known."

On the way over to Vásquez Cantina, I stopped at Sonoyta's Lotería Nacional Agency, located in a combination pharmacy and hardware store. A sign on the wall announced El Día del Billetero, the day honoring the lottery-ticket salesman. In Mexico, where almost every profession has its honorary day, that the neighborhood lottery agent should be recognized seemed more than appropriate. I chatted with the billetero and bought a ticket for the following Friday's drawing.

My lottery dealings were not as appreciated on the U.S. side, however. About this time I learned that I had been breaking U.S. law by shuffling back and forth across the border with my Mexican lottery tickets. Specifically, Title 18, Chapter 61, Sec.1301:

> Whoever brings into the United States . . . or carries in interstate or foreign commerce any paper . . . purporting to be or to represent a ticket, chance, share . . . dependent upon the event of a lottery . . . offering prizes in whole or in part upon lot or chance . . . shall be fined not more than $1,000 or imprisoned not more than two years or both.

I was a borderland outlaw! I had joined the ranks of Jacinto Treviño and all the others whose crimes straddled America's southern frontier. I was a chronic offender. Rehabilitation seemed unlikely; I'd probably meet other lottery ticket smugglers in jail and learn new tricks of the trade. Perhaps a corrido would be written about my bravery sneaking little pieces of paper into the United States past armed customs agents.

I stroll up to the bar in some small-town cantina. "What can I get you, señor?" the bartender asks. Two vaqueros shooting pool pause and stare. They whisper furtively and signal the bartender. "He is the famous lottery-ticket smuggler we have all heard so much about," they tell him. "Better be careful."

Meanwhile I'm over at the jukebox and play "El Corrido del Contra-bandista de Billetes de la Lotería Nacional Para la Asistencia Pública." The title alone takes up half the record. The bartender has my drink ready.

"I am honored to have you in my humble cantina, señor. But you must beware: Another man has been here within the week, bragging that he too carries lottery tickets into the United States."

Competition! I grit my teeth. I'll show that pinche cabrón a thing or two about bringing tickets across the line.

Back at Vásquez Cantina, Señora Vásquez introduced me to Nacho, an-other Sonoyta native, whom she insisted could lead me to the bar. Nacho took me back through the barroom, around to a deserted dance hall, and up a flight of seldom-used cement stairs. The second floor of Vásquez Cantina was an unlit, seemingly abandoned storeroom sealed off with floor-to-ceiling sheets of plastic. Nacho ripped down the plastic; behind it lay dozens of old tables, chairs, and barroom fixtures blanketed by ten years of dust. "There is the bar." He pointed. "Under those chairs."

Climbing over piles of abandoned furniture, Nacho made his way back to long slab of wood, wiped away the accumulated dust, and uncovered the twenty-foot-long mahogany showpiece from La Dorina. It was a mar-velous piece of furniture with fancy handcrafted ornaments and curlicues carved into its side. "When the bar was in place at La Dorina," Nacho recalled, "it had a mirror behind it as big as the entire wall. On a pedestal at each end of the bar was a mona," a statue of a naked lady. "The two monas are over there next to you."

At my side were two handcarved statues, handsome, with delicate features, each standing six feet high and weighing close to one hundred pounds. We carried them out to a balcony overlooking the street and Nacho began carefully dusting them off as if performing surgery. They appeared to be blinking in the sunlight.

"The monas used to be black," Nacho explained, "but the color was taken off with paint remover and a glossy finish applied to bring out the natural mahogany texture. Each part of the body was carved separately, then glued together. See this?" Nacho pointed to an indentation in the left breast of one of the monas. "It is a stab wound. Sometimes people would take target practice and throw knives at the statues from across the barroom, but they meant nothing by it.

"Leonel has had offers of five thousand dollars for the bar including the monas, but he has always turned them down. There was another bar just like this one which also came over from France; some say it is in a private home in Tucson, others say it ended up down the border in Mexicali or Tijuana."

Nacho finished dusting off the monas. Free of dust for the first time in more than a decade, the two nudes looked positively splendid. Their rich mahogany luster sparkled in the sun. One's face was slightly different from the other's. The one with the stab wound looked slightly forlorn, while her friend had a hint of mischief about her. If either of them knew about Al Capone, she wasn't talking.

Mexico's fabled gumshoe hears about a Chinese man who crossed illegally from Mexicali into the United States seven times in one day. "It's a legend with a happy ending," Macario tells him.

from *Frontera Dreams*

Paco Ignacio Taibo II

TRANSLATED BY Beth Henson

"But did *you* see him?"

"No, I'm not a local. I was born in Aguas Calientes, I lived in D.F. and I've only been here three years. But I've been told."

"And it was there at that fence?"

"Right there. Seven times the Chinese jumped that very fence."

Hector Belascoarán Shayne, being an independent and democratic Mexican private detective, which was the worst job in the world, studied the green wire that comprised the border with the United States, slicing countries like butter, the green fence, so innocuous, that rose from the Mexican side in the grass and trees of Mexicali's Park of the Revolution. He had heard the story of the Chinese three times since he arrived in town, always the same, with small variations. It was too good to be true, he told himself, looking at the little park across the street and at the nine-foot-high fence. An old water tower, like those that show up next to little train stations in the westerns of Sergio Leone, finished the fence a hundred yards before the beginning of the international bridge. On the bridge, a North American border cop smoked a cigar, shotgun in hand. On the other side Calexico, farther on, San Diego. . . .

"So, to sum up: one day there was a Chinaman who jumped that green fence. And the gringos caught him and sent him back, right there, and he tried again. Six times in one day, and on the seventh try he escaped and made it inside. That's the story?"

"That's it," said Macario. A shadow of a smile seemed to cross his face, practically hidden by a baseball cap.

"And what was his name?" asked Hector.

"Who the fuck knows—Lin Piao—How would I know. But look, guy, that Chinaman ain't just some sorry motherfucker, he holds the record around here. Seven jumps in one day, not even yours truly could fathom that. What, in D.F. you don't have heroes and legends and shit like that any more?"

An almost continuous flow of automobiles advanced toward the border. Hector watched them sleepily. The sun fell like lead. Forty degrees centigrade, they had told him. Enough to fry an egg on the hood of a car. Both of his were frying.

"And what about her?" asked the detective, as if he didn't wish to change the subject. In the first place, because he was much more interested in the story of the Chinese, the Oriental leaper of fences had invaded his thoughts. He imagined him dressed in white, advancing tenaciously through the park, barefoot (his feet on the grass), lyrical jumping Chinese, stubborn (recalcitrant is one of the favorite clichés that our popular imagination has constructed about the Chinese).

"No, she didn't leap the fence. Or at least there's no legend to that effect. How many fucking rumor mongers in this rancho would be spreading it. You can hear them now: *Wetback movie actress jumps the fence in Mexicali and heads for Hollywood.*

"She's already been there."

"No shit?"

"Four years ago, working on an Aldrich movie. She played the daughter of a Colombian drug dealer. Didn't you see it?"

"No," said Macario, rubbing his chin.

"Neither did I," said Hector, without adding that although he had not seen the movie, he had imagined it frequently during the last two weeks.

About the time the story of the Chinese smuggled itself like contraband into the conversation, he had spent three hours walking around downtown Mexicali (liquor stores, shoe stores, tobacco shops) under a Saharan sun that would have been the envy of any western filmed in Andalusia. Three hours in a strange country, neither Mexican nor North American; a land where everyone was a foreigner. It wasn't easy to be Mexican in these cities full of aggressive light, dust and billboards in English. Hector felt his mustache greying under the sun's attack.

"I like the myth of the Chinaman," said the detective. "I've been here two days and I've already heard it three times."

"The border is full of tales like that."

"He would be a Chinese-Mexican," said Hector.

"Of course. He wouldn't be a generic Chinese, he'd have to be from Sinaloa, a local from Mexicali, or someone from Chinatown in D.F. I'm going to add that the next time I tell the story," said Macario.

They headed back downtown. Hector had come in search of a woman and what he got was the legend of the Chinese.

"And why only seven times?" he asked suddenly.

"Because the last time they didn't catch him. It's a legend with a happy ending," said Macario.

Macario knew all there was to know in Mexicali. He became a journalist more out of curiosity than because he loved to divulge the news. For him the border had become a mountain of failures which he didn't really remember. Old failures. New forgettings. Hector did not know him well, but found him trustworthy, with his baseball cap shading an eagle gaze. His brother in D.F. had recommended him, saying, "Look for Macario Villalba. The 'Goose' Villalba in Mexicali. He knows everything. Moreover he tells it like it is. He's been resuscitated, he tried to poison himself with rat killer five years ago, and they saved him by pumping out his stomach. Tell him I sent you."

Hector didn't have much to go by: a postcard from a hotel in Mexicali and Macario. In the hotel they knew nothing, they didn't even remember the woman, and Macario was okay. He knew stories about Chinamen, but he didn't know anything about her.

To search for that woman was like trying to remember the names of all the characters in Tolstoy's novels. It was like trying to swim in the sticky light of that harsh, Mexicali sun. Like trying to remember who won the bicycle races in the Mexican Cup in the sixties. It was, Hector now knew the truth, not only an impossible investigation, it was also an effort of memory.

"Did she rent a car?"

"What for?" asked Hector.

"To cross the border, to get to the other side."

"Wait here," said Macario, and left him standing in the sun while he entered a hotel. Hector watched the great neon sign, turned off at the moment, like a movie marquee: *Welcome, Jarritos Inc.* Macario came back in fifteen minutes.

"She rented a car to drive to Ensenada," he said, grinning. He doffed his baseball cap and saluted the detective.

When this dictionary appeared at art galleries, it was mounted on a mojonera (a border obelisk) split into sections representing, according to Aztec legend, Corn and Humanity. Each section had many colors: European white, symbol of the brain; red from the Americas, the heart; African black, the foot—or migration; and Asian yellow, two people tied back-to-back, like border towns such as Tijuana/San Diego. A saw blade shaped like the U.S. presidential seal sliced the dictionary, whose cover resembled the sort of steel fencing built along the frontier. The dictionary sat on some very phallic plumbing releasing sewage along the border, and the entire work rested on a pre-Columbian pyramid with gold spires symbolizing material wealth and private property.

Border Dictionary/Diccionario Fronterizo

Victor Ochoa

Dedicado a las generaciones que han vivido en la zona fronteriza.	Dedicated to the generations that have survived the Border Region.
Amnestia	*Amnazty*
una quebrada más pa' jalar al otro lado, sin la migra sobres.	historical insult forgiving being exploited
Bordo	*Border*
Punto clave donde lansarse para San Ysidro	Control area of natural human migration, delineating property or perimeter
Cruzando	*Crossing*
cadaveres	*cross*
A HO2 Gados	*crusader*
Aogados	*Christianity* +
Cinco de Mayo	*TO CRUISE*
Coyote	
Chicanoz	*Chicanos*

Raza que son raza	*Fools that won't learn English well, fill our jails, and eat tacos.*
Dompe	*Dump*
Donde cae lo que espulgamos	*Unload as much junk over there*
Es nuestro	*Extradition* *Go get um . . . John.*
Frontera	*Fence*
"Frito con mermelada"	*"free trade"*
familia	*foreigners* *farmworkers* *floating population*
Gringo-Gavacho	*Gestapo*
Gacho	*Green Card*
Garita	*Guns*
Helicoptero	*Human Rights*
H-2 Bracero	Hell
Huevon	Happiness
Ilegal	*Illegal*
Independencia	*INS*
Ipocrita	*I-191 Permanant Resident Card*
Justicia	*Just U.S.* System
Jalapeño	Jeep
KKK	*Keep Out*
Linea	*Line*
Lana	*Labor*
Llantas	used tires
Llorona	crying for 500 years
Maquiladora	*Mexicans working*
Migra	*Marines*

Mota	*Maids*
Mordida	
La Mica	
Narcotraficante	*Narco trafi Can't tell*
Ñ, ñ ('eine)	17th letter of the Spanish alphabet, always ignored
Otay	*Otay*
Ya era tiempo de abrirla . . . ¿y el aeropuerto binacional?	second legal crossing what airport?
Perros	*Police*
Pollos	*Pilgrims*
Pocho	*Pocho*
Patria	*Plymouth Rock*
Quesadilla	*Que-za-di, la*
Rodillas	*Rodino*
Redadas	*Raids*
Ratas	informers
San Diego	*Sandy ego*
Suciedad	*Sewage*
chivo expiatorio	*Scape Goat*
Tijuana	*Tia who? Ana*
Trabajo	*Taco Bell*
Tragando de Libre Comerico	*Texas Rangers*
Uvas	*Grapes*
Unido	*United States*
Utopia	
Vato	*Victor*
Vagabundo	*Vagrant*
Visita	*Visit—house call*
Visa	*Visa*

W.C.	*White man*
el water	*Wet Back*
	Wall
Xenofobia	*Xenophobia*
extraño	*Strange, foreign*
	X-ray
	X-mas
	X-ing
Yonke	*Yankee*
Yerba	*Yearn*
Zona	*Zone*
Zorro	*Zero*

Part 5

Section 1

The border developed its identity decades ago. These pieces helped shaped our current biases and inclinations.

Before the turn of the last century, Presido, Texas, still had hope. But not much.

from *The Devil In Texas*

Aristeo Brito

TRANSLATED BY David William Foster

Don Pancho went into his private office and there among books and piles of newspapers, he set about struggling against his cynicism. He meditated on his life and his career, which had been a real disaster. Nothing more. Failure, crashing failure, period. The dusty newspapers and books that surrounded him were the last vestiges of a fight he'd lost. Proof of his creative age? Even the question was stupid. He remembered how his own destruction matched the town's, how the two had been reduced to an insignificant microcosm, but one replete with history. For his part, he had been spurned by both governments because of his strong sense of justice. There was nothing left of the efforts he had made during his time to ensure basic human rights, and the only thing that consoled him was unearthing his truth buried under the dust. The issues of *The Frontiersman* he had saved in his office said it all. Perhaps someone would come someday and read them, but that would be after he was dead.

He remembered very well his first year of practice, because it was in that same year when the world he had built in the air during his studies collapsed around him. Reality, damn it, was something else. Life was lived by shouting and waving hats. He had soon realized that the career of a lawyer was not quite so illustrious, and even less when it was practiced in a town of impoverished conditions. Then he came to realize that the best way to help others and to help himself would be through journalism, and he immediately began to publish *The Frontiersman*, a small newspaper that was read not only by those who needed to read it but also by other publishers in the Southwest. His undertaking grew strong when to his surprise he began to receive newspapers from California, Trinidad, Colorado, Laredo, New Mexico, and from places where he never even suspected there were Mexicans. In time, the publication became a strong voice with one concern: polemics, denunciation, and protest over the life of Mexicans in these areas. Soon his words were being picked up by newspapers in Mexico, and the Mexican government did not take long to recognize Francisco Uranga's benefit to the country. He received his appointment as consul with great enthusiasm. The exact words? "To serve as representative of our citizens abroad as appropriate in the defense of their rights and principles as designated by the treaties between Mexico and the United States." Just as soon as he had received the appointment, he began to order by priority the tasks to be undertaken. First, the clarification of the question of properties that had been usurped in the Presidio valley and to discover how to validate claims on lands that had little by little been rolled away like a rug. (But he remembered that by that time it was already too late because the legal archives were written in another language and bore another seal.) Later, he would pursue the complicated question of citizenship, and for that he would have to contact the other consuls in the Southwest. And he would have to find quickly a more efficient way of arranging the repatriation of all those individuals who wished to go home, but who thought that the Mexican government had abandoned them. Another of the causes, and here he was emphatic, was the need to combat the insolence on the part of those who considered themselves the law, and crossed the border without prior authorization. This point was one of the touchiest, because he had seen numerous cases in which the person being pursued was taken out of Mexico in order to try him in a foreign court and in a foreign language. Yes, it was necessary to clarify the law of extradition so trammeled by the conqueror, although he knew that it was a very difficult task. On other occasions, the opposite occurred: the person accused by the Mexican authorities could not prove that he was a citizen of the United States, even when the treaty said that anyone not repatriated within two years would be considered a citizen. And the papers? They had vanished into thin air. Where are you from? From the land, sir. From wherever I can make a living.

It did not take long for Pancho Uranga to realize that he was in the same whirlpool. Between the accumulation of paper and the confusion, he lived as though sick and lost at sea. He ended up with his hands tied with frustration, transformed into one of those persons who know so much about how the world works that they smirk as if to say: Jerks, what did you expect? God's blessings wrapped in a blanket? Get it straight; humanity is rotten to the core. And each time the devil won out, the thorn dug deeper, and by the time he tried to extract it, it had already poisoned his soul. By then he had taken up the pen as a sword. His writings appeared in his own paper, *The Frontiersman,* in *The Tucsonian, The Spanish American, The Zurtian, The Voice of the People* and forty other newspapers that were coming out at that time: "I roundly denounce the usurpation of the lands and I support the White Caps for having shown their weapons"; "I put my name to the resolution of the unified Spanish American press which condemns the governor of New Mexico for calling us 'greasers' in the English-language press of New York and who now has the nerve to threaten us"; "I protest the filibustering expeditions of opportunistic Yankees"; "I condemn discrimination in the workplace, in schools, and in public establishments"; "I support the defenses mounted by the Mexican Alliance"; "with anger and love I lament the dissolution of our people and I weep for its future"; "I am a partisan of the radical element of workers in San Antonio, California, and New Mexico, not because I know they have achieved something, but because it proves that we are still alive and that there will be something for us to fight"; "I am suspicious of the justice and the sentences meted out by judges that are guided by the opinions of prejudiced witnesses; moreover, I know that Manuel Verdugo was not guilty. I found out afterward that he was sentenced to die in El Paso"; "I condemn the sale of black slaves in Fayetteville, Missouri"; "for the information of the editor of the aforementioned rag in Guadalajara, my efforts to repatriate our people are genuine. And I do so because I know the sufferings experienced in a country that is considered the best example of democracy, and I also would have you understand fully, via examples, that our people here are not a bunch of tamale vendors, as you so grossly describe us. The survey I print here contains the number of persons of Mexican descent, and you should know that of all those who responded, only four are in the business of selling tamales, and not because they are lazy but because of the adverse fortunes they have experienced. I have on numerous occasions appealed to the Mexican government to provide the money to provide transport for those who want to be repatriated, as well as to allot them a parcel of land; otherwise, what guarantee is there that they would live any better if they returned to Mexico? . . .

Thus he pricked sensitivities with the tip of his pen, and it wasn't too long before both governments considered him an enemy of harmony. By the time he defended the cause of Catarino Garza, who provoked the uprising of workers in New Mexico against the landowners and the government of Chihuahua, he had ceased to be consul. It was a miracle he wasn't killed, although in those days he would have preferred it, because nothing mattered to him. The town he had defended with love now turned its back on him, and that was what hurt the most. Some, as soon as luck went their way, came down on him. "Old troublemaker, leave well enough alone. Things are going well, and you threaten our position with your stupidity. So either you shut up or . . ." *The Frontiersman* died a death without glory. People were right, history stops for no one. (History flows like water. Sometimes calm, sometimes with the devil riding it, making it swollen and rabid. Then it brings forth a deformed hand that stretches its fingers out to infinity. Then the water's hand withdraws and becomes a claw, leaving only a trickle in the bed of the Río Grande. Then the people on their eternal migration return to form a twisted cross, a miserable cross of flesh and water.) And since the history of my race is that of the river, I thought, I am going to build a launch to ferry them across. This will help me support myself, but I will charge only those who can pay. It will also give me the opportunity to guide people by setting them on the best road. "Go this way and be careful with this and that, and if he doesn't give you a job, follow the river until . . ." But before I do that, I'll gather my belongings, my books, and move to Ojinaga. I will build a house near the river on the other side, in order for our history not to be washed away in the water.

Stephen Crane in Mexico (II)

Stephen Crane

City of Mexico, July 4—

The train rolled out of the Americanisms of San Antonio—the coal and lumber yards, the lines of freight cars, the innumerable tracks and black cinder paths—and into the southern expanses of mesquite.

In the smoking compartment, the capitalist from Chicago said to the archaeologist from Boston: "Well, here we go." The archaeologist smiled with placid joy.

The brown wilderness of mesquite drifted steadily and for hours past the car windows. Occasionally a little ranch appeared half-buried in the bushes.

In the door-yard of one, some little calicoed babies were playing and in the door-way itself a woman stood leaning her head against the post of it and regarding the train listlessly. Pale, worn, dejected, in her old and soiled gown, she was of a type to be seen north, east, south, west.

"That'll be one of our best glimpses of American civilization," observed the archaeologist then.

Cactus plants spread their broad pulpy leaves on the soil of reddish brown in the shade of the mesquite bushes. A thin silvery vapor appeared at the horizon.

"Say, I met my first Mexican, day before yesterday," said the capitalist. "Coming over from New Orleans. He was a peach. He could really talk more of the English language than any man I've ever heard. He talked like a mill-wheel. He had the happy social faculty of making everybody intent upon his conversation. You couldn't help it, you know. He put every sentence in the form of a question. 'San Anton' fine town—uh? F-i-n-n-e—uh? Gude beesness there—uh? Yes gude place for beesness—uh?' We all had to keep saying 'yes,' or 'Certainly' or 'you bet your life,' at intervals of about three seconds."

"I went to school with some Cubans up North when I was a boy," said the archaeologist, "and they taught me to swear in Spanish. I'm all right in that. I can—"

"Don't you understand the conversational part at all?" demanded the capitalist.

"No," replied the archaeologist.

"Got friends in the City of Mexico?"

"No!"

"Well, by jiminy, you're going to have a daisy time!"

"Why, do you speak the language?"

"No!"

"Got any friends in the city?"

"No!"

"Thunder!"

These mutual acknowledgements riveted the two men together. In this invasion, in which they were both facing the unknown, an acquaintance was a prize.

As the train went on over the astonishing brown sea of mesquite, there began to appear little prophecies of Mexico. A Mexican woman, perhaps, crouched in the door of a hut, her bare arms folded, her knees almost touching her chin, her head leaned against the door-post. Or perhaps a dusky sheep-herder in peaked sombrero and clothes the color of tan-bark standing beside the track, his inscrutable visage turned toward the train. A cloud of white dust rising above the dull-colored bushes denoted the position of his flock. Over this lonely wilderness vast silence hung, a speckless sky, ignorant of bird or cloud.

"Look at this," said the capitalist.

"Look at that," said the archaeologist.

These premonitory signs threw them into fever of anticipation. "Say, how much longer before we get to Laredo?" The conductor grinned. He recognized some usual, some typical aspect in this impatience. "Oh, a long time yet."

But then, finally, when the whole prairie had turned a faint preparatory shadow-blue, someone told them: "See those low hills off yonder? Well, they're beyond the Rio Grande."

"Get out—are they?"

A sheep-herder with his flock raising pale dust-clouds over the lonely mesquite could no longer interest them. Their eyes were fastened on the low hills beyond the Rio Grande.

"There it is! There's the river!"

"Ah, no, it ain't!"

"I say it is."

Ultimately the train maneuvered through some low hills and into sight of low-roofed houses across stretches of sand. Presently it stopped at a long wooden station. A score of Mexican urchins were congregated to see the arrival. Some twenty yards away stood a train composed of an engine, a mail and baggage car, a Pullman and three day coaches marked first, second and third class in Spanish. "There she is, my boy," said the capitalist. "There's the Aztec limited. There's the train that's going to take us to the land of flowers and visions and all that."

There was a general charge upon the ticket office to get American money changed to Mexican money. It was a beautiful game. Two Mexican dollars were given for every American dollar. The passengers bid good-bye to their portraits of the national bird, with exultant smiles. They examined with interest the new bills which were quite gay with red and purple and green. As for the silver dollar, the face of it intended to represent a cap of liberty with rays of glory shooting from it, but it looked to be on the contrary a picture of an exploding bomb. The capitalist from Chicago jingled his coin with glee. "Doubled my money!"

"All aboard," said the conductor for the last time. Thereafter he said: "Vamanos." The train swung around the curve and toward the river. A soldier in blue fatigue uniform from the adjacent barracks, a portly German regardant at the entrance to his saloon, an elaborate and beautiful Anglo-Saxon oath from the top of a lumber pile, a vision of red and white and blue at the top of a distant staff, and the train was upon the high bridge that connects one nation with another. . . .

It was amazing. The travellers had somehow expected a radical change the moment they were well across the Rio Grande. On the contrary, southern Texas was being repeated. They leaned close to the pane and stared into the mystic south. In the rear, however, Texas was represented by a long narrow line of blue hills, built up from the plain like a step.

Infrequently horsemen, shepherds, hovels appeared in the mesquite. Once, upon a small hillock a graveyard came into view and over each grave was a black cross. These somber emblems, lined against the pale sky, were given an inexpressibly mournful and fantastic horror from their color, new in this lonely land of brown bushes. The track swung to the westward and extended as straight as a rapier blade toward the rose-colored sky from whence the sun had vanished. The shadows of the mesquite deepened.

What thoughts went through the old man's mind as he crossed a boundary, mid-revolution? A celebrated author gives us this rendering, drenched in sweat and metaphor.

from *The Old Gringo*

Carlos Fuentes

He got off the train in El Paso, carrying his folding black suitcase, what they called a Gladstone then, and dressed all in black except for the white expanse of cuffs and shirtfront. He'd told himself he wasn't going to need much luggage on this trip. He walked a few blocks through the border town; he'd imagined it drearier and duller and older than it actually was, and sick, as well, of the Revolution, of the rage from across the river. Instead, it was a town of bright new automobiles, five-and-ten-cent stores, and young people, so young they could hardly have been born in the nineteenth century. In vain, he searched for his idea of the American frontier. It wasn't going to be easy to buy a horse without having to fend off inopportune questions about the horseman's destination.

He could cross the frontier and buy a horse in Mexico. But the old man wanted to make life difficult for himself. Besides, he'd got it in his head that he needed an American horse. If they opened his suitcase at customs, all they'd find would be a few ham sandwiches, a safety razor, a toothbrush, a couple of his own books, a copy of *Don Quixote,* a clean shirt, and a Colt .44 wrapped in his underclothes. He didn't want to explain why he was traveling with such a light, if precise, array of provisions.

"I intend to be a good-looking corpse."

"And the books, señor?"

"They're mine."

"No one suggested you'd stolen them."

Resigned, the old man would offer no further explanations. "All my life I've wanted to read the *Quixote.* I'd like to do it before I die. I've given up writing forever."

He imagined this scene, and told the man who sold him the horse that he was going to look north of the city for land to develop; a horse was still more useful in the sagebrush than one of those infernal machines. The dealer said that was true; he wished everyone thought like him, because no one was buying horses these days except agents for the Mexican rebels. But that's why the price was a little steep; there was a revolution on the other side of the border, and revolutions are good for business.

"Yes, there's still a place for a good horse," said the old man, and rode off on a white mare that would be visible at night and would make life difficult for her owner when he wanted his life to be difficult.

Now he had to keep his sense of direction, because although the frontier was traced broad and clear by the river dividing El Paso from Ciudad Juárez, beyond the Mexican town there was no demarcation but the line in the distance where sky joined dry, dirty plain.

That horizon kept receding as the old man rode on, his long legs dangling beneath the mare's belly, his black suitcase cradled in his lap. Some twenty kilometers west of El Paso, he forded the river at its narrowest point while everyone's attention was diverted by the explosion on the bridge. At that instant, in the old man's clear eyes were fused all the cities of gold, the expeditions that never returned, the lost priests, the nomadic and moribund tribes of Tobosos and Laguneros that had survived the epidemics of the Europeans and then fled the Spanish towns to master the horse, the bow, and later the rifle, in an endless ebb and flow of beginnings and dissolutions, mining bonanzas and depression, genocides as vast as the land itself and as forgotten as the accumulated bitterness of its men.

Rebellion and suppression, plague and famine—the old man knew he was entering the restless lands of Chihuahua and the Rio Grande, leaving behind the refuge of El Paso, founded with a hundred and thirty settlers and seven thousand head of cattle. He was abandoning the sacred refuge of fugitives from the north and from the south: a flimsy, precarious haven in harsh desert lands: one main street, a hotel and a pianola, soda fountains and hiccuping Fords, and the answer of the invading north to the mirages of the desert: an iron suspension bridge, a railroad station, a blue haze imported from Chicago and Philadelphia.

He himself was now a voluntary fugitive, as much a fugitive as the ancient survivors of the attacks of Conchos and Apaches whom cruel necessity, sickness, injustice, and disillusion had once again driven to wandering: all this was etched in the old gringo's head as he crossed the frontier between Mexico and the United States. No wonder they had all tired of continual flight and for over a hundred years remained entangled in the thorns of the hacienda system.

But maybe he was carrying a different fear, one he voiced as he crossed the frontier: "I'm afraid that each of us carries the real frontier inside."

The bridge exploded in the distance and he headed to the right and to the south, feeling sure of his bearings (he was already in Mexico, that was enough) when about dusk he smelled warm tortillas and beans.

He approached the small gray adobe hut and asked, in his accented Spanish, whether they could offer him a meal and a blanket to sleep on. The fat owners of the smoky house said yes, ésta es su casa, señor.

He knew the ritual phrase of Mexican courtesy but suspected that after having offered him the house, his host would feel free to subject his guest to all manner of whims and insults, especially any arising from jealous suspicion. But he curbed his desire to stir up a fight; not yet, he told himself, not yet. That night, drowsing on the straw mat in his black clothes, listening to the heavy breathing of his hosts and their dogs, smelling the heavy odors of the couple, different from his because they ate differently and thought and loved and feared differently, it pleased him that they'd offered him their house. What had he lost, in four successive and irreparable blows, but that? In the end, what other reason had he, he admitted countering his own sleepy but malicious wink, for trotting off toward the south, the only frontier left to him after exhausting in his seventy-one years the other three boundaries of the North American continent, even the black frontier the Confederates had tried to establish in '61? Now all that was left was the open south, the only door open to his encounter with the fifth, blind, murderous blow of fate.

Dawn rose over the edge of the mountain.

"Is this the way to Chihuahua?" he asked his fat host.

The Mexican nodded and in turn asked with a jealous glance toward the closed door of his house: "And what takes you to Chihuahua, mister?"

Speaking in Spanish, he added a faint *ee* that made the word sound like *misteree,* and the old man thought how the first advantage a gringo always has over a Mexican is that of being a mystery, something he doesn't know how to take: friend or enemy. Although generally they didn't get the benefit of the doubt.

The Mexican continued: "The fighting is thick around there; that's Pancho Villa territory."

His look was more eloquent than his words. The old man thanked him and set off. Behind him, he heard the Mexican open the door to scold the woman, who only then had dared to peer outside. The gringo thought he could imagine the black melancholy of her eyes; a journey is painful for the one who has to remain behind, but more beautiful than it can ever be for the traveler. The old gringo tried to reject the comforting notion that his presence in another man's house might still provoke jealousy.

The mountains rose like worn, dark-skinned fists and the old man imagined the body of Mexico as a gigantic corpse with bones of silver, eyes of gold, flesh of stone, and balls hard as copper.

The mountains were the fists. He was going to pry them open, one after the other, hoping that sooner or later, like an ant scurrying along the furrowed palm, he would find what he was after.

That night he tied his horse to an enormous organpipe cactus and fell into a famished sleep, thankful for his woolen underwear. He dreamed about what he had seen before falling asleep: new bluish stars and dying yellow ones. He tried to forget his dead children, wondering which of the stars were already quenched, their light nothing more than his own illusion: a heritage from the dead stars to human eyes that would continue to praise them centuries after their extinction in an ancient catastrophe of dust and flames.

He dreamed he was crossing a flaming bridge. He awakened. He wasn't dreaming. He'd seen the bridge that morning as he crossed into Mexico. But now as he gazed at the stars the old man said to himself: "My eyes shine brighter than any star. No one will ever see me old and decrepit. I will always be young because today I dare to be young again. I will always be remembered as I was."

Steel-blue eyes beneath speckled, almost blond, eyebrows. They were not the best defense against the raging sun and the raw wind that the following day bore him into the heart of the desert, occasionally nibbling on a dry sandwich, settling a shapeless wide-brimmed black Stetson lower on his thatch of silvery hair. He felt like a gigantic albino monster in a world the sun had reserved for its favored, a people of shadow protected by darkness. The wind died down but the sun continued to burn. By afternoon, his skin would be peeling. He was deep in the Mexican desert, sister to the Sahara and the Gobi, continuation of the Arizona and Yuma deserts, mirror of the belt of sterile splendors girdling the globe as if to remind it that cold sands, burning skies, and barren beauty wait patiently and alertly to again overcome the earth from its very womb: the desert.

"The old gringo came to Mexico to die."

In the classic novel of the Mexican Revolution, the author suggests to a friend that a Mexican restaurant in El Paso would be just the ticket for social and financial reward.

from *The Underdogs*

Mariano Azuela

TRANSLATED BY E. Muguía Jr.

El Paso, Texas, May 16, 1915

My Dear Venancio:

Due to the pressure of professional duties I have been unable to answer your letter of January 4 before now. As you already know, I was graduated last December. I was sorry to hear of Pancracio's and Manteca's fate, though I am not surprised that they stabbed each other over the gambling table. It is a pity; they were both brave men. I am deeply grieved not to be able to tell Blondie how sincerely and heartily I congratulate him for the only noble and beautiful thing he ever did in his whole life: to have shot himself!

Dear Venancio, although you may have enough money to purchase a degree, I am afraid you won't find it very easy to become a doctor in this country. You know I like you very much, Venancio; and I think you deserve a better fate. But I have an idea which may prove profitable to both of us and which may improve your social position, as you desire. We could do a fine business here if we were to go in as partners and set up a typical Mexican restaurant in this town. I have no reserve funds at the moment since I've spent all I had in getting my college degree, but I have something much more valuable than money; my perfect knowledge of this town and its needs. You can appear as the owner; we will make a monthly division of profits. Besides, concerning a question that interests us both very much, namely, your social improvement, it occurs to me that you play the guitar quite well. In view of the recommendations I could give you and in view of your training as well, you might easily be admitted as a member of some fraternal order; there are several here which would bring you no inconsiderable social prestige.

Don't hesitate, Venancio, come at once and bring your funds. I promise you we'll get rich in no time. My best wishes to the General, to Anastasio, and the rest of the boys.

Your affectionate friend,

Luis Cervantes

The author dove head first into the Mexican Revolution, then gave us this short story when he surfaced.

Endymion; or, On the Border

John Reed

Presidio, Texas, is a collection of a dozen adobe shacks and a two-story frame store, scattered in the brush in the desolate sand-flat along the Rio Grande. Northward the desert goes rolling gently up against the fierce, quivering blue, a blasted and silent land. The flat brown river writhes among its sand-bars like a lazy snake, not a hundred yards away. Across the river the Mexican town of Ojinaga tops its little *mesa*—a cluster of white walls, flat roofs, the cupolas of its ancient church—an Oriental town without a minaret. South of that the terrible waste flings out in great uptilted planes of sand, mesquite and sage brush, crumpling at last into a surf of low sharp peaks on the horizon.

In Ojinaga lay the wreck of the Federalista army, driven out of Chihuahua by the victorious advance of Pancho Villa, and apathetically awaiting his coming here, by the friendly border. Thousands of civilians, scourged on by savage legends of the Tiger of the North, had accompanied the retreating soldiers across that ghastly four hundred miles of burning plain. Most of the refugees lay camped in the brush around Presidio, happily destitute, subsisting on the Commissary of the American Cavalry stationed here; sleeping all day, and singing, love-making and fighting all night.

The fortunes of war had thrust greatness upon Presidio. It figured in the news dispatches telephoned to the outer world by way of the single Army wire. Automobiles, gray with desert dust, roared down over the packtrail from the railroad, seventy-five miles north, to corrupt its pristine innocence. A handful of war-correspondents sat there in the sand, cursing, and twice a day concocted two-hundred word stories full of sound and fury. Wealthy *hacendados*, fleeing across the border, paused there to await the battle which should decide the fate of their property. Secret agents of the Constitutionalistas and the Federal plotted and counterplotted all over the place. Representatives of big American interests distributed retaining fees, and sent incessant telegrams in code. Drummers for munition companies offered to supply arms wholesale and retail to anyone engaged in or planning a revolution. Not to mention—as they put it in musical comedy programs—citizens, Rangers, deputy Sheriffs, United States troopers, Huertista officers on furlough, Customs officials, cowpunchers from nearby ranches, miners, etc.

Old Schiller, the German storekeeper, went bellowing around with a large revolver strapped to his waist. Schiller was growing rich. He supplied food and clothing and tools and medicines to the swollen population; he had a monopoly on the freighting business; he was rumored to conduct a poker game and private bar in the back room; and sixty men slept on the floor and counters of his store for twenty-five cents a head.

I went around with a bowlegged, freckle-faced cowboy named Buchanan, who had been working on a ranch down by Santa Rosalia, and was waiting for things to clear up so he could go back. Buck had been three years in Mexico, but I couldn't discover it had left any impression on his mind—except a grievance against Mexicans for not speaking English; all his Spanish being a few words to satisfy his natural appetites. But he occasionally mentioned Dayton, Ohio—from which city he had fled on a freight train at the age of twelve.

He seemed to be a common enough type down there; a strong, lusty body, brave, hard, untroubled by any spark of fine feeling. But I hadn't been with him many hours before he began to talk of Doc. According to Buck, Doc was Presidio's first citizen; he was a great surgeon, and more than that, one of the world's best musicians. But more remarkable than everything, to me, was the pride and affection in Buck's voice when he told of his friend.

"He kin set a busted laig with a grease-wood twig and a horse-hair riata," said Buck, earnestly. "And curing up a t'rantn'ler bite ain't no more to him than taking a drink is to you or me. . . . And play—say! Doc kin play any kind of a thing. By God. I guess if anybody from New York or Cleveland was to hear him tickle them instruments, he would be a-setting on the Opera House stage right now, instead of the sand at Presidio!"

I was interested.

"Doc who?" I asked.

Buck looked surprised. "Why, just Doc," he said.

After supper that night I plowed through the sand in the direction of Doc's adobe cabin. It was a still night, with great stars. From somewhere up the river floated down the sound of a few lazy shots. All around in the brush flared the fires of the refugee camps; women screamed nasally to their children to come home; girls laughed out in the darkness; men with spurs "kajunked" past in the sand; and like an accompaniment in the bass sounded the insistent mutter of a score of secret agents conspiring on the porch of Schiller's store. Long before I came near, I could hear the familiar strains of the *Tannhäuser* overture played on a castrated melodeon; and immediately in front of the house, I almost stumbled over a double row of Mexicans, squatting in the sand, wrapped to the eyes in *sarapes,* rigidly listening.

Within the one white-washed room, two U. S. cavalry officers sat with their eyes closed, pretending to enjoy what they considered "high-brow" entertainment. They had been eight months on the Border, far from the refinements of civilization, and it made them feel "cultured" to hear that kind of music. Buchanan, smoking a corn-cob pipe, lay stretched in an armchair, his feet on the stove, his glistening eyes fixed with frank enjoyment on Doc's fingers as they hopped over the keys. Doc himself sat with his back to us—a pathetic, pudgy, white-haired little figure. Some of the melodeon keys produced no sound at all; others a faint wheeze; and the rest were out of tune. As he played he sang huskily, and swayed back and forth as one rapt in harmony.

It was a remarkable room. At one end stood the wreck of an elaborate glass-topped operating-table. Behind it, a case of rusty surgical instruments—the top shelf full of pill bottles—and a book-case containing five volumes: a book of Operatic Selections scored for the piano, part of a volume of Beethoven's Symphonies arranged for four hands, two volumes on Practical Diagnosis, and The Poems of John Keats, morocco-bound, hand-tooled, and worn. There was a desk, too, piled with papers. And all around the rest of the room were musical instruments in various stages of desuetude: concertina, violin, guitar, French horn, cornet, harp. A small Mexican hairless dog with a cataract in one eye, sat at Doc's feet, his nose lifted to the ceiling, howling continuously.

Doc played more and more furiously, humming as his gnarled fingers jumped about over the keyboard. Suddenly, in the midst of a thundering chord, he stopped, turned half around to us and stretching out his hands, mumbled through his whiskers:

"M' hands are too small! Every damn thing's wrong about me somewheres. Aye!" He sighed. "Franz Liszt had short fingers, too. Hee! Not like mine. No short fingers in the head . . ." his words ran off into indistinguishable mumbling.

Buck brought his feet down with a crash, and slapped his knee.

"God, Doc!" he cried. "If you had big hands I don't know what in hell you couldn't do!"

Doc looked dully at the floor. The little dog put his feet upon his lap and whimpered, and the old man laid a trembling hand on his head. The two officers awkwardly took their leave. Presently Doc lit up a great pipe, grumbling and groaning to himself, the smoke oozing out of his mustache, nose, eyes and ears.

With a sort of reverence Buck introduced me. Doc nodded, and looked at me with bleary little eyes that didn't seem to see. His round, puffy face was covered with a white stubble; through a yellow, ragged mustache came indistinctly the ruins of a cultivated articulation. He smelt strongly of brandy.

"Aye—you're not one of these—sand-fleas umble-umble-umble," he said, blinking up at me. "From the great world. From the great world. Tell 'em my name is writ in water umble-umble."

No one knew anything about him except what he had dropped when drunk. He himself seemed to have forgotten his past. The Mexicans, among whom most of his practice was, loved him devotedly, and showed it by paying their bills. He always made the same charge for any medical service—setting a fracture, amputating a limb, delivering a child, or giving a dose of cough syrup—twenty-five cents. But he had spoken of London, Queen's Hall, the Conservatory of Music, and of being in India and Egypt, and of coming to Galveston as head of a hospital. Beyond that, nothing but the names of Mexican cities, of unknown people. All that Presidio knew of him was that he had come across the border nameless and drunk during the Madero revolution and had stayed there nameless and drunk ever since. . . .

. . . We had supper, Buchanan, Doc and I, in a one-room Mexican restaurant, whose proprietor had once owned a little ranch across the river, which Enrique Creel had sold to William Randolph Hearst, pocketing the proceeds. As big, brown men, booted and spurred, came in, each one stopped at the head of the table to say "Howdye Doc! How ya coming?" The Mexican waiter served Doc first, and when a rich cattleman who had motored in that morning began cursing him for a lazy Greaser, one of the Rangers leaned over and tapped him on the arm.

"Doc gets his first, stranger," he said quietly. "After that you kin put *your* foot in the trough."

. . . We walked over toward a little shack where a pool-table had been set up, and I tried to find out just when he had dropped out of "the great world." He responded to the name of Pasteur, but Ehrlich, Freud and the other modern medical names I knew evidently meant nothing to him. In music, Saint-Saëns was evidently an interesting youngster and no more; Strauss, Debussy, Schönberg, even Rimski-Korsakov, were Greek to him. Brahms he hated, for some reason.

There was a game on in the pool-room when we came in, but some one set up a shout "Here comes Doc!" and the players laid down their cues. Doc and Buchanan played on the rickety table, while I sat by. The old man's game was magnificent; he never seemed to miss a shot, no matter how difficult, though he could hardly see the balls. Buck hardly got a chance to shoot. Around the walls on the ground sat a solid belt of Mexicans in high wide sombreros, with *serapes* of magnificent faded colors, great boot buckles and spurs as big as dollars. When Doc made a good shot a chorus of soft applause came from them. When he fumbled and dropped his pipe, ten hands scrambled for the honor of retrieving it. . . .

In the soft, deep, velvety night we started home through the sand.

What must it have been like to confront Pancho Villa at his peak? "A man! A man!"

My First Glimpse of Pancho Villa

Martín Luis Guzmán

TRANSLATED BY Harriet De Onis

To go from El Paso, Texas, to Ciudad Juárez in Chihuahua was, to quote Neftalí Amador, one of the greatest sacrifices, not to say humiliations, that human geography had imposed on the sons of Mexico on that part of the border. Yet that night, when we arrived from San Antonio, Pani and I went through this ordeal with a certain joy that was somehow bound up with the very sources of our nationality. We realized once for all that we had been born and would die a part of the soul of our country.

Ciudad Juárez is a sad sight; sad in itself, and still sadder when compared with the bright orderliness of that opposite river-bank, close but foreign. Yet if our faces burned with shame to look at it, nevertheless, or perhaps for that very reason, it made our hearts dance as we felt the roots of our being sink into something we had known, possessed, and loved for centuries, in its brutishness, in all the filth of body and soul that pervades its streets. Not for nothing were we Mexicans. Even the sinister gleam of the occasional street-lights seemed to wrap us round in a pulsation of comforting warmth.

Hoarse, noisy Neftalí Amador acted as our guide. He walked with short and rapid steps. He talked without a pause, stringing together flat-toned words, words redolent of chewing-gum, which he ejaculated from between rigid jaws. On the street-corners the night light glanced off his pox-pitted face. Every time we had to cross the street, as our feet sank into the mud, he would repeat: "This is a pigsty. When the revolution wins we're going to clean it up. We'll make a new city, bigger and better than the one across the river."

Beams of light which were powerless to dispel the gloom filtered through the doors to the public mud. Street-cars clanged by. People and shapes resembling people crowded the streets. Occasionally above the mass of noise in Spanish—spoken with the soft accent of the north—phrases of cow-boy English exploded. The hellish music of the automatic pianos went on incessantly. Everything smelled of mud and whisky. Up and down the streets, rubbing shoulders with us, walked ugly prostitutes, ugly and unhappy if they were Mexican; ugly and brazen if they were Yankees; and all this intermingled with the racket and noise of the gambling-machines that came from the saloons and taverns. We stopped for a few minutes before the doors of a large hall where a hundred or more people sat bent over the tables, their attention fixed on a number of placards covered with figures. Raucous voices called out numbers in English and Spanish.

"They play the lottery here," said Amador.

A few steps farther on we stopped at the entrance to a long hall at the rear of which, among the groups of men and women, could be seen the gleam of green tables with piles of red, blue and yellow chips. It seemed a big place.

"That's for poker, for the roulette-wheel, for monte, for shooting craps."

And after blurting out those words, one on top of the other, Amador paused for a few seconds and then went on, as if he were answering himself: "No doubt about it, it's a low-down business; but there's nothing like it when funds are low. When the time comes, we'll get rid of it. We'll drive it out. But not now. Anyway, in the mean time it's the Yankees who keep it going. They come with their money and leave it here for us to buy rifles and ammunition. They're helping along the good cause; though I realize that, as we buy our munitions from them, in the end they get back the money they left here for a little while. Still, we have the arms. But we don't have them either, for we destroy them. And, what's worse, we destroy each other with them."

. . . We went on awhile longer until we came to a place that in the blackness of the night gave the feeling of being near the river, towards the part where the bank and the lower end of the city came together.

Amador interrupted himself: "Here it is. Right round the corner."

Saying this, he stepped a couple of paces ahead of us, straightening up his shoulders with the air of one who is conducting a party. A short throaty cough replaced his talk.

And, sure enough, just round the corner we almost bumped into a group of the rebels on guard. They were lined up along both sides of the door of one of the first houses, some squatting against the wall, some standing up. From between the two halves of the door, which was ajar, a few faint gleams of light radiated out into the thick shadows, throwing the forms of the soldiers into a kind of distorted visibility. The brim of their enormous hats seemed to weigh them down, making them still more squat. Each one seemed to have across his breast ten or twenty cartridge-belts with hundreds and hundreds of shells. The movements of their legs in their tight trousers imitated the swell and fall of a wheezy accordion. Across their shoulders, between their hands, beside their feet, gleamed the rifle-barrels, and the rifle-butts made a dark, triangular blotch.

As soon as they heard our steps, they jumped to their feet, making a brilliant play of lights and shadows in the pale rays that filtered through the door. One of them, heavy with the weight of his rifle and cartridge-belts, shuffled forward to meet us. His dark face was framed by a huge hat, the brim of which, turned up in front and down in back, buckled against the thick folds of his blanket, which he wore in a roll over his shoulders.

"Say, where are you headed for?"

Amador went towards him, assuming a friendly, somewhat familiar air, and answered him in a voice that was meant to be low, but which was toneless: "We're friends. These two gentlemen, who are revolutionists, just got here from Mexico City, and want to see the General. I'm Neftalí Amador. One of them was a minister under President Madero—"

"Not minister," interrupted Pani, "under-secretary."

"That's it, under-secretary," and Amador rambled on with a thousand unnecessary explanations.

We had stopped in front of the door. The soldiers, quiet in their places, were listening to Amador's chatter with the rapt attention of those to whom a discussion is all Greek. They had about them that air of humble pride which characterizes our victorious revolutionists.

"Then it's Mr. Amador and two ministers . . ."

"That's right. The Under-secretary of Public Instruction in President Madero's Cabinet and the director general . . ."

"Say, how do you expect me to say all that?"

"Well, then, just Mr. Amador and a minister of President Madero."

"One minister or two ministers?"

"It doesn't matter, one or two . . ."

The door was opened wider to let the soldier in and then was shut completely. In a minute it opened again:

"Well, come in, if you're who you say you are."

We went in. The door opened into a low-ceilinged square room, with a damp, dirt floor. A kerosene lamp on top of a pile of saddles and boxes shed its dim light and smoke through the room, which was nothing but a shed.

Once across the threshold, Amador turned to the left, slipping between the door and the soldier. Pani followed him. I was the last. Four or five steps more and the three of us were in the corner opposite the lamp, the darkest of all.

There was Pancho Villa.

He was lying on a cot, covered to the waist with a blanket. He had raised himself up a little to receive us, one arm acting as a column of support between his body and the bed. His right arm hung by his side; it was unbelievably long. But Villa was not alone. At the head of his bed two other revolutionists were sitting on turned-up boxes, with their backs to the light. They seemed to have cut short an important conversation. Neither of them moved as we came in, or showed more than a vague curiosity, indicated by the way they turned their heads, half-hidden in their enormous hats, towards the door.

Amador's words of introduction were as flowery as they were long. Villa listened to him unblinkingly. His mouth was a little open and there were traces on his face of the mechanical smile that seemed to start at the edge of his teeth. At last Amador stopped short, and Villa, without answering him, ordered the soldier to bring up chairs. But apparently there were only two, for that was all the soldier brought. Pani and Amador sat down. At the general's invitation I had seated myself on the edge of the cot, about an inch from him. The warmth of the bed penetrated through my clothes to my flesh.

It was evident that Villa's intention had been to rest for only a little while; he had on his hat, his coat, and, to judge from some of his movements, his pistol and cartridge-belts. The rays of the lamp shone straight into his face and brought out a gleam of copper around the brilliance of the whites of his eyes and the enamel of his teeth. His curly hair lay in a tangled bushy mass between his hat and his broad, curved forehead. As he talked the short ends of his reddish moustache made moving shadows across his mouth.

His attitude, his gestures, the movement of his restless eyes, gave him a resemblance to a wild animal in its lair; but an animal that defends itself rather than one that attacks. He looked like an animal that was beginning to feel a little confidence, but at the same time was not sure that the other animals would not leap upon him suddenly and devour him. In part his attitude was in contrast with that of the other revolutionists. Who were they?—Urbina? Medina? Herrera? Hipólito? To judge from their appearance they were perfectly calm, smoking, one leg crossed over the other, and every now and then leaning forward with elbow on knee and chin on fist.

"Why didn't you put a bullet through that son of a bitch of Victoriano Huerta?" Villa interrupted Pani in the middle of his account of Madero's death.

Pani repressed a tendency to smile, for he grasped the psychological import of the situation, and answered very seriously: "That wasn't easy."

Villa reflected for a moment.

"You're right, boy. It wasn't easy. But, believe me, it will be."

And in this way, for over half an hour, a strange conversation went on. Two absolutely opposed categories of mind were revealed. Every question and every answer from one side or the other made it plain that here were two different, two irreconcilable worlds whose only point of contact was the chance fact that they had joined forces in the same struggle. We, poor visionaries—for then we were only that—had come armed only with the feeble experience of our books and our early ideals. And into what had we walked? Full-face, and without a word of warning, into the tragedy of good and evil, which knows no compromise. One or the other had to win or be defeated; there was no middle ground. We came fleeing from Victoriano Huerta, the traitor, the assassin, and this same vital impulse, with everything that was good and generous in it, flung us into the arms of Pancho Villa, who had more of a jaguar about him than a man. A jaguar tamed, for the moment, for our work, or for what we believed was our work; a jaguar whose back we stroked with trembling hand, fearful that at any moment a paw might strike out at us.

As we were crossing the river back into the United States, I could not get the figure of Villa as I had just seen him out of my mind. It obsessed me and kept me thinking of what Vasconcelos had said to us in San Antonio: "Now we'll win all right. We've got a man !"

A man! A man!

His raid on Columbus has become mythic, but in Pancho Villa's first visit to the small New Mexico town, a novelist writes that a barber cut his dirty, unkempt hair, and he shopped at a department store seduced by "the moist smell of dreams."

from *Under the Fifth Sun*

Earl Shorris

In a little charreada outside Delicias he won twenty pesos riding a bull, at a cockfight near Santa Ysabel he turned the twenty pesos into forty-five; but a widow who sat with her children in front of the market in Chihuahua begged him to give her a peso and he gave her twenty because it comforted him. He swam and fished In San Bernabé Lake, stole two mules in Bustillos, and led them north into the ranch country. On the Terrazas Ranch he butchered cattle, dried the meat in the winter sun and carried it south to the lumbering towns to sell to camp cooks and the managers of the company stores. He bought salt, corn flour, and cooking oil and carried it down into the Copper Canyons, selling it to the Tarahumaras and the prospectors who wandered the greenwater tributaries of the Urique, the Papigochic, the Conchos, and the Mayo. From his trading he filled a sack with flakes of gold. He camped each night in an inaccessible place, a natural tower or a tiny platform among the broken edges of the mountains, sleeping soundly there, letting the horse and the mules do his watching. He wandered away the winter, and in the early spring he sold the mules in Casas Grandes and took the road north to Palomas, crossing the border there to Columbus, New Mexico, at the end of April which is the time of the long fast and the hope of the new corn.

The town lay at the foot of a round hill. To the west the mountains hid behind a brown haze of dust, to the north the land dipped and rolled along the base of a chain of sawtooth mountains, and on the east a long stretch of deadly waterless land led to the river and the great northern pass. He saw the town first in the afternoon in the harsh wind, when the streets were empty and the sound of creaking metal was all that came to a man passing the rows of barracks, mess shacks, stables, and officers' houses, riding up the road between the customs house and the tan square of the railroad station, crossing the tracks, turning east on the first street, then north at the Commercial Hotel to the block of stores, the silk and silver treasures of the rich.

The streets were made of hard clay dusted with sand. The town smelled of manure and alkaline powder that did not settle out of the wind. Soldiers passed on their high-tailed horses, their lustrous, white-hocked horses. They sat as if on parade, the reins in one hand, the other hand upon a hip. Their hats were tilted, their boots were shined, their spurs were polished; each man wore a single bandolier across his chest. The soldiers' faces were red, they squinted their eyes in the wind.

There were women in the streets, hurrying from store to store, dressed in long skirts and bonnets that hid their hair. They pulled children along with them and carried packages wrapped in brown paper and tied with rough twine. Businessmen in dark suits and white shirts stood in the streets. They kept their hands in the pockets of their trousers. They wore thin neckties that hung down to their waists. Some chewed tobacco and spit streams in the dust. The spittle did not mix with the dust but lay on it in dark globes.

Mexicans walked between the businessmen and the soldiers and the women in their bonnets. They were barefoot or wearing the poorest huaraches. The women wrapped their heads against the wind. The men wore farmers' hats and faded blue shirts and trousers. They did not raise their heads; only their eyes lifted to see who passed. They walked slowly. They did not speak. The men removed their hats for everyone, even the soldiers who passed them blindly on their high-stepping horses, as if on parade.

Villa tied his horse to a rail near the drugstore and walked along the rows of stores to look in the windows. They were richer than the stores in Torreón or Chihuahua, profusions of canned goods, sacks of beans, flour, potatoes, and onions. There were crates of eggs, slabs of bacon, fresh-killed chickens, cleaned tripe, and strips of dried beef. Bolts of cloth lay one upon another in disarrayed mountains of reds, blacks, browns, whites, and prints, checks, patterns of flowers and dots and stripes and squares and mixture of every kind. He passed barbers and gunsmiths, saddlers, feed merchants, bootmakers, assayers, bankers and cattle brokers, bartenders, bakers, waiters, and tailors. It was a town of hundreds with enough goods for thousands, a rich and dusty town, hostage to the wind.

He sold his pouch of gold flakes in the assayer's office for two hundred and six dollars. A man with a pale bald scalp counted out the money and explained in Spanish that each dollar was worth two pesos and that he could have his choice of pesos or dollars in payment for his gold. Villa took the dollars and went to the barber shop. The barber, who was sitting in a chair tilted back against the wall, said that he was too busy; he directed Villa to the Mexican barber two blocks west and one block south. "I have dollars," Villa said in Spanish. The barber directed him again to the Mexican barbershop.

"Son of a bitch," the Mexican barber said in his best English accent, and then returned to Spanish to continue his discussion of the American barber. "He says we have lice in our hair because of the grease we use on it. That's how he stays in business. The gringos won't come to me and he won't cut hair for the Mexicans. It would be all right, but the gringos have the money and the Mexicans have the hair.

"Look at yours, for example; it must be almost a year since you cut your hair. How can you wear a hat over so much hair? Thank God it's clean. If so much hair was dirty, I would send you to the baths first; it's the only thing to do with cowboys. Are you a cowboy? What ranch are you from?"

"I'm a woodcutter. I sold my wood in Guzmán and came up here to look at the Americans. They say that all the Americans are rich."

"Sure. The gringos are rich because we do the work for them, us and the blacks. The whole country is this way. I have been to California to see it there too. All rich people in America have blue eyes—it's a rule. All poor people are black or toasted—that's also a rule."

"Who makes these rules?"

The barber clipped and combed, cutting a part into Villa's hair, mumbling that he would have to charge more for so much hair. "Books," he said in answer to the question. "The rules are made by the books."

"Books don't make rules."

The barber came around to the front of the chair and waved his comb in Villa's face. "You think I don't know what I'm talking about—you think I'm just a foolish barber who only knows about hair. Well, Mr. Woodcutter, if you see a rich Mexican in America, you ask him who makes the rules."

Villa closed his eyes and let the barber continue his work without interruption. While the barber stropped the razor before shaving his beard, Villa said, "I'm not a woodcutter, I'm a prospector. I just changed a little bit of gold for dollars in the office on the main street. Now I want to buy some supplies to go back out into the mountains. Is there a store here where they won't cheat me?"

"Ravel," the barber said. "Ravel the Jew is the only one to trust. He doesn't like Mexicans, but he doesn't like gringos, either. They're hard men, Ravel and his brothers; they don't sell on credit and they don't give anything away, but you can trust them, because you know they're sons of bitches. In America, the only ones to do business with are the sons of bitches. The other ones put stones in the cheese to increase the weight, and then they sell it to you at a good price for cheese, which is a poor price for stones."

"And the gringo barber," Villa said, laughing, "isn't he a son of a bitch?"

"No, he's not a true son of a bitch; his mother likes it."

It was early evening when Villa left the barbershop. He smelled of sweet oils and his hat seemed too large; he held on to it in the wind. On the main street some of the stores were closed, music and singing came from the taverns, soldiers walked in the street, some of them already staggering. Ravel's Mercantile Store was still open; the lanterns shone yellow in the windows and there were customers inside, examining cooking utensils and picking though piles of denim overalls. Villa stepped up onto the boardwalk and looked in at the great array of merchandise; it was the store he had dreamed of in Durango, a store of sections: one for clothing, another for cloth, and another for utensils, and yet another for saddlery, and in the back a section of rifles and ammunition, and off to one side a section of spices, salt, beans, flour, and dried meat. Clothing, utensils, weapons, and meat hung from the walls; rows of bridles dangled from hooks; hats were stacked on shelves; the counters were filled with spices and boxes of ammunition, underwear, and spurs; great scales and small scales stood side by side on the counter tops; and all around the store the shelves reached to the ceiling.

The smell inside the store was so wonderful it made him dizzy: leather, spices, cotton dust, meat, gunpowder, and crude oil, the blended odor of plenty. This was not the dry, dusty smell of Valenzuela's little store; it was the moist smell of dreams. He walked among the table, touching the cloth, the cool buttons, the heavy utensils, the carefully oiled metal of rifles, the soaped and oiled leather.

A small, thin, very neat man moved away from a group of people at the spice counter and came to Villa's side. "Good evening," he said in Spanish.

• He was of the size and bearing of a young man, but there was a large pink inflammation in the corner of his right eye and the flesh around both eyes was dark and wearily fallen. His hair was thin, his mouth was tight; he did not smile. "Sam Ravel at your service."

"I want a suit," Villa said. "And a white shirt and a long tie. And a pair of low shoes in two colors of leather. And an American hat."

"There are seven-dollar suits and twelve-dollar suits and thirty-dollar suits—which do you want?"

"I don't know." Villa said. "I want to compare them."

"That's what I would do," Ravel said, and for the first time his mouth softened at the corners.

The seven-dollar suit did not have a vest and the thirty-dollar suit was too thick for the coming summer; Villa chose a brown wool suit for twelve dollars. Ravel was disappointed by the choice, and he showed his feelings in the pursed curve of his lips. Villa asked what was wrong, and he answered: "I thought you were a smarter man; the seven-dollar suit is all you need. That's what I wear. In the other suit you pay five dollars for style, and the style will change before the suit wears out."

"It's the vest, my friend. An American, like you, doesn't need a vest. But a Mexican country boy needs vests and perfume and shoes made of two colors of leather."

"For what?"

"I don't know yet. But I think that on this side of the river a man who carries a Colt pistol should hide it with a gold chain across his vest."

"A gold chain will cost you twenty dollars."

Villa made an innocent mask of his face. "Maybe a friend will give one to me," he said. "A man never knows where he is going to meet a friend."

Ravel's speech quickened. "I'm not only in the mercantile business. We deal in cattle too, all kinds of cattle. Some of the cattle we sell aren't even branded because they come off the big ranches. They're not stolen, you understand, just not branded, because the ranches are so big they can't brand them all; especially some of the big ones in Mexico are that way. We buy them here, fatten them, and drive them to El Paso or load them onto trains right here at our own loading platforms. Our prices are good, sir, very good. We'll pay in dollars, pesos, or gold."

"And if they're branded?"

"It spoils the hides, so we pay a little less. But there's no need to worry, our prices are still good, and we'll buy as many as you can deliver.

No change in the price, whether you bring in one or one hundred thousand."

"Well, that's good to know," Villa said. "I'm just a poor prospector now, panning a little gold out of the streams wherever I find it. But if I should ever get into the cattle business, I'll know where to sell my beef."

The clothing cost nineteen and a half dollars. Ravel included two pairs of socks and a suit of underwear as a bonus. "And stay in my hotel tonight," he said, "as my guest. You know the Commercial Hotel? It's the best in town."

"You must be a rich man," Villa said.

"No, no. I'm only a shopkeeper, a middleman; I make other men rich."

The great educator and philosopher reveals surprising recollections of his youth in border towns on both sides of the river.

from *A Mexican Ulysses*

José Vasconcelos

TRANSLATED BY W. Rex Crawford

In Piedras Negras business was good. Public buildings were going up, the railroad shops were being mechanized, shops dealing in luxury goods and jewelry and big stores were numerous, but there was no decent school. In search of one, we moved for a while to the neighboring American town of Eagle Pass.

My first experience in the school there was a bitter one. There I saw North American and Mexican children sitting in front of a teacher whose language I did not understand. Suddenly my nearest neighbor, a bilingual Texan, stuck his elbow into my side and said, "Hey you! How many of them can you lick?" I didn't understand, and he went on, "Can you take on Jack?" and he pointed to a red-haired boy. After looking him over, I replied modestly that I couldn't. "And Johnny, and Bill?" Finally, worn out by his insistence, I answered at random, "Yes." The boy in question was more or less my size.

As soon as we went out for recess, they formed a circle. Some boys came over to take a close look at me; others grabbed my books; one shook hands, and several gave me a push. Then my benchmate shouted, "This guy says he can lick Tom!" They put us face to face; they drew a line on the ground between us; the first to step over it was the braver. We rushed at each other, not at the line, and we fought. We stepped back and looked each other over; we fought again; after a while they pulled us apart. "O.K.," said my neighbor, "you come after him," and to me, "You're number seven." Puzzled and offended, I couldn't do anything but submit. The whole episode made me angry and I withdrew further into myself. I was a timid, sad child, subject to sudden fits of rage.

Anxious fears would come over me; for no good reason, I became profoundly sad; for long hours I stayed alone, wrapped in the darkness of my own mind. Paralyzing fears overwhelmed me, and then suddenly I would be a prey to reckless, frenetic impulses. "Go slow about making a decision, because when you do, you will be its slave." If someone had whispered this advice in my ear, it might have made life a lot easier for me. Darkness, helplessness, terrible fears, self-centeredness, such is the summary of the emotional life of my childhood.

As soon as we could find a decent place to live, we went back to Piedras Negras. It is in this house that my conscious life begins. I must have been about ten. We were glad the time in Eagle Pass was over. My mother had suffered a great deal from neuralgia there. Then, too, she was bothered by one of those things that leads to jealousy and recrimination. My father never failed to come home to sleep, but he began to arrive late at night.

My mother's elder brother, Esteban, was paying us a visit at the time, and he managed to calm her down. He had just finished his engineering course, and he spent a lot of time with books. He impressed me so much that I thought his learning quite unlimited. He used to discuss religion with Mother, and they would both get worked up. Uncle soon returned to the capital. A few days after he left, Mother sent me to gather some kindling. I lit a big fire and then I helped her throw into it a lot of bound and paperback books. A whole pyre of print went up in flames. "These books," explained my mother, "are heretical books!"

The most innocent of the games, and the most often played, was baseball. It never attracted me. I kept away from it, or contented myself with watching. At the most, if no one else was available, I undertook to be a fielder.

School had been winning me over gradually. Now I would not have exchanged it for any pastime. I never missed a class. All things considered, the school was very permissive and the teachers fair. The year we had a woman teacher I got my first punishment. I don't remember what I had done, but I was forced to hold out my hand. The blow I received was given with a will, but still without anger.

The fair-mindedness of the teachers stood out in connection with the arguments arising from Texas history. The independence of Texas and the war of 1847 divided the class into rival camps. We Mexicans in the class were not numerous, but we stood our ground. When I say Mexicans, I include the many who lived in Texas, and whose fathers had become naturalized, but who made common cause with us because of their descent. And if they had not, it would have turned out just the same, since the Yankees put us all in the same category. When it was said in class that a hundred Yankees could put to flight a thousand Mexicans, I got up and said, "That isn't so!" And it made me still more angry if some pupil compared the customs of the Mexicans to those of the Eskimos, and said, "Mexicans are a semi-civilized people." At our house, on the other hand, we believed that Yankees had just recently acquired culture. I would get up in class to argue, "We had printing before you did." And the teacher would chime in, "Yes, look at Joe. He's a Mexican. Isn't he civilized? Isn't he a gentleman?"

For the moment, this fair observation established a cordial relationship, but soon our passions were aroused again. We made a date for recess; blows were exchanged. The fight became a personal one. We went to the neighboring field. A large group followed us. We began to fight in earnest. From the beginning, I got the worst of it. My opponent beat me up methodically. Next day, at lunch time, while I was brooding over my defeat of the previous day, a Mexican fellow-student, one of those born and brought up beside the river, came up. "Here, take this," he said, handing me a sharp razor. "I'm lending it to you. These gringos are afraid of the blade. Keep it for this afternoon."

When we came out of school, my foe took up a position in front of his gang. I came closer, with my friends. I made him a sign, inviting him to fight, and at the same time showed the open blade in my right hand. "Not that way," said Jim, "the way we did yesterday." "No, not like yesterday," I said, "like this." My Mexican friend told me, "Now these gringos won't bother you." It was lucky that I managed to make myself respected in this way, for I loved the classes.

"Mama, what is a philosopher?" I asked; and she, as laconic as the catechism, replied, "A philosopher is a man who by the light of reason tries to find the truth." The word *philosopher* sounded to me full of satisfaction and mystery. I wanted to be a philosopher. When would I become a philosopher? . . .

Certain scholastic triumphs and the isolation forced upon me by my work had made me not only the best-read boy in town but the most famous as a good student. So on one of the holidays, the Patriotic Committee decided to include me among the orators.

In short pants and with a few sheets in my hand, feeling very important, I marched in the procession beside my father. It seemed obvious to me that when I reached the years of those about me, I would be immeasurably superior to them. Even as a boy, I regarded myself as something apart. Visions of future glory appeared and disappeared, kicked up by the dust of our feet. The hour of my debut was at hand; my hands were cold, and I had a lump in my throat.

At the same hour, with the very same patriotic trappings, the same oratory, the same popular "enthusiasm," similar ceremonies were being celebrated in every village and city of the country. No wonder that I, too, felt moved. My weak, dull voice counted against me. An exaggerated timidity inhibited my movements and was in painful contrast to my inner conviction about the value of what I had written. In reality, the audience did not worry me; but gradually, as I read my composition, I lost interest in it; I saw defects in it and was mentally correcting them. I wanted to say, "This isn't good; it must be done over." But somehow or other I kept on reading, in a hurry to get it over, since no one was listening and the hisses were beginning. My father began to make signs, telling me to cut it short, but I didn't know how. I felt a flame burning in each ear. At last I finished. What I had written was not too long, but I had not known how to deliver it; perhaps it was just not in the right style for a speech. One thing was sure, I lived through agony. The crowd soon forgot me, but I kept thinking of my failure. My mother, hours later, found some consoling words, "You are not made for oratory; you'll be a writer, and that is better."

We left there, you might say, without any apparent reason except an unspoken agreement within the bosom of the family. The pretext may have been dissatisfaction with the new boss. The dominant motive, however, was our desire to find better schools for my sisters and to prepare me for a professional career. Taking advantage of the two months of paid vacation that the regulations allowed my father after I don't know how many years of work, we decided to move without knowing exactly where we would go. We wanted a job in the customs office in a place where there were good secondary schools. In this way, the family could remain united without standing in the way of our educational progress. By consulting our geography, we found that only two ports filled the bill: Vera Cruz and Campeche. No use thinking about Vera Cruz; only the pets of the government went there, and my father was not cast in that role. With absolute conviction, father began to assert, "We are going to Campeche."

Although I was very eager to go, to broaden my horizons and my destiny, I used to wake up at night crying; I dreamed of returning to Piedras Negras after years of absence. I could see the streets transformed; people I did not know would look at me with indifference. Hanging around in the shade of the doorways, not a single friendly face. Bigger and higher buildings, but I hardly recognized the places I had loved. Showy construction, smooth pavements, a new and sumptuous Piedras Negras, no longer mine, had replaced the city of my childhood, a part of my soul.

As war clouds gathered over Europe for a second time, the author traveled to Mexico to write his epic *The Power and the Glory*. On his way he paused just long enough to fan his peculiar prejudices and moisten his literary tastebuds.

from *Another Mexico*

Graham Greene

The border means more than a customs house, a passport officer, a man with a gun. Over there everything is going to be different; life is never going to be quite the same again after your passport has been stamped and you find yourself speechless among the money-changers. The man seeking scenery imagines strange woods and unheard-of mountains; the romantic believes that the women over the border will be more beautiful and complaisant than those at home; the unhappy man imagines at least a different hell; the suicidal traveller expects the death he never finds. The atmosphere of the border—it is like starting over again; there is something about it like a good confession: poised for a few happy moments between sin and sin. When people die on the border they call it 'a happy death.'

The money-changers' booths in Laredo formed a whole street, running downhill to the international bridge; then they ran uphill on the other side into Mexico, just the same but a little shabbier. What makes a tourist choose one money-changer rather than another? The same prices were chalked up all the way down to the slow brown river—'3.50 pesos for a dollar'; '3.50 pesos for a dollar.' Perhaps they look at the faces, but the faces were all the same too—half-caste faces.

I had imagined a steady stream of tourist cars going across from America on this side into Mexico over there, but there wasn't one. Life seemed to pile up like old cans and boots against a breakwater; you were part of the silt yourself. A man in San Antonio had said I'd be sure to find a car going down, and an agent near the bridge-head said that was right—he knew for a fact that there was a Mexican driving down from San Antonio ('in a fine German car') who would give me a seat to Mexico City for a few dollars. I waited and waited and of course he never turned up; I don't think he even existed, though why they should have wanted to keep me on *their* side of the river I don't know. They weren't getting any money out of me.

Every half-hour I walked down to the river bank and looked at Mex-

ico; it looked just the same as where I was—I could see the money-
changers' booths running uphill through the heat and a kind of mass of
people near the bridge-head—the silt washing up on their side of the
breakwater too. I could imagine them saying over there, "There's an
American going from Monterrey to New York in a fine German car. He'll
give you a seat for a few dollars"; and people like me were waiting on the
other side, staring across the Rio Grande at the money-changers and
thinking, 'That's the United States,' waiting for a traveler who didn't exist
at all. It was like looking at yourself in a mirror.

Over there—one argued to oneself—were Chichen Itzá and Mitla and
Palenque, the enormous tombstones of history, the archaeologists' Mexico; serapes and big hats and Spratling silver from Taxco to delight the
tourist; for the historian relics of Cortés and the Conquistadores; for the
art critic the Rivera and Orozco frescoes; and for the business man there
were the oilfields of Tampico, the silver mines of Pachuca, the coffee
farms in Chiapas, and the banana groves of Tabasco. For the priest prison,
and for the politician a bullet. You could buy a great deal for your dollar,
everyone said.

I walked back up to the plaza and bought a paper. It was my unlucky
day. The paper was being edited by the high school students—guest editors
and guest reporters; it was full of small-town gossip and what was muttered on the campus. Impatient, revolutionary young men and women? Not
a bit of it. The platitudes of age are often the main discoveries of youth.
Geneva . . . democracy . . . popular fronts . . . the threat of Fascism. One
might as well have been in the Albert Hall. As for Mexico, there wasn't as
much news of it here as in New York. In New York there had been stories of
fighting across the border from Brownsville—a man called General Rodríguez had organized discontented farmers, they were losing their land to
the Indians under the Agrarian Laws, into a Fascist body called the Gold
Shirts. The New York papers had sent down special reporters: one of them
had taken a taxi from Brownsville to Matamoros and back and reported
he'd seen no fighting but a lot of discontent. One pictured the earnest tough
face peering through the glass at discontent on the dry plain. Somebody in
New York told me General Rodríguez had forty thousand trained men on
the Texas border—I'd be missing everything if I missed Rodríguez.

You get used in Mexico to disappointment—a town seems fine at
evening and then in daylight the corruption seeps through, a road peters
out, a muleteer doesn't turn up, the great man on acquaintance becomes

strangely muted, and when you get to the gigantic ruins you are too tired to see them. It was that way with Rodríguez. He came to nothing.

Then I went down to the river bank again and had a look at Mexico; the lights were coming out on the other side of the Rio Grande; it seemed absurd to wait any longer on *this* side; the side of the freak show and the paper edited by the local high school and the coloured comic supplement —Mr. Gump, with the horrible missing jaw and the stuck-out nose, quarrelling with Mrs. Gump week by week, year after year; Moon Mullins and Kitty Higgins; Tarzan eternally young and brave and successful; Dick Tracy, the G man, for ever on the track.

I went back to the agent's and got a taxi; he no longer tried to pretend that a fine German car was on the way from San Antonio. We drove slowly between the money-changers to the bridge-head, I deposited five hundred pesos at the customs, and then we drove past the other bridge-head, uphill between the money-changers. This was Mexico, that was the United States. The only difference was dirt and darkness: there weren't so many lights in Mexico. They called this Nuevo Laredo to distinguish it from the town in Texas, but as so often happens the son looked older than the father, more acquainted with the seamy side of life. The streets were dark and unsurfaced, the little plaza stuffy with greenery; all the life there was went on behind the swing doors of the cantinas and billiard parlours. There was a large cockroach dead on the floor of my room and a sour smell from the water-closet. Thunder came rolling up from Texas and rain splashed and dug and churned the unmade roads. I tried to read myself to sleep with *Barchester Towers* . . . but I couldn't concentrate. The world is all of a piece, of course; it is engaged everywhere in the same subterranean struggle, lying like a tiny neutral state, with whom no one ever observes his treaties, between the two eternities of pain and—God knows the opposite of pain, not we.

There was nothing to do all morning but wait around for the man from San Antonio, who I knew would never turn up. The side streets were ankle-deep in mud, and there was nobody to talk to. It was a small town and it sank every way you walked but one into the muddy plain. That one way was the bridge: I was in looking-glass land now, staring back at the United States. The tall Hamilton Hotel stood up clearly above Laredo; I sat in the Mexican plaza and had my shoes cleaned and looked at it. The morning was like a replica of yesterday, only reversed: the walk down to the river and back to the plaza, the morning paper. Several people had been shot by a police chief in a quarrel—that was the regular feature of a Mexican paper; no day passed without somebody's being assassinated somewhere; at the end of the paper there was a page in English for tourists. That never included the shootings, and the tourists, as far as I could see, never read the Spanish pages. They lived in a different world, they lived in a few square inches of American territory; with *Life* and *Time* and coffee at Sanborn's, they were impervious to Mexico.

Lunch was awful, like the food you eat in a dream, tasteless in a positive way, so that the very absence of taste is repellent. All Mexican food is like that: if it isn't hot with sauces, it's nothing at all, just a multitude of plates planked down on the table simultaneously, so that five are getting cold while you eat the sixth; pieces of anonymous meat, a plate of beans, fish from which the taste of the sea has long been squeezed away, rice mixed with what look like grubs—perhaps they are grubs—a salad (dangerous, you are always warned, and for a long while you heed the warning), a little heap of bones and skin they call a chicken—the parade of cooling dishes goes endlessly on to the table edge. After a while your palate loses all discrimination; hunger conquers; you begin in a dim way even to look forward to your meal. I suppose if you live long enough in Mexico you begin to write like Miss Frances Toor—'Mexican cooking appeals to the eye as well as to the palate.' (It is all a hideous red and yellow, green and brown, like art needlework and the sort of cushions popular among decayed gentlewomen in Cotswold tea-shops.) 'The artistic instinct is alive even in the humblest cook.'

In the afternoon I caught a train to Monterrey—couldn't wait any longer for the car.

Jacinto Treviño

Los Pingüinos del Norte

Ya con esta van tres veces
en que se ve lo bonito
la primera fue en McAllen
en Brownsville y San Benito.

This makes it the third time
that he has been seen,
first it was in McAllen
Then in Brownsville and San Benito.

En la Cantina de Beca
se agarrarón a balasos
por donde quiera volaban
botellas hechas pedasos.

In the Cantina de Beca
here began all the shooting,
broken bottles were flying
all around.

Esa Cantina de Beca
Al momento quedó sola
no más Jacinto Treviño
de carabina y pistola.

In the Cantina de Beca
For a moment there was
only Jacinto Treviño
With his rifle and his pistol.

Entrenle rinches cobardes
Validos de la ocasión
creián que era pan blanco
con tajadas de jamón.

Ok, you cowardly Rangers,
You have always been opportunists,
you thought this would be
a piece of cake.

Entrenle rinches cobardes
el pleito no es con un niño
que bien conocen su padre
yo soy Jacinto Treviño.

Okay, you cowardly Rangers,
You are not fighting with children,
come and meet your father.
I am Jacinto Treviño.

Decía el cherife mayor
Como era un americano
Ay que Jacinto tan hombre
no niega ser mexicano.

The sheriff was heard saying
For he was an anglo,
"Jacinto is very brave,
Proud of being a Mexican."

Decía Jacinto Treviño
no me pueden agarrar
Me voy para el Río Grande
Allá los voy a esperar.

Jacinto Treviño was saying,
"You'll never catch me,
I am going to the Río Grande
I will wait for you there.

Ya con esta me despido
Aquí a presencia de todos
Yo soy Jacinto Treviño
Nacido de Matamoros.

This is to say farewell
in presence of all here"
I am Jacinto Treviño,
born in Matamoros.

Section 2

The following pieces will take you so far inside the borderland you won't know which way is out.

From its opening sentence, this 1889 account reveals the revulsion and undeniable attraction an eastern lady felt on confronting "the witchery of a foreign land."

Over the Border

Cora Hayward Crawford

El Paso surpasses all of our expectations of the horrors of a border-town. It is desolation, dreariness and dust personified. The hotels are vile. Gambling is carried on as openly and much more generally than church-going in the East. We were one day much impressed by the lofty air with which a man came into the dining-room, seating himself near our table. On one side of his plate he laid a large revolver and a bowie-knife; on the other a bag of jingling coins. Then he proceeded to give his order with the importance of a lord. We supposed he must be a revenue officer, or some other dignitary, but upon inquiry we learned that he was a bunko-steerer or decoy-duck for one of the gambling dens. These places are said to realize an income greater than that of a prosperous gold mine, and with much less capital. In western parlance, "they make money hand over fist," and are, indeed, dens of iniquity.

The town is totally without shade or verdure of any kind, and the country about is barren as a desert. There is not even pasturage enough in the vicinity to tempt a venturesome dairyman to settle here, notwith-standing the adjacent river, and the fact that the entire supply of milk, except the condensed article largely used in this town, is brought here from a distance by train. As traffic, in the winter-time especially, is always more or less obstructed by snows and wash-outs farther north, and as the trains are often more than twenty-four hours late, the supply is somewhat uncertain.

The climate is the only redeeming feature of the place; it is delightful, quite cold in the midwinter season, but always bright, sunshiny and dry. For this we are thankful as we are waiting for passes, letters of introduction, and other necessary papers, before venturing farther south, strangers in a strange land; and we find ourselves fated to spend some little time here.

Naturally we hasten to visit Paso del Norte at the first opportunity, a Mexican town just across the river from El Paso, and connected with it by a tramway. Paso del Norte, or, as its name indicates, the "pass to the north," was an important fording place across the Rio Grande, a deceitful river and difficult to cross, long before the railroads had built up the American town. To us it is fascinating chiefly because it is over the border; and the witchery of a foreign land is upon us as we step from the car into the narrow streets of the quaint little village. It is a mere collection of *adobe* huts lying in a somewhat luxuriant valley which, during the summer season, is green with outlying fields of clover and wild-grass, and gardens of vegetables. Its *acequias* are embowered with shade and fruit trees, and rich with clustering vines that yield abundantly, for the sandy soil is well suited to grape-raising. Great quantities of purple grapes are here converted into a variety of wines said to be of the richest quality and equal in flavor to any of the California wines.

The town seems always wrapped in the haze of a lazy afternoon. Here for the first time we see the native Mexican on his native soil. The men are arrayed in their gay *serapes* and wide-brimmed *sombreros;* and the women are wrapped, head and shoulders, in their *rebosas.* A few of these poor creatures offer images for sale, but, generally speaking, the people sit before their mud dwellings industriously doing nothing. In the little plaza, or park, found in every Mexican village however humble, we see groups of men, women, and children half-reclining on the rickety benches, and basking in the rays of the winter sun, or seated on the scattering grass, gambling at dice. In the old church we find at work a few elderly women, their faces as wrinkled, yellow and leathery as the parchment bearing the records of the early days of New Spain, which for a small consideration they bring out for our inspection. . . .

On crossing the river a fierce-looking Mexican in official dress and carrying a brace of revolvers almost as long as his arm, somewhat after the style of our horse-pistol, entered the car, eyeing each passenger, and opening every suspicious-looking bundle or basket, to the sorrow of any would-be smuggler. This incident only heightened our desires to try our own good fortune in attempting to elude the tariff laws of our country. So, on our return, the men filled their pockets with choice weeds, and we made liberal use of every receptacle that would hold a piece of the quaint pottery we found for sale in the little den-like shops. Fortunately we had been warned that the American officials are in civilian dress, and quietly perform their duties without making themselves known; otherwise, some of our party, might have had an experience similar to that of a gentleman who, having crossed the river, thought himself safe with his box of smuggled cigars, and on bringing them out to treat his friends an officer from the corner of the car quietly requested his company to the custom-house. This smuggling by means of the street-car, however, is very small, the natives doing their work by fording the river at night, and even though under constant surveillance they often succeed in safely landing whole wagon loads of contraband goods. At less exposed points along the river the business of smuggling is said to be carried on extensively. The excessive rates of duty on the necessities of life, and the high prices of home-products make it a temptingly profitable, though precarious industry. . . .

Paso del Norte is the northern terminus of the Farrocarril Central Mexicano. The construction of this road was an event of vast importance to Mexico, connecting, as it does, in one continuous line the City of Mexico with the northern borders giving an impetus long needed to its commerce and making an easy, pleasant voyage for the tourist, who desires to visit that noble city with its relics of a fallen race. This road was built by American capital and received from the Mexican government some grants of land along the line, and promises of subsidies to be obtained from a certain percentage of the import taxes. This contract, however, has been a source of discussion and trouble ever since the first train started, the government being more generous in promises than prompt in payment. . . .

Through the gathering dusk of evening we can see on each side of our track a vast stretch of desert rising into barren sand-hills, and spotted with deposits of alkalies white as snow. A few mesquite bushes and occasional yuccas, or cacti, are the only signs of vegetation.

Living in World War Two San Diego, a teenager accepts her father's invitation for a day in Mexico. "I feared that I would never get back to America, civilization, English and wide streets again."

from *I Know Why the Caged Bird Sings*

Maya Angelou

In the morning, we set out on the foreign adventure. The dirt roads of Mexico fulfilled all my longing for the unusual. Only a few miles from California's slick highways and, to me, tall buildings, we were bumping along on gravel streets that could have competed in crudeness with the worst paths in Arkansas, and the landscape boasted adobe huts or cabins walled with corrugated metal. Dogs, lean and dirty, slunk around the houses, and children played innocently in the nude or near nude with discarded rubber tires. Half the population looked like Tyrone Power and Dolores Del Rio, and the other half like Akim Tamiroff and Katina Paxinou, maybe only fatter and older.

Dad gave no explanation as we drove through the border town and headed for the interior. Although surprised, I refused to indulge my curiosity by questioning him. After a few miles we were stopped by a uniformed guard. He and Dad exchanged familiar greetings and Dad got out of the car. He reached back into the pocket of the door and took a bottle of liquor into the guard's kiosk. They laughed and talked for over a half hour as I sat in the car and tried to translate the muffled sounds. Eventually they came out and walked to the car. Dad still had the bottle but it was only half full. He asked the guard if he would like to marry me. Their Spanish was choppier than my school version but I understood. My father added as an inducement the fact that I was only fifteen years old. At once the guard leaned into the car and caressed my cheek. I supposed that he thought before that I was not only ugly but old, too, and that now the knowledge that I was probably unused attracted him. He told Dad that he would marry me and we would have "many babies." My father found that promise the funniest thing he had heard since we left home. . . . The guard was not discouraged by my attempts to get away from his probing hands and I would have squirmed to the driver's seat had not Dad opened the door and got in. After many *adiós*'s and *bonitas* and *espositas* Dad started the car, and we were on out grimy way again.

Signs informed me that we were headed for Ensenada. In those miles, along the twisted roads beside the steep mountain, I feared that I would never get back to America, civilization, English and wide streets again. He sipped from the bottle and sang snatches of Mexican songs as we climbed the tortuous mountain road. Our destination turned out not to be the town of Ensenada, after all, but about five miles out of the city limits. We pulled up in the dirt yard of a *cantina* where half-clothed children chased mean-looking chickens around and around. The noise of the car brought women to the door of the ramshackle building but didn't distract the single-minded activity of either the grubby kids or the scrawny fowls.

A woman's voice sang out, "Baylee, Baylee." And suddenly a claque of women crowded to the door and overflowed into the yard. Dad told me to get out of the car and we went to meet the women. He explained quickly that I was his daughter, which everyone thought to be uncontrollably funny. We were herded into a long room with a bar at one end. Tables sat lopsidedly on a loose-plank floor. The ceiling caught and held my attention. Paper streamers in every possible color waved in the near-still air, and as I watched a few fell to the floor. No one seemed to notice, or if they did, it was obviously unimportant that their sky was falling in. There were a few men on stools at the bar, and they greeted my father with the ease of familiarity. I was taken around and each person was told my name and age. The formal high school "Cómo está usted?" was received as the most charming utterance possible. People clapped me on the back, shook Dad's hand and spoke a rat-a-tat Spanish that I was unable to follow. Baylee was the hero of the hour, and as he warmed under the uninhibited show of affection I saw a new side of the man. His quizzical smile disappeared and he stopped his affected way of talking (it would have been difficult to wedge *ers* into that rapid Spanish).

It seemed hard to believe that he was a lonely person searching relentlessly in bottles, under women's skirts, in church work and lofty job titles for his "personal niche," lost before birth and unrecovered since. It was obvious to me then that he had never belonged in Stamps, and less to the slow-moving, slow-thinking Johnson family. How maddening it was to have been born in a cotton field with aspirations of grandeur.

In the Mexican bar, Dad had an air of relaxation which I had never seen visit him before. There was no need to pretend in front of those Mexican peasants. As he was, just being himself, he was sufficiently impressive to them. He was an American. He was Black. He spoke Spanish fluently. He had money and he could drink tequila with the best of them. The women liked him too. He was tall and handsome and generous.

It was a fiesta party. Someone put money in the jukebox and drinks were served to all the customers. I was given a warm Coca-Cola. The music poured out of the record machine as high-tenored voices wavered and held, wavered and held for the passionate rancheros. Men danced, at first alone, then with each other and occasionally a woman would join the foot-stomping rites. I was asked to dance. I hesitated because I wasn't sure I'd be able to follow the steps, but Dad nodded and encouraged me to try. I had been enjoying myself for at least an hour before I realized it. One young man had taught me how to put a sticker on the ceiling. First, all the sugar must be chewed out of Mexican gum, then the bartender gives a few slips of paper to the aspirant, who writes either a proverb or a sentimental remark on the strip. He takes the soft gum from his mouth and sticks it to the end of the streamer. Choosing a less densely covered area of the ceiling he aims at the spot, and as he throws he lets out a bloodcurdling scream which would not be out of place in a bronco-busting rodeo. After a few squeaky misses, I overcame my reserve and tore my tonsils loose with a yell that would have been worthy of Zapata. I was happy, Dad was proud and my new friends were gracious. A woman brought *chicharrones* (in the South they're called cracklings) in a greasy newspaper. I ate the fried pig skins, danced, screamed and drank the extra-sweet and sticky Coca-Cola with the nearest approach to abandonment I had ever experienced. As new revelers joined the celebration I was introduced as la niña de Baylee, and as quickly accepted. The afternoon sun failed in its attempt to light the room through the single window, and the press of bodies and scents and sounds melted to give us an aromatic and artificial twilight. I realized that I hadn't seen my father for some time. "Dónde está mi padre?" I asked my dancing partner. My formal Spanish must have sounded as pretentious to the ears of the paisano as "Whither goeth my sire?" would have sounded to a semiliterate Ozark mountaineer. In any case it brought on a howl of laughter, a bear-crushing embrace and no answer. When the dance was finished, I made my way through the squeeze of the people as unobtrusively as possible. A fog of panic nearly suffocated me. He wasn't in the room. Had he made an arrangement with the guard back at the pass? I would not put it beyond him. My drink had been spiked. The certainty made my knees weak, and dancing couples blurred before my eyes. Dad was gone. He was probably halfway back home with the money from my sale in his pocket. I had to get to the door, which seemed miles and mountains away. People stopped me with "Dónde vas?" My response was something as stiff and double meaning as "Yo voy por ventilarme," or "I am going to air out." No wonder I was a big hit.

Seen through the open door Dad's Hudson sat in lonely splendor. He hadn't left me, after all. That meant, of course, that I hadn't been drugged. I immediately felt better. No one followed me into the yard where the late afternoon sun had tenderized the midday harshness. I decided to sit in his car and wait for him since he couldn't have gone far. I knew he was with a woman, and the more I thought about it, it was easy to figure which one of the gay señoritas he had taken away. There had been a small neat woman with very red lips who clung to him avidly when we first arrived. I hadn't thought of it at the time but had simply recorded her pleasure. In the car, in reflection, I played the scene back. She had been the first to rush to him, and that was when he quickly said "This is my daughter" and "She speaks Spanish." If Dolores knew, she would crawl up in her blanket of affectations and die circumspectly. The thought of her mortification kept me company for a long time, but the sounds of music and laughter and Cisco Kid screams broke into my pleasant revengeful reveries. It was, after all, getting dark and Dad must have been beyond my reach in one of the little cabins out back. An awkward fear crept up slowly as I contemplated sitting in the car all night alone. It was a fear distantly related to the earlier panic. Terror did not engulf me wholly, but crawled along my mind like a tedious paralysis. I could roll up the windows and lock the door. I could lie down on the floor of the car and make myself small and invisible. Impossible! I tried to staunch the flood of fear. Why was I afraid of the Mexicans? After all, they had been kind to me and surely my father wouldn't allow his daughter to be ill treated. Wouldn't he? Would he? How could he leave me in that raunchy bar and go off with his woman? Did he care what happened to me? Not a damn, I decided, and opened the flood gates for hysteria. Once the tears began, there was no stopping them. I was to die, after all, in a Mexican dirt yard. The special person that I was, the intelligent mind that God and I had created together, was to depart this life without recognition or contribution. How pitiless were the Fates and how helpless was this poor Black girl.

I made out his shadow in the near gloom and was about to jump out and run to him when I noticed that he was being propelled by the small woman I had seen earlier and a man. He wobbled and lurched but they held him up firmly and guided his staggering toward the door of the *cantina.* Once he got inside we might never leave. I got out of the car and went to them. I asked Dad if he wouldn't like to get into the car and rest a little. He focused enough to recognize me and answered that that was exactly what he wanted; he was a little tired and he'd like to rest before we set out for his place. He told his friends his wishes in Spanish and they steered him to the car. When I opened the front door he said No, he'd lie down on the back seat for a little while. We got him into the car and tried to arrange his long legs comfortably. He began snoring even as we tugged at him. It sounded like the beginning of a deep and long sleep, and a warning that, after all, we were to spend the night in the car, in Mexico.

Ciudad Juárez in the 1950s: Catholic school in El Paso, hunting for Montezuma's treasure outside town, streets with "industrial quantities of dumb gringos," and real fights over imagined girlfriends. Care to dance?

Cloister

Ricardo Aguilar-Melantzón

TRANSLATED BY Irene del Corral

We were just kids, fresh out of elementary school, when they took us to that unfamiliar, strange brick building, four floors counting the basement, set on a sandy mound overlooking most of the valley. The floors, class-rooms, corridors, stairs, doorframes, desks, lockers, papers, pencils and pens were constantly coated with a fine dust that crunched underfoot and stuck to the heel of your hand when you tried to write. The place was absolutely austere, not a single picture on any of the walls, everything designed for some functional and practical purpose. They even painted all the furniture the same color, an odd tone, something like a Sunday hang-over, as if they'd mixed together whatever was left over in a lot of different paint buckets, I'll bet the paint was a gift from some hardware store. Long ago, they told us later, the building had been a refuge for Jesuits escaping from Mexico during the anti-Church movement. It was built in the shape of an M. The right leg of the M and part of the upper angle held class-rooms and offices. The cloister was on the other side. A chapel stood in the center, with the cafeteria in the basement. A coat of arms was set in the floor just outside the chapel, beneath the letters AMDG *(Ad Majore Dei Gloriam)* BVMH *(Beata Virgine María Honorem)* were a two-headed eagle, byzantine-style with no crowns, and a brown and white striped shield, the symbol of the San Ildefonso School. The schoolyard was unattractive too, with only a couple of listless bay trees and some scraggly grass. Every-thing was so ashen that it produced an overwhelming thirst we tried to slake at the water fountains. Eventually we got used to the horrible taste of the water because we were too parched to be finicky. On the first day, they gave us an exam, supposedly to test our intelligence. It was ridicu-lous because those of us who didn't know enough English flunked, not because we didn't know the answers, but because we couldn't understand the questions. To this day I remember how one of the priests led me to his office and, doing his best to console me, told me that I shouldn't be too upset over my test score, that although my low intelligence showed I wasn't cut out for a profession, I could get along very nicely as a policeman, a fireman or working with my hands, besides, I'd probably make a good artisan because everyone knew that Mexicans are especially good at any kind of manual work. (All the groundkeepers and most of the cooks and janitors at the school were Mexicans.) The first regulation to be learned by those of us from Juárez and the chicanos who by some miracle had survived the U. S. school system without forgetting their Spanish was that it was forbidden to speak that language in school, just think about that, lots of us had never had a single English lesson. Of course there was discipline, you had to stay after school and walk around a bare field. Each demerit, three for speaking Spanish, cost you three laps around the field and each lap took about 10 minutes. So when you piled up a lot of demerits, not only did you give your leg muscles a good workout, but it would get dark while you were still shuffling around in the sand. You weren't allowed to speak during your stroll. How often I meditated there about the reasons why crabs should be immortal and other profound principles. . . . Some of the carpool "friends" came from Juárez high society. Their parents spoiled them, bought them the latest model cars and forked over plenty of cash. Others, like me, barely got enough for a movie on Sundays and wore the same clothes until the shirts didn't fit and the pants reached mid-calf. And I was the smallest, the butt of the others' jokes. Unfortunately I hadn't yet learned enough curses to answer the chain of obscenities heaped on me, and could only count on a small repertory of shits and hells. So the only goddamn thing I could do was sit and take it, although two or three times, when I got good and fed up, I reacted with my fists. All I got to show for that was a couple of black eyes and long-term trouble. I learned then that the middle class in Mexico is shit, that chicanos are more noble, that the Mexican bourgeoisie raises their kids to be bullies. Somehow I realized that I didn't fit in with that group of boys who were supposed to be my peers, that I found their company disgusting. There were two terrific exceptions: Luis and Charlie Boy. I still love those guys even though I hardly see them any more. Maybe what made them different was that they were poorer and were part of the group only by chance, not choice. One of the crowd was a queer, but I didn't even suspect that until much later, I must have been naïve with a capital N. He was the worst bully of all, I know now that he probably picked on me because the others wouldn't have stood for it. Anyway, most of the insults had to do with homosexuality. The group spoke of nothing but sex during the four years of my adolescence and theirs. They invented girlfriends, gabbed endlessly about the tea-dances, about the parties in their homes, about the clothes they'd wear to the dances, about what a hot number that blond X was, about how she'd let you paw her, "in the movies, in the dark, you've never done it?, well I have, thousands of times, and to different girls, you're an asshole, no girl would ever look at you." I can't recall a single instance when they spoke well of anyone or when there was a conversation about any other subject. But Luis and Charlie Boy, well, that was different, those kids were decent. Once Luis got the brilliant idea of starting a Science Club, Charlie and I got all excited about it (though I hated science), and we set up a laboratory in my grandmother's attic. Charlie brought a few things from his old man's furniture store, Luis some instruments, and my Dad gave us some old tables we set up in the kitchen for our lab. We really got into it, and we'd even do our homework there, repeating the experiments we'd done in class. One day Charlie decided that we ought to manufacture some nitroglycerine—get this—by mixing glycerine with nitric acid. No, not that way, more of this and less of that, or less of this and more of that. Then that skunk Charlie leaves me alone and suddenly I hear a son-of-a-bitch of a blast. Charlie Boy had set me up, the bastard. I had to go change my underwear. Another day we had another marvelous inspiration, we'd make an ice bomb. Charlie and little Luis (he always got the biggest kick out of everything) went to the ice cream stand and got some dry ice and a container with a good strong cap. Trembling with fear, we put the ice in water and screwed on the cap. It began to build up pressure, Charlie tossed it into my grandmother's yard, and nothing happened, it didn't break, it didn't explode, it didn't do anything. It just lay there on the grass. We ran down, dumb kids, it could have exploded in our faces, and Charlie picked it up and threw it over the fence. The neighbor's dog started to bark, he knew what was going on, he must have been sniffing it. The thingamajig blew up and killed the stupid dog. . . . At the time we were just unbridled and determined to run wild. We were great buddies, we'd go out beyond the airport, cross-country among the brambles. He had his .22, and I had the target pistol I'd steal from my aunt Estela, poor thing, she always seemed to understand the fury burning inside me. We had energy to spare, we were convinced nothing was impossible, there was nothing we couldn't do. We hunted hares, rabbits, birds, and anything else that crossed our path. We climbed all the hills, crossed the deserts. . . . Agapito Mendoza, heaven help humankind, was the class comedian. He could make the sphynx laugh. Tall, fat, dark-skinned, he always wore Levis, suede shoes and the most fantastic collection of T-shirts I've ever seen, from one with a picture of Einstein to one with Mickey Mouse and another with Donald Duck. He had trouble-making down to a science. Nacho told me that one day at about four o'clock in the afternoon they're standing on a corner downtown where a bunch of people are waiting for the bus, and Agapito suddenly pipes up, "Jesus, it just got hard!", everybody glares at him. Nacho feels like crawling into the path of the approaching bus. Agapito, cool as a cucumber, goes on, "My bubble gum! It just got hard as a rock! What dirty minds!" . . . Agapito was in hot water most of the year he spent in Phillipot's class. He was a pain in the ass, a black from Louisiana with two doctorates, one in Philosophy and one in foreign languages, and at the time he was working on another in Theology, his classes were really brilliant. I got my first taste of French from him, and literature too, because he made us read, read and read, and expected us to know all the answers. We wrote our first poems, we did our first play. Phillipot spoke with incredible clarity, it was hard not to get wrapped up in what you were hearing. But Agapito acted up as usual. At first Phillipot ignored his wisecracks, then answered him with withering sarcasm. He threatened him, but the threats went over Agapito's head, then he sat him in the back corner, facing the wall. There he remained the whole semester, but he never improved, putting his feet against the wall. "Agapito!" said Phillipot, "When will you grow up?" Probably never. We all knew it. . . .

The kids from around here were bastards too, with a couple of exceptions, the same spoiled kids, the ones from Los Nogales, from the Country Club, they lived like kings, dressed in the latest style, went to all the dances, played golf, their fathers gave them plenty of money so they could get drunk and not bother them, and so they could get themselves girl-friends of their own high class, hell, there was never any high class in Juárez unless you were a descendant of Fray García de San Francisco. Juárez was a lively place, all along Mariscal street down to the river and on all the side streets. Floor shows, good, cheap booze, lots of dames and industrial quantities of dumb gringos. In those days, the place to go was Curley's Club, and that's where Pedro and I used to sneak off to at night. He'd bought an old gray and black Mercury, fixed it up like new, it looked great, little lights in each door, plush upholstery and carpeting. From Curley's we'd go to the Noa Noa, then to Don Felix Club, the Reno, from there to the strip tease at the Follies or Waikiki, and then to the untitled movies at the Taxco Bar. That was supposed to be a kid's initiation, he'd pick up a hooker, and when it was all over, he'd come out a man. You were expected to dance with the whores to prove your manhood, even if they stank like hell you had to put up with it just the way they put up with the whiff of brandy on your breath, the stench of your sweat and cheap after-shave. That must have been the best the world had to offer because people came from miles around, even Parral, to have fun. The low-class places were always packed with gringo soldiers and others of their kind who invariably admired the strippers and their suggestive poses, cheering when the women assumed positions never before seen, they were with their wives who clapped and hooted as loud as they did. . . . But all that's gone now, the city's grown, a million and a half to the south and half a million on the other side. Mariscal Street is done for, business shot to hell, no customers, they're all in the fashionable discotheques, they don't go to the bars any more. When the center of the city moved, Sodom was left on the outskirts. With all those maquiladoras, single women have jobs nowadays. No more professional hookers, just affairs, they don't sweep the streets the way they used to but nowadays that's where people make love.

Another of our nutty buddies was Panayote. I was stunned when I heard that crazy guy had gotten married, and my eyes popped one day when I saw him giving his baby a pacifier. The poor kid just sucked it. I should have known that couldn't turn out well. One day, very calmly, Panayote shot himself while he was cleaning a pistol.

He couldn't even stand himself, we met him at the Reno Bar, he'd buy us all beers, and we were a little afraid of him because he was one of those guys who won't listen to reason, who don't give a damn about anything. Dangerous at dances and parties. Once we were cruising on 16th street, on Sundays the kids would ride back and forth from one end of the street to the other, up and down from noon until three, everyone happy, honking horns, yelling to each other, gossiping, a real blast. There was a gang we called the Flintstones because they were a rough bunch, they carried switchblades, chains, tire irons and were always looking for trouble. Panayote hated them, especially one of their leaders. There we were having a helluva good time when suddenly a rickety black Cadillac full of long-haired thugs drove up right next to our car. Panayote gave them the finger, they wanted to get out and fight. Panayote took out a Derringer he always carried and started shooting right there in the street. He didn't give a damn that there were people on the sidewalks and a bunch of kids in their cars. The Flintstones just ducked down and put the pedal to the floorboard. When it was all over we discovered two big bullet holes in the trunk, that damn fool Panayote, after that we didn't want to go anywhere with him for fear of getting ourselves killed because of some stunt he'd pull.

He didn't go to school, and that surprised us because our parents made us toe the line, like it or not. His old man had him tending bar at the Reno, but he'd come along when we went mountain-climbing. In those days we liked to play at being explorers, supposedly to see if we could find the treasures said to be hidden in the hills, the gold Benito Juárez had brought during the Reforma wars, all the money Maximilian had sent to keep his enemies from getting it, Montezuma's treasure, and all the other treasures the legends said were buried around there, near what had been a post house behind the mountain, to the west, the stopping place for the stage coaches that crossed toward the north along the Camino Real through Mesilla, Socorro, Belén, Albuquerque and Santa Fe, following the river, through Dead Man's Pass and the plains. What we found was a cave three-quarters of the way up the hillside, it looked like hoboes or hikers stayed there because there were lots of ashes and bits of charcoal on the ground, the cave was beautiful because it was like a miniature mine, the walls studded with clusters of white and purple quartz crystals, we also found a whole damn lot of pain, we came back all bruised and scratched by cactuses on the way up, by thorns and more cactuses on the way down, not counting our slips and falls and the suffering of our tobacco-filled lungs. When we got home we had to use brushes all over to get the sticky filth off our bodies. . . .

We were always on the make, even at the dances, and all real machos, "I like this one," or "I like that one and you'd better not ask her to dance because you'll have to answer to me, and then we'll see who cries uncle." Huddled in a corner, drinking and drinking to get up our nerve and whispering among ourselves, we'd let three songs go by while the girls sat and waited because these idiots didn't ask them to dance, just stared, finally when some other guy came to ask them to dance, the jackasses got burned up, then we'd insult the girls, "what a pill she is, ugly too, not worth a second glance, besides I like that one better," or, "I didn't really feel like dancing just now anyway," there were always a couple of guys at those dances who loved to spoil things for everyone else, "why did you dance with so-and-so, as if you didn't know she's my girl, she's mine and I don't share her with anybody", and pow, a fist, right there, to the jaw or the stomach and a free-for-all would start. You always went to the dances neat and tidy, but you knew you might leave in tatters. Once a bunch of idiots started fighting on the second floor of the casino, it was like a balcony around the dance floor, three stairways and a very nice railing, so you could sit and watch the dancers from there. There were tables, and it was the favorite spot for the fellows who didn't know how to dance and spent their time getting drunk instead. One night, in the middle of the dance, when the Aceves orchestra was playing Ramona, a brawl broke out, fists flying all over the place, one of the pugilists shoved another against the railing, he lost his balance and went over, fell on top of one of the couples on the dance floor, in spite of all the yelling, the dancers pretended not to notice and just ignored the childish antics and boorishness of the upstairs crowd. That was the end of the party, everybody got into it, they threw out the people from upstairs, how embarrassing, my friend. Whenever the subject of dances comes up in a conversation I always remember the joke about the casino, that one night when there was to be a dress ball a guy showed up at the door without an invitation, with three women who were obviously prostitutes. The doorman didn't want to let him in because "The gentleman's companions are ladies whose reputation is questionable," to which the man shouted "There's no question about these ladies' reputation, they're whores, the ones with the questionable reputations are the ones in there, on the dance floor . . ."

from *The Autobiography of a Brown Buffalo*

Oscar Zeta Acosta

In January of 1968 the main Juárez jail had no ceiling. There was an earthen floor. They had neither toilet, running water nor electricity. Dark kerosene lamps showed up cockroaches the size of the pirate's thumb running willy-nilly on urined walls. The stench of shit wasn't nearly as bad as standing in the stuff in the first place. They stripped me of my clothes and searched for knives and dope up my ass. Three times, standing in darkened rooms while the freezing wind came in from above, on three separate occasions Mexican soldiers in black mustaches gave me a skin search from head to toe. The third time around I told the man I was cold and his two buddies had already searched me. He grabbed my balls and squeezed while his partner laughed and stuck a ten-foot-long rifle into my kidneys. They pushed me into another room which was completely dark. Not even the hole in the ceiling showed the bodies of the men I could hear coughing and spitting and shuffling around.

"¡Cabrón!" someone shouted in dungeon-tones as I started to move.

"¡Oye, puto!" another, garbled tequila voice screamed at me. I was trapped. I couldn't move. The door opened slightly and another man was shoved in behind me. In that split second I saw the room was completely covered with men stretched out on the floor. There was only room to stand around the bodies of the ugliest pirates I have ever seen. Men with whiskers bristling with lice. Men with mustaches uncut for a century. Men without hands, without arms, with black patches over depraved faces. Prisoners of war, God damn it. The black hole of Calcutta. The dungeon. Deep in the cavern of some sewer beneath the spittled streets of Juárez.

Three hours of standing and they finally led us all into a court yard. For breakfast they gave us a cup of hot coffee. Period. They lined us up and warned that if we so much as uttered one single word we'd have to wait until the following week when the magistrate came around again. I was silent and rehearsed my speech to the judge.

It is very simple, your honor, I'd say. I am an attorney. An American citizen. From California. I don't have my Bar license with me, but as you can tell from my speech, I am an educated man. A quick phone call to the

American Embassy will do. If you don't accept my word, that is. But surely you can tell from . . . well, I know I don't exactly *look* like an attorney . . . but you see, the hair styles are longer in San Francisco . . . no, of course I'm not a hippie. I'm an attorney at law, your honor. A member of the bar, just like you . . . it was just a misunderstanding . . . a breakdown in communication . . . he didn't speak English. He didn't understand that I'm accustomed to heat. I'm from sunny California . . . and would you believe that your sergeant actually tried to get me to *bribe* him? I don't want to create an international incident, your honor . . . but the man actually told me that I could square it with him without the necessity for an arrest. Can you imagine that? I, an attorney, a citizen of the United States, should I become a partner to the corruption of justice in my very own father's country?

I didn't have a chance to translate my speech into Spanish before they led me into the magistrate's courtroom, a small cubicle with a single lightbulb dangling from a black cord over a simple desk which was her bench. She had grey hair and wore a plain black business suit. A soldier with a rifle in hand stood on either side of her . . . Jesus H. Christ, I was being courtmartialed by woman! In Spanish, at that!

"The papers say you insulted the hotel clerk?" Her voice was calm, business-like. . . .

"Forgive me, madam, I don't speak Spanish too well . . ." I began.

"¿Que dice?" she snapped at the fat soldier with the rifle.

"Soy abogado . . ." I started.

She kept thumbing through a bunch of papers. Clearly the report could not be so long. There was simply an argument, a slight shove when the man ordered me out of his hotel for cursing him.

"Dice también que usó palabras malas," the magistrate kept on.

Is there no constitution here? I wondered. I'm charged with using *bad words?* Don't they understand that I'm an attorney! What happened to due process? Where's the Goddamned First Amendment around here?

"Madam, I'm an attorney . . ."

"¿Sí o no?" she stopped me cold. Just yes or no. That's what it all comes down to eventually. This is my trial. Yes or no?

"I am a citizen of the United States and an attorney at law, your honor," I said in English.

"Well, counselor, in that case you should be able to answer questions . . . yes or no?" she answered in perfect English.

I hesitated. The fat soldier with the ten-foot long rifle stuck it in my ribs. "¡Conteste la señora!"

There was no mistaking the real meaning of that order. I entered my plea immediately. "Si, soy culpable." I answered. I am guilty of all those nasty things, vile language, gringo arrogance and *americano* impatience with lazy *mexicanos*. Yes, take me away to, the guillotine right now! . . .

"If you're a lawyer, you should act like one. Cut your hair or leave this city. We get enough of your kind around here. You spend your money on the putas and then don't even have enough to pay for your fines when you're caught with your pants down."

"I am truly sorry, madam."

"That'll be 1,200 pesos. 300 for each offense."

"But, madam, your honor, that would be 900, no?"

"It says here you also cursed at the arresting officers . . . next."

As I was being led out by the soldier, she looked me directly in the face and said to me, "Why don't you go home and learn to speak your father's language?"

My father's language? What does she mean? I shuffle behind the soldier, I pay my fine and the man behind the tall, black desk hands me back *diez centavos,* which is something like two cents, American. I look up at him and stare.

"And the rest?" I say meekly.

"Ah, yes. I forgot," he smiles through black teeth under a huge brooch. He nods to a young man in wrinkled khakis. He brings out my suitcase and hands it to me. They both show me their teeth.

"Gracias. . . . But where is the rest of my money?" I speak with humility for I can see the light of day through the window. We are a stone's throw from freedom. "As I understood the judge . . . the multa was to be 1,200 pesos, no?"

"Yes, that was my understanding of the matter. . . . But of course we have to add the tax and, of course one has to pay for his bed and food, no?"

His smile was so broad, his eyes so deeply set into the furrow of his forehead that I knew better than to press my luck. I began to walk away when the young man said, "Say, mister . . . I could really use that knife you have in your suitcase."

"A *knife,* you say?" the fat sargeant spoke loudly.

"It's a gift from a friend. A hunting knife," I said.

"You'd better let me see it," he shook his head in sadness.

Of course, I thought. You can't have a criminal running around Juárez with a knife in his suitcase.

When it was over, the young man thanked me for the present. I took a deep breath when I stepped into the sunlight outside the fort.

I walk slowly in the late morning hours through the city of sin and colored lights. Gone are the finely shaped women with mascara and ruby lips. The bars are silent. I see no pimps. The city is grey. Dust covers all the walls of cheap paint. The streets are filthy with corn husks, corn leaves from tamales, apple cores, empty beer cans and dog shit. Juárez in the morning, when you have two cents in your pocket and been ordered out of town at gun point, is as depressing a city as you can find.

With my head bent to my chest I walk to the guard on the Mexican side of the border and pay my two centavos for the toll. I cross over the bridge with my suitcase to the international boundary. The border patrol empties the contents of my suitcase.

A tall blond with a .357 Magnum says, "Where you born?"

"El Paso."

He investigates my feet, analyzes my turtle neck and looks me straight in the eye. "You americano?"

"I'm from San Francisco." My heart is pounding.

"Thought you said you was from Paso."

"I'm a lawyer. I was born in El Paso. I practice in Frisco."

He smiles at that one. He looks to his partner who is pulling out a bag of avocados from an old Mexican woman's straw shopping bag.

"Got your papers?" the tall bounty hunter asks.

"I lost my wallet. . . . I'm a citizen, man."

"Well . . . can you prove it? What you got to show me?"

Jesus Christ, I think, what *do* I have to prove who I am? I squint my eyes tight. There's nothing in my pockets but eight *centavos.* I've got a clarinet and a camera with a few rags in my traveling bag. I nod slowly.

"Nothing. I've got nothing on me to prove who I am . . . just my word."

He carefully inspects the contents of my bag, fingering the camera and the b-flat clarinet. He finally looks up and says, "Okay, buddy. Next time I suggest you have some I.D. on you. You don't *look* like an American, you know?"

Three blocks from the border I pawn my camera and my clarinet. The greasy pimp gives me fifteen dollars. I take a green room at the Grand Hotel in downtown El Paso. I sit on the edge of the single bed and remove the cockroach-infested clothes from my lice-eaten body. . . .

I stand naked before the mirror. I cry in sobs. My massive chest quivers and my broad shoulders sag. I am a brown buffalo lonely and afraid in a world I never made. I enter the womb of night and am dead to this world of confusion for thirty-three hours. . . .

My eyes open to the sun splitting window panes into colored jewels. It's a new day. I jump up and stretch to feel the juice of lemon blood. I pound my chest and shriek the call of Tarzan swinging through the jungle. I didn't eat all that protein and lift those weights for nothing. I mastered Charles Atlas at the age of ten and no beach bully will ever again kick sand in my face, God-damn it!

I rush down the stairs and call my brother from the pay phone in the lobby. I've got to sober up and come home, he tells me. I am clear, I say. I've checked it all out and have failed to find the answer to my search. One sonofabitch tells me I'm not a Mexican and the other one says I'm not an American. I got no roots anywhere.

With a friend, the author set out to cross the harshest desert borderland. The two "followed tracks of tennis shoes, running shoes, soccer shoes, huaraches, and boots. . . . This is the fabled border." Some fable.

from *Blue Desert*

Charles Bowden

We are twenty-odd miles into the passage. Around us are all the places I studied on the wall maps back at the apartment. If you have enough water, the names have a picturesque ring. If you do not have enough water, they sound like the lid opening on a crypt. The Lechuguilla Desert is at our backs, the Tule Desert sprawls to the south, and the dunes of the Mohawk Valley yawn before us with the sands glowing under a full moon. We are stopped on the east flank of the Copper Mountains, just north of the Cabeza Prietas. Behind us, Big Pass opens with jaws seven miles wide. Fifteen miles to the southeast, the Tinajas Altas look near enough to touch. All these places are creosote, bare ground, dry washes, stunted trees. This earth is too dry for the deer, too dry for the javelina. This is the furnace room of the Sonoran Desert.

I cannot get the map out of my head with its names, tidy brown contour lines, blue strands hinting at drainages and babble of Spanish words and prospector lingo, all struggling to nail down the land. On my faithful map, this country appears as tidy and organized as a city park. . . .

We are two specks on an ill-defined strand of migrant trails, faint footpaths that start at truckstops just over the line in Mexico and then lance north thirty to sixty miles, depending on the angle chosen, to Interstate 8. Yuma is more than forty miles to the west and Ajo eighty to the east and in between there is not much at all. There are no springs or streams and no one lives here, no one. A few rock holes hold puddles for desert bighorns for weeks or months at a time and the rains average three inches a year and sometimes forget to come for years at a time. In the summer, say from Memorial Day to mid-September, daytime temperatures scamper right past 100 and sometimes touch 120, 125 degrees or more.

This is the basic desert of folklore, one uncluttered with annoying twentieth-century rest areas, water fountains, trail signs, and short cuts. For me, this is clearly part of the draw. I don't have to think much here because everything is stated very plainly. I have found a place that skips the big words.

We do not know how many are out here with us this night. Before we left El Saguaro truckstop in Mexico hours ago, we watched men glide off in twos and threes and head north. But there are other spots for departure and many more are walking this desert. We are all heading for towns and points along the Interstate, places like Wellton, Tacna, or a roadside rest area at Mohawk Pass. Little dots of flesh inching north and probably by now all hurting.

We go up against seven border patrolmen who work days, the random war games of the gunnery range and full-time companions like hunger and thirst and heat.

Score-keeping is a bit haphazard. The Border Patrol body count runs anywhere from two to twelve dead a summer but no one pretends to find all the bodies or have any real sense of how many rot undiscovered. There is a range here littered with bones and the desire to recover them is slight since a pauper burial costs the county $400. Over the past decade, I calculate at least 200 people have died on this stretch. . . .

Now Bill and I are deep into this nowhere and by 2 A.M. we are facing our hurts. Our shoulders ache, our backs ache, our legs ache, and our feet ache. We drink constantly and nibble candy bars and yet our thirst never seems to end and our energy continues to decline. And we are maybe halfway. . . .

Something is happening at a deep level in our bodies, a revolt in the cells, a shift in the chemical juices, in the intricate synapses that fire information through our flesh and that organize our muscle into motion and purpose. Our will is dissolving as our tissue loses tiny trace elements, things with names I do not even know. . . . We do not trust our minds any longer. They seem fine and even more interesting than is usually the case but there is something different now about the way thoughts come and go. And we do not want to speak of this feeling of unreliability. How can we even trust our perceptions of warning?

I drift back to our start yesterday afternoon. In that beginning there is warmth, confidence, and good spirits. We sprawl in the shade at El Saguaro truckstop, a dot along the Mexican highway between Sonoyta, eighty miles to the east, and San Luis forty miles to the west. A man, a woman, and a baby rest on pads under a flatbed truck and wait out the aftenoon heat. The man is about thirty and he stretches out and smokes.

His woman nuzzles against him. The baby gurgles and plays with the man's finger.

It is 105 degrees in the shade and rising.

The truck bears Sinaloa plates, a Mexican state 600 miles south and I imagine them homeward bound. El Saguaro has no electricity, no cooling, no well. A few miles to the east is La Joya truckstop, another place of dreams. There electric lights hang from the ceiling, a television is mounted in a corner, and at La Joya also there is no electricity, no cooling, no well. Once I was there and I saw a dog eating a dead dog. The food in the cafe is simple but filling.

These two spots are the principal launching pads for the walks of *los mojados* northward. Water is sold to these travelers at about a buck and a half a gallon. At times Mexico can seem a little weak on compassion. . . .

El Saguaro attracts people willing to give it a shot. Around 12:30 two men start north. They wear caps and each carries his gallon of water. Three hours later, some men get off a flatbed truck that has stopped. They carefully fold up the tarp for the driver as payment for the ride. Each of these men also has a one-gallon milk container and heads north. They wear no hats; their shirts do not cover their arms and are dark colors. For shoes, they favor sneakers.

Bill and I watch them depart into the heat. The Border Patrol has found that the men who die are usually in their twenties and quite strong. They do not fear the desert or the sun. They walk right through the heat of the day. And they die. We are both on the edge of forty. We wait.

I content myself with watching the people who must live with heat. They are drinking beer, sleeping in hammocks under trucks, sprinkling water on squawling babies. . . .

Our packs tip the scales at a little over thirty pounds and hold three gallons of water, some raisins, nuts and candy bars, extra socks, medicine, swatches of material for plastering blisters, flashlights, trousers and long-sleeved shirts, a sheet to stretch out for shade. Also, we have buried water along the route just in case we need it or run into someone else who does.

We wear hats, running shorts, t-shirts, and light boots. . . .

The Mexicans . . . arrive after long truck rides and hitchhikes and carry their one gallon of water and little or no food. They wear shabby shoes or sandals, skip hats as often as not and sometimes are decked out in black from head to foot. According to the Border Patrol, about sixty percent have made the passage before and presumably know what they are getting into. The other forty percent are virgins.

The first-timers are often dropped here by coyotes, the border's smugglers of humans, and are told that the border is a few miles away and they will meet them on the other side. The other forty or fifty miles of the route is apparently considered a detail by these smugglers. The people ignorant of the area tend to come from the interior, from jungles full of parrots or Sierras full of pines. They amble off into the hard desert and discover a different kind of world. . . .

It is 5:30 P.M. when we step off and there will be some light for three hours. The border waits five or six miles ahead and many trails streak northward to the line. We follow tracks of tennis shoes, running shoes, soccer shoes, *huaraches,* and boots. The way is lined with empty cans of fish, nectarine juice, and chiles. Black ash marks where fires fought back the night.

The trails braid and wander and cross each other, a kind of stuttered beginning to a long walk. We move along the stone walls of the Tinajas Altas mountains, walking fast, eager to leave the Mexican immigration official behind and powered like all travelers on this path by the pull of the El Dorado to the north.

Then a white masonry obelisk spikes upward a couple of hundred yards to the east. A bunch of stones on the ground at our feet spell out MEXICO/USA, and nearby a huge wooden sign stands there with its surface weathered and perfectly blank. Another and smaller sign warns that motor vehicles are forbidden.

This is the fabled border. There is no fence, just this boast of an imaginary line and footprints, everywhere footprints, and all heading one direction.

We move through the low hills, a gentle roll of land, and after a half hour, the view opens up and we can see across the Lechuguilla to Big Pass. Beyond Big Pass, puffs of smoke rise from fields being burned off near Tacna. Everything looks close enough to touch. It seems impossible that the hike will take more than two, maybe even three hours. The light weakens from white to gold, the valley shines with perfectly spaced creosote and is lanced down the center by ironwood and palo verde lining Coyote Wash. We hardly speak now. The rhythm of our footsteps constitutes our language and to a degree, we are struck dumb by the order and hugeness of the landscape. The big valley could serve as the garden of a Zen monastery.

Two and a half hours out of El Saguaro truckstop, we reach a fork in the trail that leads off to Tinajas Altas, a series of nine rock tanks. All human footprints arc away from the water. All coyote tracks race left toward the water. The small pools lie hidden from view on the steep rock side of the mountain. The rains fill them and historically they have been the only sure water between Agua Dulce spring sixty miles to the east, and Yuma, forty miles to the west. Once hundreds of graves were visible around the tanks and the path was lined on both sides with the mummified carcasses of upright horses and mules. The federal boundary survey of the 1890s found a prospector dead just below the first tank. His fingers were worn raw from trying to climb the rock. He had been too weak to make it to water and died a few yards from his salvation. . . .

We pass Tinajas Altas without stopping and strike out across the desert for Big Pass, following the footprints of Mexicans. A little after 8 P.M. we stop and eat and drink. We have been drinking steadily, making no effort to conserve water. The problem is not running out of water but pouring it into our bodies fast enough. We sweat like beasts but we can only drink like human beings. . . .

The Lechuguilla wears the marks of many journeys. Aboriginal trails cross car tracks, tank tracks, game tracks, Mexican tracks, our tracks. Pieces of spent military hardware litter the ground. I can see traces in the sand of lizards, rats, and sidewinders.

Big Pass is so near, so very near. We joke that this walk may be too easy, that Big Pass will be ours in an hour or so. But from Tinajas Altas to the Big Pass is 13.5 miles as the raven flies. We are not ravens. We dodge clumps of creosote, fall into rat holes, stumble down into washes, detour ironwoods, watch for cactus, and zigzag across the terrain. . . .

We stumble across the valley. The heat ceases to matter, not because it goes away, but because we go into it and join with it and can imagine no life separate from it. The night is soft with warmth, the moon is up, and I feel my sweat as the air brushes against my flesh with a light touch. I have no desire to be cool and no desire to be elsewhere. I do not think of the Border Patrol or of snakes or of thirst, fatigue, thorns, blisters, hunger, and pain. . . .

A flare bursts over our heads. The military sharpens itself for war. We enter a cleared strip of ground, a target area. Something finned like a bomb fragment squats on the sand. And then everything turns blue. The mountains rise azure, the ocotillo waves blue wands, the creosote whispers by my feet, and everything is awash with a rich, bright blue. At first the color is ahead and then I enter it like water and the blue is everywhere. It does not coat the surface but seems to come from the center of things. I look at my hand and the skin glows with blue pigment.

I do not hesitate or wonder. I do not speculate that the sugar flow to my brain has declined, that the pangs of dehydration have addled my mind, that some vast chemical change in my body is altering my perceptions. I have entered this blue world and I accept it totally. It means peace. I long to see a coyote cutting across the flats on a night hunt, to see a blue coyote and hear a blue yell under a blue moon. . . .

After Big Pass, the drag roads begin. The Border Patrol pulls old tires on chains to wipe the dirt clean. Then they know any tracks are fresh. The drag roads are checked often, on the ground and from the air. When a new sign is spotted, the hunt begins.

Tonight, no one seems interested in hiding their tracks. The road shows clear sign. It is now 1 A.M. and the Border Patrol shift will not begin until 6 A.M. Perhaps, everyone counts on being past the Interstate by then. Or perhaps everyone is too weary to care.

The game is played seriously but without anger. If a Mexican cannot make it, his companions often go to the Border Patrol and turn themselves in so that help can be sent to the person left behind. The Border Patrol responds. If someone is trapped in the desert, they say he is down. And that is serious business. . . .

We gaze ahead at Tacna, at the big road, at Mohawk Pass, at the twinkling lights of other people and the promise of shade, water, food, rest. We have twenty miles more.

We have entered the killing ground. . . .

The night is still a blue dream. The desert can never be better than what greets my eyes. The forms cannot be questioned. The night world brings no fears. Bats fly just over our heads and they are friends. I am certain of this. An owl lifts off a saguaro and I stop and stare with worship. Nighthawks sweep just off the ground. . . .

At 4 A.M., we strike another drag road, wide and clean and hungry for our footprints. The moon is down and our pace is two miles an hour. We drift closer to the Coppers where we have cached water, all part of our grand strategy. Six gallons lie buried under the sand. We do not touch them and are amused by their uselessness. The water mocks our thirst. We possess this treasure but we cannot get it into our bodies.

We fall down on the road and eat and drink and watch a red glow grow in the east. We empty our packs of canteens and keep only a gallon. The rest we set out for whoever needs it, whoever comes after us. The brotherhood.

Originally, we thought we might stop at dawn in this area, wait out the murderous heat of the day and finish the following evening. We reject this idea now. We want out; that is part of it. But also we want to beat the Border Patrol. We want to win, to gain the big road before they can catch us. We have been playing the game too hard to be indifferent to the final score. . . .

I feel like I can walk no farther. My body, my tired, sore body, is simply something I drag along and I cannot imagine the trip ever ending.

The traffic on the Interstate can now be seen clearly, trucks storming toward Los Angeles markets, cars cruising with the air conditioning blowing hard. I hear the rumble of the engines and delight in the sound of machines.

Bill and I get up and trudge on. We must go twelve miles. We must. We cannot beat the dawn, but we will fight the sun; we will war against the rays. We refuse to stop. Every hour, we pause briefly, drink, snack, and lie down. Then we stagger up, our legs stiff as boards. Tacna seems just ahead but hour by hour comes no nearer. We dream of Tacna, a hamlet of 100 people. Bill sees iced tea, and ice cream; he makes out a waitress holding up a cone and beckoning. We shuffle more than walk, our feet scraping across the soil.

The sun comes up with unbelievable force. I shudder under the rays like a vampire caught far from my coffin. All around us are the unmarked spots where the last dramas of the dying take place. One man went down a mile south of the Interstate. He set fire to a tree in hopes that the smoke would bring help. They found his body. . . .

We walk on. We must have walked on. But there is no memory of this. We walk on.

We reach Tacna at 9:48 A.M. We have made the crossing in sixteen hours, seventeen minutes, drunk a gallon and half of water each, and have nothing to say. We have probably walked forty-five miles, but this figure, like our careful recording of the time elapsed, means very little. The weather has been very cool for this country, surely no more than 110. . . .

We enter a cafe and eat a breakfast and drink iced tea after iced tea. The food is flat. The cool drinks lack pleasure. We consume coffee, pop, ice cream, eggs, sausage, hash browns, beef, lamb, soup, beer. The gorging continues for hours.

Part 6

Border writing has an edge. The poetic contributions here are both sharp and edgy.

On U.S./Mexico Relations

FROM THE BATTLE OF EL ALAMO TO THE SIGNING OF NAFTA

Guillermo Gómez-Peña

Dear ex-friend,
I'm saddened by the fact that we simply couldn't agree
in our first meeting
I wanted to talk about everything with a good cup of coffee
you wanted the meeting to be over quickly
I was too suave and talkative
you were plain rude & too direct for my chilango taste
I called you "gringo" de cariño
you called me "minority" twice
we didn't mean it, of course
but we were somehow damned by History
I politely overstated our differences
you tried to overlook all of them
I despised your lack of affection
you hated my touching you unnecessarily
I made you feel guilty
you made me feel inferior
I truly thought you needed some therapy
you thought I wanted a job real bad
we just couldn't reach a consensus
you kept looking at your watch
wondering why I was so flamboyant
—there is a certain strength in exhibitionism, ¿que no?
I wondered why you were so measured
—there is unquestionable power in being reserved
& when it came to cultural politics
we just couldn't see eye to eye
you pontificated that multiculturalism was rightfully dead
I replied that you were avoiding the crucial matters of race
you felt I was implying that you were a racist
& changed the subject & your tone of voice, just like that

you then placed too much importance on ecology
while I put too much emphasis on immigration
you were clearly unwilling to discuss colonial privilege
while I was unwilling (or perhaps unable) to discuss aesthetics
& worst of all, we simply couldn't laugh together
my jokes were too baroque & had no punchline
and yours were too brief & simplistic
we parted feeling utterly misunderstood

II

in our second encounter I arrived a half-hour late
you were pissed but didn't express it
you ordered raw vegetables & juice
I ordered pork, rum, and a humongous dessert
you were horrified
at the end of the dinner I pulled out my cigarettes
& you proceeded to lecture me on lung cancer & nonsmokers' rights
I was pissed but didn't express it
we simply couldn't find any common ground
during coffee—you had chamomile tea, by the way—
you finally expressed your resentment of my fame
you felt it had everything to do with the fact that I am Mexican
you said that in fact I was a "a bad actor and a worse poet
who finds refuge in the fashionable kilombo of performance art"
I responded by bringing up the fact that you had tenure
in a system where only 3 percent of professors are people of color
you thought I had made up the statistics
I thought to myself: "this ex-sweet, liberal güerito
is in fact un backlasher de aquellas," but I swallowed my words
you then insisted I was a mere token for white liberals
I reminded you that more than half of my work
takes place in Chicano/Mexicano venues
you said, "that's not good enough"
I replied sarcastically, "sure, we're never good enough
you want me back in the margins
where no one can hear my voice, ¿que no?"

stuttering in anger you said I was "ungrateful to an art world
which had embraced me unconditionally"
I suggested you could read a mountain of reviews
by critics accusing me of the same things you were
but you said you needed no proof of anything
since there were probably twice as many reviews
complimenting me a-critically
at that point I pulled out my conceptual knife & stabbed you
I called you "a broken white male
with an acute case of compassion fatigue"
I didn't mean it, but I was pissed
you left the restaurant fuming
I had a Catholic guilt attack
and called you the next day to apologize
but you said our friendship was over
a week later, NAFTA was finally approved by Congress
& you were on vacation to Mazatlán
per omnia saecula saeculorum, amen.

Crossing Over

Demetria Martínez

1.

Somebody threw a baby
into the Rio Grande.

We scrub the scum off him
in the back of the station wagon
as we leave El Paso.
We tuck him, sleeping,
in a picnic basket
as we near the check point.
Officers see our fishing rods
and nod us through.
At midnight south of Albuquerque
we invent a name, a date of birth,
singing rock-a-bye-baby in English,
burying the placenta of his past.

2.

When grandma left the Catholic Church
and joined Assemblies of God,
they dipped her in the Rio Grande,
she stood up and cried.

Grandma, grandma, the river's not
the same. Sweet Jesus
got deported, this baby
bruised and hungry, my nipples red and pained.

3.

Who's throwing babies
in the river?

What bastard
signs the release?

Who will break
the bastard's brains
and let this baby
keep his name?

Surrender

María Herrera-Sobek

Lights flashing
flashing lights
from smoking
cigarettes
pupils
excited
solitary
figures
walking
throbbing
like whores
waiting
eyes inviting
to an hour's delight
by only crossing
advancing
to the other side.

Poem for the Young White Man Who Asked Me How I, an Intelligent, Well-Read Person Could Believe in the War between Races

Lorna Dee Cervantes

In my land there are no distinctions.
The barbed wire politics of oppression
have been torn down long ago. The only reminder
of past battles, lost or won, is a slight
rutting in the fertile fields

In my land
people write poems about love,
full of nothing but contented childlike syllables.
Everyone reads Russian short stories and weeps.
There are no boundaries.
There is no hunger, no
complicated famine or greed.

I am not a revolutionary.
I don't even like political poems.
Do you think I can believe in a war between races?
I can deny it. I can forget about it
when I'm safe,
living on my own continent of harmony
and home, but I am not
there.

I believe in revolution
because everywhere the crosses are burning,
sharp-shooting goose-steppers round every corner,
there are snipers in the schools. . . .
(I know you don't believe this.
You think this is nothing
but faddish exaggeration. But they
are not shooting at you).

I'm marked by the color of my skin.
The bullets are discrete and designed to kill slowly.
They are aiming at my children.
There are facts.
Let me show you my wounds: my stumbling mind, my
"excuse me" tongue, and this
nagging preoccupation
with the feeling of not being good enough.

These bullets bury deeper than logic.
Racism is not intellectual.
I can not reason these scars away.

Outside my door
there is a real enemy
who hates me.

I am a poet
who yearns to dance on rooftops,
to whisper delicate lines about joy
and the blessings of human understanding.
I try. I go to my land, my tower of words and
bolt the door, but the typewriter doesn't fade out
the sounds of blasting and muffled outrage.
My own days bring me slaps on the face.
Every day I am deluged with reminders
that this is not
my land
and this is my land.
I do not believe in the war between races
but in this country
there is war.

Speaking of My Tongue

Janet Arelis Quezada

accentless english
español sin accento
i could be anyone
from anywhere
but then how to explain my personal geography;
the tongue full of cuts
balancing the razor edges of english
accentless
and spanish
sin acento.
the hips that dance to the silence of the city
and can hold baskets full of nickel refunds,
the climbing legs
because there never is an elevator
that works,
the hands that can hold the purse in a grip of calculated
stillness
and the eyes which can see in every direction and must.

i cannot pass for borderless sophisticate:
my conversation is oily with the repetition of crimes that must be
remembered.
i only speak resistance
and if you listen carefully
verás que mi español a veces quema tu piel
and that sometimes my english thickens with a rage that you cannot
place.

La Frontera

Alicia Gaspar de Alba

La frontera lies
wide open, sleeping beauty.
Her waist bends like the river
bank around a flagpole.
Her scent tangles in the arms
of the mesquite. Her legs
sink in the mud
of two countries, both
sides leaking sangre
y sueños.

        I come here
mystified by the sleek Río Grande
and its ripples and the moonlit curves
of tumbleweeds, the silent lloronas,
the children they lose.
In that body of dreams,
the Mexicans swim for years,
their fine skins too tight to breathe.
Yo también me he acostado con ella,*
crossed that cold bed, wading
toward a hunched coyote.

*I, too, have slept with her.

La Frontera

Oscar J. Martínez

It is the best and it is the worst,
la frontera, the borderlands,
a world of acute contradictions,
a place of pungent human drama.

It lifts the spirit and sinks the heart,
for *la frontera* is laced with intense passions.
Devotees feel exuberance, vitality, zest;
detractors see drabness, ugliness, crassness.

On one side dollar power, freeways,
skyscrapers, malls, radiant suburbs.
On the other boom and bust, gaudy tourism,
maquiladora sprawl, shantytowns

A land of abundant sunshine
that keeps the body warm, the soul aglow.
Yet that same *frontera* sun
turns summer into scorching hell
an inconvenience for the fortunate,
a life-threat for the destitute.

Generations of poor migrants from the south,
driven by poverty and despair,
have headed to the imagined desert paradise,
enticed by the promise of a better life.

Embraced by those who profit from their labor,
quite dependable, plentiful, and cheap.
Abhorred by those who see social blight,
economic threat, cultural menace, demographic peril.

Affluent and leisure-conscious northerners,
captivated by *la frontera*'s mildness,

its picturesque scenery, its relaxed way of life,
gleefully descend upon its cities, towns, and trailer parks.

These settlers and sojourners reverse this land,
its desert beauty, its resplendent sunsets,
and some hold dear the indigenous human landscape,
the Indians, the Spaniards, the Mexicans.

But far too few of the northern newcomers
find enchantment in the native heritage;
indifference and token recognition are more the norm,
and all too often contemptibility and overt hostility.

Los fronterizos: people of one, or more, identities,
mono or multi—national, ethnic, lingual, cultural.
Borderlanders: neglected, misunderstood, disdained,
at once defensive and proud of their aberrant world.

Yes, *la frontera* has them all:
those who live behind their cultural wall,
and those who wish to see it fall;
those who would keep foreigners out,
and those who want them all about;
those inclined to alienate,
and those who prefer to ameliorate;
those driven by a nationalistic bent,
and those committed to a global tent.

On a cross-country trip, the poet—whose name itself implies a border—walked with friends from El Paso to Juárez. He returned personally disgusted, culturally enlightened, and poetically invigorated.

The Desert Music

William Carlos Williams

—the dance begins: to end about a form
propped motionless—on the bridge
between Juárez and El Paso—unrecognizable
in the semi-dark

        Wait!

The others waited while you inspected it,
on the very walk itself   .

       Is it alive?

           —neither a head,
legs nor arms!

     It isn't a sack of rags someone
has abandoned here   .   torpid against
the flange of the supporting girder   .   ?

       an inhuman shapelessness,
knees hugged tight up into the belly

    Egg-shaped!

        What a place to sleep!
on the International Boundary. Where else,
interjurisdictional, not to be disturbed?

How shall we get said what must be said?

Only the poem.

Only the counted poem, to an exact measure:
to imitate, not to copy nature, not
to copy nature

NOT, prostrate, to copy nature
                              but a dance! to dance
two and two with him—
                    sequestered there asleep,
                                right end up!

       A music
supersedes his composure, hallooing to us
across a great distance   .   .

                              wakens the dance
who blows upon his benumbed fingers!

                         Only the poem
only the made poem, to get said what must
be said, not to copy nature, sticks
in our throats   .

The law? The law gives us nothing
but a corpse, wrapped in a dirty mantle.
The law is based on murder and confinement,
long delayed,

  .   .   .   .
                  —it looks too small for a man.
A woman. Or a very shriveled old man.
Maybe dead. They probably inspect the place
and will cart it away later   .

                    Heave it into the river.
A good thing.

Leaving California to return east, the fertile desert,
                  (were it to get water)

surrounded us, a music of survival, subdued, distant, half
            heard; we were engulfed
by it as in the early evening, seeing the wind lift
           and drive the sand, we
passed Yuma. All night long, heading for El Paso to
           meet our friend,
we slept fitfully. Thinking of Paris, I waked to the tick
           of the rails. The
jagged desert   .

. . . .
The Old Market's a good place to begin:
Let's cut through here—
                     tequila's only
a nickel a slug in these side streets.

Keep out though. Oh, it's all right at
this time of day but I saw H. terribly
beaten up in one of those joints. He
asked for it. I thought he was going to
be killed. I do
my drinking on the main drag   .

               That's the bull ring
Oh, said Floss, after she got used to the
change of light   .
               What color! Isn't it
wonderful!

       —paper flowers *(para los santos)*
baked red-clay utensils, daubed
with blue, silverware,
dried peppers, onions, print goods, children's
clothing   .   the place deserted all but
for a few Indians squatted in the
booths, unnoticing (don't you think it)
as though they slept there   .

       There's a second tier. Do you
want to go up?

         What makes Texans so tall?
We saw a woman this morning in a mink cape
six feet if she was an inch. What a woman!

Probably a Broadway figure.

—tell you what else we saw: about a million
sparrows screaming their heads off
in the trees of that small park where
the buses stop, sanctuary,
I suppose,
from the wind driving the sand in that way
about the city   .

                         Texas rain they call it

—and those two alligators in the fountain   .

There were four

              I saw only two

                         They were looking
right at you all the time   .

Penny please! Give me penny please, mister.

              Don't give them anything.

                         .   instinctively
one has already drawn one's naked
wrist away from those obscene fingers
as in the mind a vague apprehension speaks
and the music rouses   .

                         Let's get in here.
                    a music! cut off as
the bar door closes behind us.

We've got
another half hour.

                    —returned to the street,
the pressure moves from booth to booth along
the curb. Opposite, no less insistent
the better stores are wido open. Come in
and look around. You don't have to buy: hats,
riding boots, blankets   .

            Look at the way,
slung from her neck with a shawl, that young
Indian woman carries her baby!
                    —a stream of Spanish,
as she brushes by, intense, wide-
eyed in eager talk with her boy husband

—three half-grown girls, one of them eating a
pomegranate. Laughing.

                        and the serious tourist,
man and wife, middle-aged, middle-western,
their arms loaded with loot, whispering
together—still looking for bargains   .

                        and the aniline
red and green candy at the little booth
tended by the old Indian woman.
            Do you suppose anyone actually
buys—and eats the stuff?

My feet are beginning to ache me.

                    We still got a few minutes.
Let's try here. They had the mayor
up last month for taking $3000 a week from
the whorehouses of the city. Not much left
for the girls. There's a show on.

Only a few tables
occupied. A conventional orchestra—this
place livens up later—playing the usual local
jing-a-jing—a boy and girl team, she
confidential with someone
off stage. Laughing: just finishing the act.

So we drink until the next turn—a strip tease.

Do you mean it? Wow! Look at her.

You'd have to be
pretty drunk to get any kick out of that.
She's no Mexican. Some worn-out trouper from
the States. Look at those breasts

There is a fascination
seeing her shake
the beaded sequins from
a string about her hips

She gyrates but it's
not what you think,
one does not laugh
to watch her belly.

One is moved but not
at the dull show. The
guitarist yawns. She
cannot even sing. She

has about her painted
hardihood a screen
of pretty doves which
flutter their wings.

Her cold eyes perfunc-
torily moan but do not
smile. Yet they bill

and coo by grace of
a certain candor. She

is heavy on her feet.
That's good. She
bends forward leaning
on the table of the
balding man sitting
upright, alone, so that
everything hangs for-
ward.
    What the hell
are you grinning to yourself about? Not
at *her?*
    The music!
I like her. She fits

the music   .

Why don't these Indians get over this nauseating
prattle about their souls and their loves and sing
us something else for a change?

This place is rank
with it. She
at least knows she's
part of another tune,
knows her customers,
has the same
opinion of them as I
have. That gives her
one up   .   one up
following the lying
music   .

There is another music. The bright-colored candy
of her nakedness lifts her unexpectedly
to partake of its tune   .

                    Andromeda of those rocks,
the virgin of her mind   .   those unearthly
greens and reds

                in her mockery of virtue
she becomes unaccountably virtuous   .
             though she in no
way pretends it   .

Let's get out of this.

             In the street it hit
me in the face as we started to walk again. Or
am I merely playing the poet? Do I merely invent
it out of whole cloth? I thought   .

       What in the form of an old whore in
       a cheap Mexican joint in Juárez, her bare
       can waggling crazily can be
       so refreshing to me, raise to my ear
       so sweet a tune, built of such slime?

       Here we are. They'll be along any minute.
       The bar is at the right of the entrance,
       a few tables opposite which you have to pass
       to get to the dining room, beyond.

       A foursome, two oversize Americans, no
       longer young, got up as cowboys,
       hats and all, are drunk and carrying on
       with their gals, drunk also,

       especially one inciting her man, the
       biggest, *Yip ee!* to dance in
       the narrow space, oblivious to everything
       —she is insatiable and he is trying

       stumblingly to keep up with her.
       Give it the gun, pardner! *Yip ee!* We

pushed by them to our table, seven
of us. Seated about the room

were quiet family groups, some with
children, eating. Rather a better
class than you notice
on the streets. So here we are. You

can see through into the kitchen
where one of the cooks, his shirt sleeves
rolled up, an apron over
the well-pressed pants of a street

suit, black hair neatly parted,
a tall
good-looking man, is working
absorbed, before a chopping block

Old fashioneds all around?

        So this is William
Carlos Williams, the poet   .

        Floss and I had half consumed
our quartered hearts of lettuce before
we noticed the others hadn't touched theirs   .
You seem quite normal. Can you tell me? Why
does one want to write a poem?

      Because it's there to be written.

Oh. A matter of inspiration then?

                Of necessity.

Oh. But what sets it off?

     I am that he whose brains

are scattered
                aimlessly

                                —and so,
the hour done, the quail eaten, we were on
our way back to El Paso.

                            Good night. Good
night and thank you   .   No. Thank you. We're
going to walk   .

—and so, on the naked wrist, we feel again
those insistent fingers   .

                        Penny please, mister.
Penny please. Give me penny.

                        Here! now go away.

—but the music, the music has reawakened
as we leave the busier parts of the street
and come again to the bridge in the semi-dark,
pay our fee and begin again to cross   .
seeing the lights along the mountain back of El
Paso and pause to watch the boys calling out
to us to throw more coins to them standing
in the shallow water   .   so that's
where the incentive lay, with the annoyance
of those surprising fingers.

                        So you're a poet?
a good thing to be got rid of—half drunk,
a free dinner under your belt, even though you
get typhoid—and to have met people you
can at least talk to   .

                        relief from that changeless, endless
inescapable and insistent music   .

What else, Latins, do you yourselves
seek but relief!
with the expressionless ding dong you dish up
to us of your souls and your loves, which
we swallow. Spaniards! (though these are mostly
Indians who chase the white bastards
through the streets on their Independence Day
and try to kill them)   .
                                 What's that? . . .

In *You Are There* fashion, the Uruguayan author chronicles Mexico's pain looking north.

from *Memory of Fire*

Eduardo Galeano

1835: COLUMBIA

Texas

Fifteen years ago, a wagon train creaked across the desert prairie of Texas, and the mournful voices of owls and coyotes bid them illcome. Mexico ceded lands to these three hundred families that came from Louisiana with their slaves and plows. Five years ago, there were already twenty thousand North American colonists in Texas, and they had many slaves purchased in Cuba or in the corrals where the gentry of Virginia and Kentucky fatten up little blacks. Now, the colonists hoist their own flag, the image of a bear, and decline to pay taxes to the government of Mexico or to obey Mexican law which has abolished slavery in all the national territory.

The vice president of the United States, John Calhoun, believes that God created blacks to cut wood, pick cotton, and carry water for the chosen people. Textile factories demand more cotton and cotton demands more land and more blacks. *There are powerful reasons,* said Calhoun last year, *for Texas to form part of the United States.* At that time President Jackson, who breathes frontiers with an athlete's lungs, had already sent his friend Sam Houston to Texas.

The rugged Houston forces his way in with his fists, makes himself an army general, and proclaims the independence of Texas. The new state, soon to be another star on the United States flag, has more land than France.

And war breaks out against Mexico.

1836: SAN JACINTO

The Free World Grows

Sam Houston offers land at four cents an acre. Battalions of North American volunteers pour in by every road and weapons arrive by the shipload from New York and New Orleans.

The comet that announced calamity in the skies over Mexico was no news to anybody. Mexico has lived in a perpetual state of calamity since the murderers of Hidalgo and Morelos declared independence in order to grab the country for themselves.

The war does not last long. Mexican General Santa Anna arrives calling for a bloodbath, and makes one at the Alamo, but at San Jacinto loses four hundred men in a quarter of an hour. Santa Anna gives up Texas in exchange for his own life and returns to Mexico City with his beaten army, his personal chef, his seven-thousand-dollar sword, his countless decorations and his wagonload of fighting cocks.

General Houston celebrates his victory by naming himself president of Texas.

Texas's constitution assures the master perpetual rights over his slaves, as legitimately acquired property. *Extend the area of liberty* had been the slogan of the victorious troops.

1836: HARTFORD

The Colt

Samuel Colt, engineer, registers in Hartford, Connecticut, the patent of the "revolving pistol" he has invented. It is a pistol with a revolving cylinder of five shots, which kills five times in twenty seconds.

From Texas comes the first order.

1848: VILLA OF GUADALUPE HIDALGO

The Conquistadors

In Washington, President Polk proclaims that his nation is now as big as all Europe. No one can halt the onslaught of this young voracious country. To the south and to the west, the United States grows, killing Indians, trampling on neighbors, or even paying. It bought Louisiana from Napoleon and now offers Spain a hundred million dollars for the island of Cuba.

But the right of conquest is more glorious and cheaper. The treaty with Mexico is signed in the Villa of Guadalupe Hidalgo. Mexico cedes to the United States, pistol at chest, half of its territory.

1908: CIUDAD JUÁREZ

Wanted

A few years ago, at the request of Porfirio Díaz, North American Rangers crossed the border here to crush the striking copper miners of Sonora. Later, the strike in the Veracruz textile plants ended in arrests and executions. Still, strikes have broken out again this year in Coahuila, Chihuahua, and Yucatán.

Striking, which disturbs order, is a crime. Whoever does it commits a crime. The Flores Magón brothers, agitators of the working class, are criminals of the highest order. Their faces are plastered on the wall of the railroad station in Ciudad Juárez as in all stations on both sides of the border. The Furlong detective agency offers a forty-thousand-dollar reward for each of them.

For years, the Flores Magón brothers have flouted the authority of eternal president Porfirio Díaz. In journals and pamphlets they have taught the people to lose respect for him. With respect once lost, the people begin to lose their fear.

1914: CIUDAD JIMÉNEZ

Chronicler of Angry Peoples

From shock to shock, from marvel to marvel, John Reed travels the roads of northern Mexico. He is looking for Pancho Villa and finds him at every step.

Reed, chronicler of revolution, sleeps wherever night catches up with him. No one ever steals from him, or ever lets him pay for anything except dance music; and there's always someone to offer him a piece of tortilla or a place on his horse.

"Where do you come from?"

"From New York."

"Well, I don't know anything about New York, but I'll bet you don't see such fine cattle going through the streets as you see in the streets of Jiménez."

A woman carries a pitcher on her head. Another, squatting, suckles her baby. Another, on her knees, grinds corn. Enveloped in faded serapes, the men sit in a circle, drinking and smoking.

"Listen, Juanito, why is it your people don't like Mexicans? Why do they call us 'greasers'?"

Everyone has something to ask this thin, bespectacled, blond man who looks as if he were here by mistake.

"Listen, Juanito, how do you say 'mula' in English?"

"Goddamn stubborn—fathead mule . . ."

1916: COLUMBUS

Latin America Invades the United States

Rain falls upward. Hen bites fox and hare shoots hunter. For the first and only time in history, Mexican soldiers invade the United States.

With the tattered force remaining, five hundred men out of the many thousands he once had, Pancho Villa crosses the border and, crying *Viva Mexico!* showers bullets on the city of Columbus, New Mexico.

1917: THE FIELDS OF CHIHUAHUA AND DURANGO

Eagles into Hens

A punitive expedition, ten thousand soldiers with plentiful artillery enter Mexico to make Pancho Villa pay for his impudent attack on the North American city of Columbus.

"We'll bring back that assassin in an iron cage," proclaims General John Pershing, and the thunder of his guns echoes the words.

Across the drought-stricken immensities of northern Mexico, General Pershing finds various graves—*Here lies Pancho Villa*—without a Villa in any of them. He finds snakes and lizards and silent stones, and campesinos who murmur false leads when beaten, threatened, or offered all the gold in the world.

After some months, almost a year, Pershing returns to the United States. He brings back a long caravan of soldiers fed up with breathing dust, with the people throwing stones, with the lies in each little village in that gravelly desert. Two young lieutenants march at the head of the humbled procession. Both have had in Mexico their baptism of fire. For Dwight Eisenhower, newly graduated from West Point, it is an unlucky start on the road to military glory. George Patton spits as he leaves *this ignorant and half-savage country.*

From the crest of a hill, Pancho Villa looks down and comments: *"They came like eagles and they leave like wet hens."*

Part 7

Section 1

These pieces, which date from the mid-twentieth century, show agitation and vigor, struggle and animation

from *The Edge of the Storm*

Agustín Yáñez

TRANSLATED BY Ethel Brinton

I

"It's worse when they come back," most people say.

"And they gain nothing from their experience."

"Even those who come back with money aren't satisfied here any longer."

"Many of them don't want to work anymore; they just strut around, air their opinions, and criticize everything."

"They're a bad example, making fun of religion, the country, the customs."

"They sow doubt, undermine patriotism, and encourage others to leave this 'filthy, poverty-stricken country.' "

"They're the ones who spread ideas of Masonry, Socialism, and Spiritism."

"They've no respect for women."

"Nor sense of obligation at all."

"They're vicious and quarrelsome, always ready to pick a fight."
"They've lost the fear of God, that's the sum of it."

"And there are more and more of them all the time. Nobody gets any peace. They meddle with everything—with the rich for being rich and the poor for being poor. They have no respect for anyone."

"Miserable people! Poor country!"

"They think because they can roll off a few strange words they know more than anybody else and are a cut above other people, but they can't read a bit better than when they went away."

"Just because they have some gold teeth and are always ready for a fight."

"Because they come back with round-toed shoes, felt hats, wide-legged trousers, and shirts with wristbands and shiny cuff-links."

"With their hair bushy in front and shaved behind."

"They don't even have a mustache."

"They're ridiculous."

"They certainly are. When poor old Don Pedro Rubio's son-in-law came back and saw them stirring atole, he said he couldn't remember the word for it!"

"But he remembered how to stir up trouble all right."

"They're ridiculous."

"What gets me most is the way they laugh and brag."

"How can anybody forget the language he's been brought up with?"

"They're traitors, that's all there is to it. Whether they know it or not, they're the advance scouts of the gringos, sent to take our land away from us."

"How the women put up with them is more than I can see."

II

"No, Padre, I'm sorry to say so, but when we come back, we realize what the people here have to put up with, the injustice and the living conditions. Why should a man have to sweat all day to earn a few cents? And sometimes not even that. The rich are past masters at juggling accounts, and put the peasants off with promises they don't mean to keep, stop their mouths with enough corn and beans that they won't die of hunger, and just say, 'We'll see . . . at harvest time . . . next year . . .' If they struggle for it they may get a few yards of coarse cotton cloth, and a few more of cheap percale, but their debts are never paid, they're handed on from father to son. You never have a house of your own, and if you do manage to get a little plot of land, you're forced to sell it for less than you paid for it, tricked out of it. The family lives in a hovel, the children grow up there, they have nothing to wear when they're alive and when their time comes, nothing to die in.

"I tell you, Padre, it can't go on like this; sooner or later the worm will turn, and for better or worse, things will change. To be frank, it would be better if the gringos did come and teach us their way of life than for us to stay the way we are now, living no life at all. Who enjoys it? Tell me. The poor? No. Nor the rich either; they don't even know how to spend their money. The women work all the time like slaves, raising families, always wearing black, always afraid to move. What are we working for? The next life? That's all right, but I believe we ought to make this one a little better and live like human beings. Why can't we eat our fill and enjoy it, have a drink now and then, have some fun for a change, sing, visit, speak our minds, talk to women, wear decent clothes that fit us, work in freedom like the gringos? They at least aren't hypocrites. Here life is always sad, we sigh without knowing why, we don't even dare to draw a free breath. We take pleasure in making ourselves suffer.

"This is no life, Padre, forgive me. Those of us who have known what freedom is will never be satisfied with these customs again. No. The worst sin is exploiting others, and the sin is greater when it's hand in hand with hypocrisy. Don't tell me that the men here don't feel like men, or feel their gorge rising, just because, outwardly, they pretend to be meek. Don't even try to tell me that about the women. The saint that slips is soon a devil, as the saying goes, begging your pardon. You can do anything if you go about it the right way, but pretense and the use of force make matters worse; a rope strained too much will break. Many of the women who have run away, so many unhappy women, might have had a happier lot if they'd been allowed to behave according to their feelings and hadn't been forced to pretend.

"We who have been away are criticized because we see how things are and speak out. But this state of affairs can't go on. Oh, I agree that nobody here dies of hunger, but don't tell me that most people are doing more than barely living. You know as well as I do how they struggle and worry for half enough to live on. But go to Cuernavaca, Puebla, Chihuahua, where I worked, and you'll really see hell let loose, on the sugar farms, the huge estates. The people live worse than slaves. If anyone so much as opens his mouth, he's stabbed to death or beaten till he's half-dead. I saw tortures worse than the Christian martyrs went through. You don't realize what's going on in other parts of the Republic; when the Revolution starts it will catch us unawares here. Mexico isn't just our region, and you priests, begging your pardon, ought not to pull the wool over the people's eyes.

"I won't deny that life can be hard in the United States; but you can live in comfort and freedom. I'm not denying, either, that in some parts of the United States, especially in Texas and California, there are people who think Mexicans are no more than animals; there're a great many Mexicans there and they have our Mexican faults. But if you go a little farther north, you'll see how different it is; besides, even in Texas and California it depends on the place you make for yourself. I could live there comfortably enough. They say that the money we earn there has wings; the truth is, it's in our blood to spend it as fast as we get it and we can't keep our hands on it; the poorest earns four times as much as he earns here—in ready cash too, not in promises. And when you come back, the minute you reach the border you get a different treatment even from your own fellow countrymen, and you feel let down. That's why so many fellows won't work when they get back but only dream of going away again. Call it whatever you like—Socialism, or Liberalism—but that's the truth. The Church doesn't deny human nature, does it, or want a man to spend all his time praying? Well, then . . . ?"

1945: Franklin Roosevelt died, we dropped atomic bombs on Japan, and racism continued in South Texas unabated. Mexicans waged "a bloody fight for liberty," writes the author in this forgotten gem of frontier fiction.

from *Border City*

Hart Stilwell

Down in the patio of the hotel an orchestra was tuning up. Waiters were arranging tables, and the hotel manager stood on the small dance floor, the lord of all he surveyed. He passed on an order now and then, but most of the time he merely watched, occasionally rubbing his hands together as though the mild friction stimulated his thought processes.

I put my drink down on the window ledge and pulled my chair up close so I could see everything that was going on below me. At times I watched the people and was conscious of what they were doing. Then again I forgot them and my thoughts wandered back to the events of the day, back to the Moreno family and their troubles, to the girl with the frightened eyes—the girl who had been raped.

Just what was the psychological reaction to rape, anyway? Was it as much of a shock as some people would have you believe? It usually came suddenly, and there was little opportunity to build a tense aversion to it in advance. Was it possible it was in some cases the easiest introduction to certain phases of life? . . .

It had undoubtedly been a severe shock to the Moreno girl, however. The look in her eyes still haunted me. They were striking eyes. They sparkled under the long lashes that so many Mexican girls have. But behind the sparkle was that expression of a wounded being.

I finished my drink, dismissed rape with the thought that no matter what the reaction of the woman in the case might be it would be of small pleasure to me, and began watching the activity in the patio once more. The crowd was beginning to gather.

Then the telephone rang.

"Dave," came the voice on the line, "there are three people down here to see you." It was the hotel clerk calling.

"Who are they?"

"I wouldn't know. All I know is they have your name on a piece of paper and they want to see you. And, Dave—you know how we feel about the—about the Mexican people."

"I don't recall your explaining your attitude to me."

"I mean you know we don't have any prejudice or anything like that. We—"

"Say, Steven, just what's the idea? Why the lecture on international relations if there are people down there waiting to see me? Send them up.

"What I was saying, Dave, is we can't have people like these running around here in the lobby, especially on a night like this with the big dance—"

"What dance?" I asked, as though I didn't know.

"The Inter-American Ball."

"The one where we meet our neighbor from across the river and explain to him that we are his busom pal?"

"You needn't try to kid me about it. These people—"

"Are they women?" I asked, doing some rapid reflecting.

"Two of them are. I'm sending them up."

"If they're disturbing you, don't blame me. I didn't ask them to come here. I'll try to get them out without international incident."

I opened the door in response to a light knock, and there before me stood the old women, the man, and the girl whom I had encountered earlier in the day at the office of the district attorney.

"Enrique sent us," the old woman said.

"Sent you for what?" I asked, still standing in the door. Then I asked them in and finally got them distributed in the little room, the girl and the woman sitting on the bed and the man in the extra chair. He sat on the edge of the chair, holding his big white Stetson in both hands. The big Stetson is the one luxury in the way of clothing indulged in by Mexican working people in this border country, particularly those who work on farms. All the clothes on his body cost less than fifteen dollars, but the Mexican laborer will usually wear a hat that costs almost twice as much.

"Enrique said you would help us," the woman said, then she rattled off a string of Spanish so rapidly I couldn't follow. I told her to please slow down so I would be sure to understand.

The old woman told me the story of their troubles, adding now and then that Enrique said I could help them.

"But why does he think I can help?" I asked her, cursing the deputy sheriff who had apparently unloaded them on me out of sheer spite in revenge for the remarks I had made to him earlier in the day.

"Enrique said you would help us," was the best I could get out of the old woman, but I got a lot of other conversation from her dealing with the family troubles. There was another son, Tito, who was sick. The doctor said he had tuberculosis, which wasn't surprising since it was almost as prevalent as head colds among these Mexican working people. Since Tito was sick and had to quit working, the family had to take Chelo out of school just before she graduated from high school, where she was making fine grades, for Chelo had to work to help support the family.

She got a job in the home of an American family, and the lady at the house was kind to her. The lady taught her to cook the way Americans cooked and was helping her with her English accent. And the lady sent the family washing to the Morenos, which helped them still more, and they were now making enough money to pay the doctor part of what they owed him and to buy medicine for Tito.

Then one day, when all the people were gone from the house except Chelo, the man came back home and wronged her—ruined her life, the old woman said. All the time the old woman was telling the story the girl sat without moving. Occasionally she would glance at me, then look quickly away.

These were strange people, all right. I couldn't understand their coming to me, a stranger, unloading their troubles, then sitting there waiting for me to wave a wand and produce some sort of miracle. I had not been in contact with the Mexican laboring people long enough to understand this attitude—an attitude that stems from centuries of existence as a subject people. For centuries these people have gone quietly to the *patrón,* stated their woes, and then stood patiently waiting, hoping that this representative of the ruling race, whether he be of Spanish or English or any other European origin, might do what should be done.

That they stand quietly and speak softly should never lure anybody into overlooking the bitterness that wells up in their brown bodies— bitterness that in recent generations has flared into a bloody fight for liberty.

I finally asked them just exactly what they expected me to do.

"Enrique said you could write something for the newspaper and the man would be sent to jail," the old woman said.

"I can't do that," I assured her. "It is against the law."

"That is a strange law," she replied, implying that I had made it up for the occasion.

"It is," I admitted, "but it is the law."

"Enrique said if you would talk to the lawyer at the courthouse, then the man would be punished," she insisted.

"Look," I said, "Enrique has been telling you a lot of lies. I have talked to the lawyer at the courthouse. I talked to him after you left. He is not going to do anything. Nobody is going to do anything to punish Billings. They are afraid."

"Enrique said you are not afraid."

"Enrique is a fool."

"You mean you will not help us?" the old woman said, moving slightly as if to go. "Tito said you would not help us. He said you were like all the others. He said we were fools for coming here. But Enrique said you were an honest man and would help us."

"But I tell you there is nothing I can do. If you wanted to sue him and try to get some of his money—"

This brought a sudden outburst from Antonio, the brother, who had remained silent until then. "What I would like to do is kill him," he said, and the old woman turned rapidly to him and told him to quit talking that way, that he would ruin them all. Then she added, turning to me, "But we believe the man should be punished."

I was frankly puzzled. But I started out trying to explain some of the workings of the law to them.

"In this country," I said, realizing that the situation was about the same in any other country, "you have different forms of justice. Sometimes you put a man in prison. Sometimes you make him pay a fine, or damages. The more money a man has, the harder it is to put him in prison. But sometimes it isn't so hard to make him pay damages. That is a form of punishment, and it works two ways. It hurts the man who pays it, and it helps the people who get the money, the people who have been wronged and who are entitled to it."

They remained silent.

"Of course if you insist on filing a charge against him, then you can file a charge. The justice of the peace has to take it."

"But the lawyer at the courthouse said he would not do anything about it," the old woman put in. "He said we could not do anything that way."

"You could get it filed, all right. But do you know what would happen then?"

They didn't answer, so I went on. "They would probably put it off and put it off and never try it at all. But if they ever did try the case, they would put a lot of men on the stand who would swear that Chelo was a bad woman—" I stopped there because Antonio came halfway out of his chair and said savagely, "That is a filthy lie."

"I know it," I put in quickly, "but I am telling you what would happen. You ought to know beforehand. They would put men on the stand who would swear that Chelo was a bad woman. All of you would suffer. Chelo would suffer terribly. And the man would not be punished at all. That is how it would be."

"Ah God, is there no justice in this land?" the old woman muttered.

"Is there much justice in any land for the poor?" I said, having a pretty clear idea of the kind of justice they would get under similar circumstances in their native land.

"All we ask is justice," the old woman repeated.

"You can punish him, all right," I went on. "He loves money because it gives him power. His heart bleeds when he loses it, even if he does like to throw it around and make a show. He has plenty of money. You could make him pay. You could take the money and send your sick son to the hospital. You might even send Chelo to a college so she wouldn't have to work in the homes of other people."

I walked over to the window and glanced down into the patio where the guests at the Inter-American Ball were eating at a long banquet table. Then I turned back to the family, who had been talking among themselves in low voices.

"You could make him pay you thousands of dollars," I went on, beginning to work up some entirely unnecessary enthusiasm over my own ideas, which is a fault that I seem unable to cure. "He has plenty of money."

"Thousands of dollars—that is impossible;" the old woman said.

"No, it isn't impossible at all. He can pay it. And he will."

"But—but if we wanted to punish him that way," she said hesitantly, watching Antonio as she talked, "how would we get it? Would we go ask him for it?"

"No, no. That would be against the law. You would hire a lawyer."

"But we have no money," she explained. "We have only twenty-three dollars. We are saving that." I didn't have to ask what they were saving it for. They were saving it to bury Tito. I had learned that much about the Mexican people.

"I know a lawyer will want money," I told her, and then I began running over in my mind the list of lawyers in our town, trying to think of one who might handle the case for them. There were some Latin-American lawyers in Border City, but most of them had a finger in politics, which wasn't so good. Then it probably would not be wise to have a Mexican lawyer represent them anyway, I figured. Too much prejudice—an Anglo-American should represent them.

"I think I know one," I said at last, recalling Sol Bloomfield, an old bachelor who was known in our town for his disturbing ideas and rough manner more than for any purple passages poured forth to juries or victorious verdicts in court. For some reason which I didn't bother to analyze at the time, I decided he would be the man.

I wrote his name on a piece of paper and handed it to the woman.

"Now you go see this man in the morning. Don't say a word—" I checked myself. What difference did it make? If I was going to stick my nose into their affairs, I might as well do it openly. "Tell him I sent you," I went on. "Tell him I will come by his office tomorrow afternoon when I get through work. He will get the money for you, and you can send Tito off to a hospital and send Chelo to college. That is the way to punish Billings. That's the best thing to do."

Before they left they insisted that I come out to their home so they could thank me some more. I told them I would, although I had no intention of doing so. What I wanted mainly was to get them off my hands. The girl's eyes haunted me.

After they left I moved my chair back to the window, poured another drink—a stiff one—and started watching the crowd again. They were milling around now, some of them dancing. They were the people of my town and the people of Santander, across the Rio Grande.

They were well dressed and looked prosperous. Some of those who came from the other side of the Rio Grande were as dark as Chelo. One or two were real Indian types, much darker than Chelo—darker even than Antonio. But most of them were not dark at all. Many of them, particularly the women, were fairer than some of the sun-tanned Anglo-Americans with whom they were talking. Mexican women who are fair are careful never to let the sun shine on them.

"Hands across the border," I muttered to myself. "I guess it's a lovely thing. We, welcome them, then when they come and stay—"

I picked up the telephone, and the hotel clerk answered.

"Those Mexicans are on the way down," I said.

"Yes, they've gone already."

"You got them out all right? No international incident? They didn't disturb the good will going on down there between the two nations?"

"Now listen, Dave—"

"O.K.," I said. "Tell me about it some other time. I just wanted to be sure I didn't mess things up for you."

Nacho Ramírez has taken leave of his family to slog his way north for the Bracero Program and the pot of gold it portended. In this excerpt from one of the finest and least known English language novels about that era, Nacho learns fast what it means to join the parade.

from *Bracero*

Eugene Nelson

"What's your name?" asked the ragged friendly youth presently, smiling coaxingly at Nacho as if extracting a secret of the greatest intimacy from him.

Nacho told him his name. "And yours?"

"Chucho Peréz, at your orders," said the other, tipping his tattered sombrero with a gallant gesture. His smile flashed whitely.

"Mucho gusto—very glad to make your acquaintance," said Nacho, shaking the youth's hand. "Are you going to the United States as a bracero?" he pursued, striving to make friendly conversation.

"¡Sí!" said Chucho with a smiling emphatic roll of his head, as if the idea had just occurred to him. "¿Usted también?"

"Sí," affirmed Nacho. "I'm going as a bracero too," feeling suddenly closer to the youth beside him.

"Ah, bien, some of them come back with a lot of money." Chucho rolled his eyes.

"Some of them?" asked Nacho apprehensively.

"Sí, creo que sí," said his companion. "I believe so."

"You mean all of them don't come back with money?" Nacho asked. He remembered the drunken man singing the song about going to the United States in huaraches and coming back barefoot.

"Well, you know how it is. Some of them get a bad contract or spend their money on wine and women." Chucho rolled his eyes again, as if contemplating what a delightful fate that would be. He took off his hat, adjusted it, and put it back on at an even more rakish angle than before, so that when he tilted his head it seemed about to slide off in the dust.

"What do you mean by a bad contract?" said Nacho. "What kind of bad contract?"

"Well, I only know what I've heard. Sometimes there is not much work or maybe in some parts of the Estados Unidos they do not pay so

well as in other parts. But then some of them come back very rich."
Chucho smiled, walking along with his rollicking rolling gait, his head
rolling continually from side to side as if he had not a care in the world.
Nacho walked along beside him deep in thought, a faintly worried look on
his face. It occurred to him that the youth beside him didn't seem to know
much about the situation for one who was going as a bracero. But then
he himself knew even less, he considered, tramping along desultorily
through the already stifling heat. . . .

He stopped at a vendor's stand to buy a glass of bright red jamaica
juice for fifteen centavos. He paid for the drink and went to sit at one of
the open-air tables. Several other men in work clothes sat about nearby,
and he listened to their confused conversation as he sat sipping his drink.

"On your way back home?" one man was asking another at a nearby
table.

"Ha!" said the other, a man about forty. "Listen, I had to borrow
twelve hundred pesos at home to go up to the States six months ago. In
six months I've only been able to save fifty dollars. I don't intend to return
until I can pay the debt. Pues, I'm just waiting out my twenty days until I
can go north again . . ."

"Well at least you are saving a little," said the other man. "I have been
away from home for twelve weeks, and on the six week contract I just
finished in Arizona I only made enough to pay for my room and board. My
family is begging right now, on the streets." He sighed deeply. "Where I
was working in Jalisco the boss at least gave me food to feed my family. In
the United States you make only money; you do not make food. I am going
to return home to make sure that my family eats." The man sat with a
weary distraught expression on his face.

"But at least you still have a family to return to," another man said
sadly. He was a small very dark man with a wall eye. "I started coming up
here as a bracero from my home in Penjamillo, Michoacán, during World
War II," he went on. "I came in first in 1943. I stayed four years that time.
Then the Mexican government objected to the bad treatment up there and
wouldn't send any more workers for a while, so I went in as a wetback.
Pues, remember, pues? The United States government legalized the wetbacks during that time in spite of the objections of our own government. I
went as a wetback seven times between '47 and '50. Then in '50 when the
ban was lifted I started going as a bracero again. My wife abandoned me
because I was away from home trying to get contracted. I do not know

what she did with our three children. I have not seen them in seven years."

"My wife has become a prostitute since I have been away from home," put in another man, leaning unsteadily in his chair.

As if the word "prostitute" had been a signal, a small handsome man in a loud shirt sidled up to Nacho and whispered in his ear, "You want to go with a girl, amigo—only twenty-five pesos for one stick." He nodded to a woman sitting alone at a table nearby.

Nacho was taken by surprise; it was the first time he had ever been propositioned in this way. He set his glass down and looked first at the man and then shyly at the woman sitting nearby; she was a dowdy-looking woman of about forty with sagging breasts and a paunch emphasized by an extremely tight-fitting skirt. She looked over at Nacho and blinked her heavily-mascaraed eyes coaxingly.

"No, gracias, señor, but—" Nacho blushed, uttering the words with difficulty.

A middle-aged man at the next table said to the pimp in a joking voice, "Jesus God, man, he doesn't want to sleep with somebody's grandmother."

The pimp frowned archly and said, " 'An old hen makes good broth,' hombre." With his small hand he described an exaggerated curve down the woman's side.

"He doesn't want the broth, hombre, he wants the meat!" said the man at the next table with a coarse laugh.

The pimp ignored the interloper and whispered frantically, "Come on, hombre—only fifteen pesos for one stick; she's got her room right around the corner." The woman sitting at the nearby table pursed her orange lips suggestively and flared her calf out where it crossed her knee.

"No, gracias, but I am a married man, señor," Nacho said.

" 'A married man!' " The pimp burst out in shrill laughter, his small body rocking. "He says he's a married man!" he said to the man at the next table, and emitted another shrill burst of laughter.

Nacho blushed deeply. He thought longingly of China and was filled with a nagging loneliness. The pimp walked on to one of the other tables and sat down by two men. Presently one of the men got up and followed the pimp and the woman down the street and they disappeared in the gathering darkness.

A boy who looked not over thirteen or fourteen walked up to the counter and ordered a beer. He took the beer bottle and sat down familiarly near the group of men.

"Don't tell me that you are going as a bracero?" said one of the men, looking over at the boy with a bemused look.

The boy took a gulp of the beer and wiped his lips with a loud smack of satisfaction. "What do you mean 'going,' man?" he said in a rough indignant voice. "I've just come back from a three months' contract in Santa Barbara. Now I'm on my way north again."

"So they're letting babies through now," one of the other men put in a voice of mock incredulity. "How old are you, anyhow?"

"Fourteen," the boy said matter-of-factly, taking another long gulp of the beer.

"Isn't this life a little rough for you at your age?" one of the other men asked.

The boy scowled, setting his beer bottle down with a loud thud on the scarred tabletop. "Ai, chinga." He swore. "All they would let me do was sweep up the barracks and help in the kitchen. There was nothing to it. This time if they don't let me work in the fields I'm going to tell them to go fuck themselves." He sat with a broad scowl on his face, sneering into his beer.

"I thought you were supposed to be eighteen to go north," someone said.

The boy laughed. "You must be a newcomer," he snorted.

"Cabrón. They don't care where the mordida comes from, hombre. A woman could pass through here if she paid her bite!"

"That's true," agreed another with a cynical smile. "I've known several boys of only fifteen or sixteen who have gone; and once near Bakersfil there was a man working next to me in the cotton who was over seventy. Enough mordida will buy anything." . . .

. . . Nacho finished his drink and slowly got up to leave, filled with uneasiness by what he had heard. He walked back the way he had come in the gathering dusk, making small detours from time to time to avoid the outstretched hands of beggars. Twice as he walked along men sidled up to him and tried to get him to give them money so that he could be shipped north the following day; a third man, almost in rags, tried to sell him some forged papers. He shrugged the men off and continued on his way. He was overcome by a deep sadness, seeing the way his fellow Mexicans were trying to cheat one another; he had not realized before that there were such people in the world, or at least not in such numbers. He suddenly felt a great loss of confidence in people, and therefore felt less secure himself, and hurried faster through the teeming avenue, holding his hand in the pocket that contained his money and papers. Everywhere he turned men seemed to be moaning bitterly about some calamity or other; and yet, among all the misfortune, other men rushed by shouting and singing and laughing as if it did not exist or as if they saw none of it—rode the ferris wheel, ate cotton candy, drank tequila, went with the "bad women," and deported themselves as if the entire world were engaged in a fiesta to end all fiestas. He decided perplexedly that Empalme was at the same time the gayest and the saddest place he had ever seen. . . .

Nacho awakened with a start. It was early dawn. Already the men were rousing themselves and milling about the newly-revived campfire, and he could smell the pungent odor of coffee mingling with the smells of his own body and the cold earth. . . .

"Aiiieee! This is the day!" his neighbor Roberto exclaimed with a little subdued cry of joy, reaching over to pinch Nacho on the arm with an ecstatic grin. "Mañana we are rich gringos!"

"Ojalá que sí," said Nacho sleepily, folding his serape carefully, then looking about with shivering interest at the uproar of activity about him in the still dim light.

"Pues, since we are all going to be so rich soon, we'll let you cabrones have some of our coffee," grinned Pablo Gonzales, placing atop the grate a battered tin can filled with water and a handful of bulk coffee. . . .

"Listos? Ready?" Refugio Mejía said to no one in particular, rising from beside the doused coals. With a nod of his head he turned and started across the barren stretch of desert toward the highway, his bedroll under one arm, and the others slowly took out after him, forming into a loosely-organized group.

The men came to the highway and turned and trooped along its shoulder to the north in the rising light, a ragged but eager army. Their voices lost the caution of night and grew gradually louder with the increasing light from the east. . . .

"The day of justice has arrived!" ejaculated one of the men swinging along jauntily.

"Tomorrow we will be in the land of honey!"

"We'll all be rich cabrones soon!"

"Sí, we'll all be rich businessmen with Cadillacs and a mistress in Guzmán!"

"Maybe I'll stay in California and marry a rich pocha."

"What—why not a gringa?"

"Oh, I'll have two or three of them for mistresses—and to wash my wife's lace panties!"

Nacho walked silently at Roberto's side, shuffling along painfully over the loose gravel in his disintegrating huaraches, but nonetheless suffused with a joyous confidence. The Gonzales brothers followed behind, laughing and snickering at the crude jokes of the others.

" 'Mañana salgo pa'l Norte,' " sang one of the men,

"Dijo un ranchero a su chata;

'Ya tengo mi pasaporte

Para ganar mucha plata . . .' "

" 'Tomorrow I leave for the North,'

Said a farmer to his sweetheart;

'I already have my passport

To earn a great deal of loot . . .' "

The crude wooden shacks of Empalme began to take shape sharply in the cool dawn as the dome of the sky became suffused with shimmering light. The morning sounds wafted through the shining firmament the same as anywhere else in México: a cock crew, a burro brayed, a distant radio blared a strident ranchera song, plaintive and bittersweet. A truck roared past to the north, emitting a cloud of choking diesel fumes, and two youths clinging to its tailgate threw them a shrill greeting.

After several minutes of rapid walking they came to the bracero installation. Already several hundred men were waiting under the huge ramada, while hundreds more milled about restlessly in the great dusty yard adjoining. Bedrolls and cheap suitcases were strewn about everywhere, their corners glinting in the long horizontal rays of sunlight. Beyond the ramada lay, stockade-like, another large dusty yard enclosed by a high fence topped by barbed wire which completely enclosed the huge installation. Past the enclosure stood the processing building itself, a vast crumbling structure of yellow stucco which had once served as an army barracks; beside it two helmeted soldiers stood stiffly at attention with rifles at present arms, while half-a-dozen of their colleagues lolled about nearby in various attitudes of relaxation.

At the sight of the huge army of men, more numerous than on the previous occasions he had passed the installation, Nacho's newly-found courage suddenly drained out of him.

"Un montón de hombres!" exclaimed Pablo Gonzales, baring his white teeth in a grimace of amazement that was half smile and half alarm. "I didn't know there were so many Mexicans in the whole world!"

The ragged crowd paused for a moment at the edge of the highway, like a sightless centipede-like creature feeling its way uncertainly, then surged forward across the dusty yard toward the ramada, Refugio Mejía at its head. As they approached the crude ramada a few of the men already jammed together in its scant shade yelled greetings at them, or taunted the newcomers genially.

"Hola. What is this ragged-looking bunch?—countrymen or some tribe from the lower depths of hell?"

"Puros pelados obviously, since they did not arrive in taxis like us!"

"Greetings—there are apparently even more fools in México than I thought!"

"More slaves for the gringos—I thought we were the only ones fool enough to be suckered into this tontería!" . . .

"That man on the train—the one who was knocked off when it went into the tunnel—was he not one of us?" Nacho asked concernedly.

"Ah, no—he was from over in Michoacán someplace," Pablo Gonzales said. "He was going as a wetback."

"And now he is going as a broken-back," his brother offered with a laugh.

"Perhaps we could sell the three vacant places to some other men who do not have certificados," it occurred to a man down the line a ways.

"Ah, sí—all they would have to do is give false names," said a companion.

"But what if the men show up—then there would be trouble," said a third man.

After what seemed an interminable period of waiting two soldiers and a couple of civilians walked leisurely to the gate in the high fence that led to the enclosure within, and the thousands of men in the dusty yard immediately sprang to attention, the deafening wave of their voices sank to an excited murmur, and all faces strained toward the approaching figures. . . .

"Chinga!" exploded Pablo Gonzales with subdued obscenity. "What are they talking about—their last night's conquests?"

"Cállate, cállate, shut up for the love of God!" immediately hissed several other men nearby, turning to look reprovingly at the fat youth, then returning their eyes scrutinizingly to the officials beside the gate.

After several more minutes one of the men finally seated himself at a small table within the enclosure, grasped a microphone that rested on the tabletop before him, and cleared his voice into it raspingly. At the sound of the official's voice a new surge of excitement swept through the men, then they cautioned one another to silence, straining their eyes and ears more anxiously than ever toward the small group of officials who held their destinies in their hands.

"Municipio of Guadalupe," the official's voice finally boomed out like fate, and a huge sigh of disappointment rushed like a fluttering of invisible wings over the vast assemblage, while from a distant corner of the ramada there arose a flurry of excitement, wild shrieks of joy, and a scramble of ragged men galvanizing themselves into action and surging forward with suitcases and bedrolls toward the open gate.

"Alfredo Nuño—" the long list of names commenced, and the chosen men began to rush forward toward the gate like forgotten souls belatedly summoned to Paradise.

from *In Search of Bernabé*

Graciela Limón

Luz and Arturo arrived at the Tijuana bus terminal forty hours later, exhausted and bloated from sitting in their cramped seat. As soon as they stepped out of the bus, they were approached by a woman who asked them if they wanted to cross the border at night. Without waiting for an answer, she told them she could be their guide. The price was five hundred American dollars apiece.

Luz stared at the woman for a few moments, caught off guard by the suddenness of what was happening. More than her words, it was the woman's appearance that caught Luz's attention. She was about thirty-five. Old enough, Luz figured, to have experience in her business. The woman was tall and slender, yet her body conveyed muscular strength that gave Luz the impression that she would be able to lead them across the border.

The coyota returned Luz's gaze, evidently allowing time for the older woman to make up her mind. She took a step closer to Luz, who squinted as she concentrated on the woman's face. Luz regarded her dark skin and high forehead, and the deeply set eyes that steadily returned her questioning stare. With a glance, she took in the coyota's faded Levi's and plaid shirt under a shabby sweatshirt, and her eyes widened when she saw the woman's scratched, muddy cowboy boots. She had seen only men wear such shoes.

Luz again looked into the woman's eyes. She was tough, and Luz knew that she had to drive a hard bargain. She began to cry. "¡Señora, por favor! Have a heart! How can you charge so much? We're poor people who have come a long way. Where do you think we can find so many dólares? All we have is one hundred dollars to cover the two of us. Please! For the love of your mamacita!"

The woman crossed her arms over her chest and laughed out loud as she looked into Luz's eyes. She spoke firmly. "Señora, I'm not in the habit of eating fairy tales for dinner. You've been in Mexico City for a long time. I have eyes, don't I? I can tell that you're not starving. Both of you have eaten a lot of enchiladas and tacos. Just look at those nalgas!"

She gave Luz a quick, hard smack on her behind. Then, ignoring the older woman's look of outrage, the coyota continued to speak rapidly. "Look, Señora. Just to show you that I have feelings, I'll consider guiding the both of you at the reduced rate of seven hundred dollars. Half now; the rest when I get you to Los Angeles. Take it or leave it!"

Luz knew that she was facing her match. She answered with one word. "Bueno."

The coyota led them to a man who was standing nearby. He was wearing a long overcoat, inappropriate for the sultry weather in Tijuana. The coat had a purpose, though, for it concealed deep inner pockets which were filled with money. The coyota pulled Luz nearer to the man, then whispered into her ear. "This man will change your pesos into American dollars. A good rate, I guarantee."

When Arturo began to move closer, the coyota turned to him. "You stay over there!"

Arturo obeyed.

Even though she felt distrust, Luz decided that she and Arturo had no alternative. However, she needed to speak with him, so she pulled him to the side. "Hijo, we're taking a big chance. We can be robbed, even killed. Remember the stories we've been hearing since we left home. But what can we do? We need someone to help us get across, so what does it matter if it's this one, or someone else? What do you say?"

Arturo agreed with her. "Let's try to make it to the other side. The sooner the better. I think you made a good bargain. We have the money, don't we?"

"With a little left over for when we get to Los Angeles."

Before they returned to where the others were waiting, she turned to a wall. She didn't want anyone to see what she was doing. Luz withdrew the amount of pesos she estimated she could exchange for a little more than seven hundred American dollars. She walked over to the money vendor, and no sooner had the man placed the green bills on her palm than she heard the coyota's sharp voice. "Three hundred and fifty dollars, por favor!"

She signaled Luz and Arturo to follow her to a waiting car. They went as far as Mesa Otay, the last stretch of land between Mexico and California. There, the coyota instructed them to wait until it got dark. Finally, when Luz could barely see her hand in front of her, the woman gave the signal. "Vámonos!"

They walked together under the cover of darkness. As Luz and Arturo trekked behind the woman, they sensed that they were not alone, that other people were also following. Suddenly someone issued a warning, "¡La Migra! ¡Cuidado!" The coyota turned with unexpected speed, and murmured one word, "¡Abajo!"

All three fell to the ground, clinging to it, melting into it, hoping that it would split open so that they could crawl into its safety. Unexpectedly a light flashed on. Like a giant eye, it seemed to be coming from somewhere in the sky, slowly scanning the terrain. No one moved. All that could be heard were the crickets and the dry grass rasping in the mild breeze. The light had not detected the bodies crouched behind bushes and rocks. It flashed out as suddenly as it had gone on.

"¡Vámonos!" The coyota was again on her feet and moving. They continued in the dark for hours over rough, rocky terrain. The coyota was sure-footed but Luz and Arturo bumped into rocks and tripped over gopher holes. Luz had not rested or eaten since she had gotten off the bus. She was fatigued but she pushed herself, fearing she would be left behind if she stopped. Arturo was exhausted too, but he knew that he still had reserves of energy, enough for himself and for Luz.

Dawn was breaking as they ascended a hill. Upon reaching the summit, they were struck with awe at the sight that spread beneath their feet. Their heavy breathing stopped abruptly as their eyes glowed in disbelief. Below, even though diffused by the dawn's advancing light, was an illuminated sea of streets and buildings. A blur of neon formed a mass of light and color, edged by a highway that was a ribbon of liquid silver. Luz and Arturo wondered if fatigue had caused their eyes to trick them because as far as they could see there was brilliance, limited only in distance by a vast ocean. To their left, they saw the lights of San Diego unfolding beneath them, and their hearts stopped when they realized that further north, where their eyes could not see, was their destination.

Without thinking, Luz and Arturo threw their arms around one another and wept.

The lights of San Diego receded behind them. The coyota had guided Luz and Arturo over an inland trail, taking them past the U.S. Immigration station at San Onofre, and then down to connect with the highway. A man in a car was waiting for them a few yards beyond Las Pulgas Road on California Interstate 5.

The driver got out of the car as they approached, extending a rough hand at first to Luz, and then to Arturo. "Me llamo Ordaz."

Ordaz turned to the coyota and spoke in English. His words were casual, as if he had seen her only hours before. "You're late. I was beginning to worry."

"The old bag slowed me down."

The coyota spoke to the man in English, knowing that her clients were unable to understand her. Then, she switched to Spanish to introduce herself to Luz and Arturo. "Me llamo Petra Traslaviña. I was born back in San Ysidro on a dairy farm. I speak English and Spanish."

There was little talk among them beyond this first encounter. The four piled into a battered Pontiac station wagon, and with Ordaz at the wheel, they headed north. The woman pulled out a pack of Mexican cigarettes, smoking one after the other, until Ordaz started to cough. He opened the window complaining, "Por favor, Petra, you wanna choke us to death?"

"Shut up!" she retorted rapidly, slurring the English *sh*.

The phrase engraved itself in Luz's memory. She liked the sound of it. She liked its effect even more, since she noticed that Ordaz was silenced by the magical phrase. Inwardly, Luz practiced her first English words, repeating them over and again under her breath.

Luz and Arturo were quiet during the trip mainly because they were frightened by the speed at which Ordaz was driving. As she looked out over the coyota's shoulder, Luz knew that she didn't like what she was feeling and hearing. She even disliked the smell of the air, and she felt especially threatened by the early morning fog. When the headlights of oncoming cars broke the grayness, her eyes squinted with pain.

The hours seemed endless, and they were relieved when Ordaz finally steered the Pontiac off the freeway and onto the streets of Los Angeles. Like children, Luz and Arturo looked around craning their necks, curiously peering through the windows and seeing that people waited for their turn to step onto the street. Luz thought it was silly the way those people moved in groups. No one ran out onto the street, leaping, jumping, dodging cars as happened in Mexico City and back home. Right away, she missed the vendors peddling wares, and the stands with food and drink.

Suddenly, Luz was struck by the thought that she didn't know where the coyota was taking them. As if reading Luz's mind, the woman asked, "Do you have a place you want me to take you to?"

Rattled by the question, Luz responded timidly, "No. We didn't have time to think."

"I thought so. It's the same with all of you."

The coyota was quiet for a while before she whispered to Ordaz, who shook his head in response. They engaged in a heated exchange of words in English, the driver obviously disagreeing with what the coyota was proposing. Finally, seeming to have nothing more to say, Ordaz shrugged his shoulders, apparently accepting defeat. The coyota turned to her passangers.

"Vieja, I know of a place where you two can find a roof and a meal until you find work. But . . ." She was hesitating. "¡Mierda! . . . just don't tell them I brought you. They don't like me because I charge you people money."

What she said next was muttered and garbled. Luz and Arturo did not understand her so they kept quiet, feeling slightly uneasy and confused. By this time Ordaz was on Cahuenga Boulevard in Hollywood. He turned up a short street, and pulled into the parking lot of Saint Turibius Church, where the battered wagon spurted, then came to a stand-still.

"Hasta aquí. You've arrived."

The coyota was looking directly at Luz, who thought she detected a warning sign in the woman's eyes. "It was easy this time, Señora. Remember, don't get caught by la Migra, because it might not be so good the next time around. But if that happens, you know that you can find me at the station in Tijuana."

Again, the coyota seemed to be fumbling for words. Then she said, "Just don't get any funny ideas hanging around these people. I mean, they love to call themselves voluntarios, and they'll do anything for nothing. Yo no soy así. I'll charge you money all over again, believe me!"

The coyota seemed embarrassed. Stiffly, she shifted in her seat, pointing at a two-story, Spanish-style house next to the church.

"See that house?"

Luz nodded.

"Bueno. Just walk up to the front door, knock, and tell them who you are, and where you're from. They'll be good to you. But, as I already told you, don't mention me."

She turned to Arturo. "Take care of yourself, muchacho. I've known a few like you who have gotten themselves killed out there."

With her chin, she pointed toward the street. When Arturo opened his mouth to speak, the coyota cut him of curtly. "My three hundred and fifty dollars, por favor."

She stretched out her hand in Luz's direction without realizing that her words about other young men who resembled Arturo had had an impact on Luz. "Petra, have you by any chance met my son? His name is Bernabé and he looks like this young man."

The coyota looked into Luz's eyes. When she spoke her voice was almost soft. "They all look like Arturo, Madre. They all have the same fever in their eyes. How could I possibly know your son from all the rest?"

Luz's heart shuddered when the coyota called her madre. Something told her that the woman did know Bernabé. This though filled her with new hope, and she gladly reached into her purse. She put the money into the coyota's hand, saying, "Hasta pronto. I hope, Petra, that our paths will cross again sooner or later."

. . . Feeling apprehensive, they were silent as they approached the large house that their guide had pointed out. They didn't know that the building had been a convent and that it was now a refuge run by priests and other volunteers. Neither realized that they were entering a sanctuary for the displaced and for those without documents or jobs. When they were shown in, Luz and Arturo were surprised at how warmly they were received. No one asked any questions. Afterwards, they were given food to eat and a place to sleep.

"The Child" from *Iguana Killer*

Alberto Alvaro Ríos

The bus station in Guaymas was crowded with friends and relatives of the few people coming or going. The wordless singing of tears, *abrazos,* laughter, and hand-shaking was common on Sundays and Wednesdays. These were the two days that the bus from Mexico City stopped here on its way to Nogales. It was for this Wednesday's trip that the widows Sandoval and García had purchased tickets and had come several hours early to make sure they would not miss the bus.

The two ladies shared a single face, held together by an invisible net, made evident by the marks it left on their skins. They wore black, more out of habit than out of mourning for their husbands, both of whom had been dead for more than ten years. Ten or eleven, it was difficult to say. Time was different now. Each of the ladies carried roughly woven bags with deep purple and yellow stripes. Aside from more black clothing, particularly black shawls, the bags both contained food—lemons, tortillas, sweet breads, cheese, sugar, all gifts. In their free hands, the women carried rosaries made of hard wood and their tickets. On their heads they wore black veils and on their legs black stockings with lines up the back and through which the leg hair showed. These stockings were rolled up just past their knees, worn in the manner of most of the other ladies their age who were at the bus station just then.

The bus arrived at about eleven-thirty and was not yet running too far off schedule. Some of the people coming from Mexico City got off to stretch, but the majority remained. The widows Sandoval and García said goodbyes to those who had come with them, crossed themselves, and got on the bus, which was not crowded this Wednesday, not as crowded as on Sundays, when people had to stand in the aisle. The two ladies found a pair of seats near the back. It took them some time to get the seats because bags and suitcases cluttered the aisle. Their own bags were stretched beyond their original intentions and knocked into people, especially the men who wore straw cowboy hats with wide brims for traveling. After many *excuse me*'s and *con permiso*'s, the ladies got to their places. Although they had gotten on first, they were the last to get settled. Both were shaped like large eggs, formless and mostly bottom-halved, so bus seats never seemed to be quite big enough.

The bus driver with green-tinted glasses and a thin-thin moustache watched and waited with much patience until they were accommodated to start the bus. As it pulled away, relatives and friends waved and shouted last minute messages, very long, but the two ladies even after considerable effort could not get their window open. The embarrassment was short-lived as smoke from the bus soon covered their view.

The two women were uncommonly quiet as the bus hurtled along. Mrs. Sandoval looked out the window and fanned herself with a magazine she had already read many times, the kind with brown pictures on newsprint that never gets thrown away. Mrs. García, the more talkative and gossipy of the two, held her brown bead rosary and looked around at the other people. In front of her she could see only the backs of heads and cowboy hats. One little girl, her lips white from candy, was standing up on a seat and looking back at her. Across the aisle a man sat pulling a blanket around the head of a little boy. The boy was asleep, and Mrs. García was envious because she had always found sleeping on a bus impossible. Behind her sat another man with a cowboy hat who was reading a magazine. Brown pictures on newsprint. The other few seats were empty.

It was almost noon now, and the bus was getting very hot. The black clothes of the two ladies did not help matters, but they had grown quite used to sweating. Each agreed, this was their lot. They complained to each other now, after many years of friendship and funerals, only with large sighs. No words. Sometimes they would shake their heads, and this said all the words. Everyone on the bus today seemed uncommonly quiet, not just the ladies, as if these people all knew why the two were making the trip. The man across the aisle began to smoke. Mrs. García sighed, and Mrs. Sandoval understood. The other words.

"Excuse me. Is the child all right?" asked Mrs. García. The man next to her was thin and moved like an ostrich, not smooth but in jerks, so that he almost could not light the newest in a line of cigarettes he had kept in his hand. He had green-tinted glasses on, too.

"Well, no, he is sick," answered the man. He did not seem very talkative either, like Mrs. Sandoval, thought Mrs. García. One would think the Republic was at war again, or somesuch. Mrs. García waited for more but the man said nothing.

After a few minutes, Mrs. García, as was her habit, asked him, "What is wrong with the child?" Her custom was not necessarily to ask about the health of children, but rather, simply to *ask*.

"I don't know exactly. We are going to see a doctor, a specialist in Nogales, maybe Tucson."

"Weren't there any specialists in Mexico City? I have heard of some very good doctors. Dr. Olvera. Do you . . ."

"Well, yes, but they have advised me to go to Nogales and see an American doctor. You know."

"Oh, I see, of course," said Mrs. García. She nodded her head to say yes in the other language. He understood clearly, with his head, also.

Mrs. Sandoval nudged her. "You should stop talking so much, you are going to wake the child," she whispered.

"Yes, yes, you are right. Poor thing." More words to the man, "I'm sorry" with her eyes.

"Poor Agustín," said Mrs. Sandoval.

"What?" said Mrs. García. Spoken words were not always understandable.

"Agustín, poor Agustín," repeated Mrs. Sandoval. She raised her eyes to the roof of the bus. Quickly, and back down.

"He has gone to fine things. All we can do is pray for him," said Mrs. García. Both woman gripped their rosaries and immediately began praying. They prayed the rosary several times together. It did not take them long because they had become very fast at it from many dragging years of practice. When they finished, Mrs. Sandoval went back to looking out the window and Mrs. García looked around at the people again.

She decided to talk to the man once more because there was no one else within speaking range. In any language. This time she was careful to whisper.

"Have you been to this doctor before?"

"What? Oh, no. This is the first time."

"I thought you had because I could not help noticing your American cigarettes. They smell different."

"Oh, uh, yes. No I've never been. A friend . . ." He offered the cigarettes. Mrs. García shook her head. It said no.

"Did you try giving him some yerba buena tea?"

"Pardon me?" said the man. He was surprised at her whispering and showed effort in turning his head to hear her again.

"Oh, I am whispering because I don't want to wake, you know, the boy."

"Oh," he said. And yes with his head.

"What I asked was, did you try giving him some yerba buena tea?" Eyebrows up.

"Oh, uh, yes, we did." Eyebrows down, clearly.

"Did you try honey and lemon? Maybe with a little bit of tequila? That always helps." Still up.

"Yes we gave him everything, but nothing helps. Really." Brows, if possible, even lower.

"That is very strange. He must be very sick. Does he have a fever?" Still.

"No, no, he gets chills. That's why I wrapped him in this blanket. I think it helps him to sleep better, too, and the doctor said that he needs lots of sleep." The ostrich in his body was uncomfortable.

"Yes, then that is the thing to do, of course. Keep him well wrapped. Chills can be very terrible, especially if you have arthritis. I have this bracelet for arthritis and it helps a little. Copper. It is the only thing the doctor has given me that helps. Dr. Valenzuela. Do you know him? Sometimes it helps the pain I get in my left shoulder, too. And a lot of liquids. Don't they always say that."

"Pardon me?" He almost was not turning his head to listen.

"And you should give him a lot of liquids, no doubt." Lips pressed.

"Yes, yes, that's right. Excuse me, I am going to try and sleep." He smiled a smile faster than the moment he had taken previously to light a match.

"Oh, of course, go right ahead. I hope you can," said Mrs. García. She let go of him with her eyes. She wished that she could get to sleep. Bus rides always seemed to be endless and her neck always ached, as it did now, a great deal. They would at El Sopilote soon and she could get out and stretch. She sighed, but Mrs. Sandoval was asleep, and did not hear. . . .

Mrs. García, tired of looking at the desert scrub and occasional mesquite trees, read the magazine that Mrs. Sandoval had fanned herself with earlier. Read it, really, for the third time. The man next to them stared out of his window and from time to time fixed the blanket around the still sleeping child. . . .

"How old is the child?" asked Mrs. García. She could only see his short hair from her angle.

"Oh, he is five years old." His head nodded yes.

"He will be starting school soon." Her eyebrows made this a question.

With the side of his face he heard the eyebrows rise. "Yes, I suppose he will." He almost shrugged his shoulders. His body was moving so much, just a little but all over, that perhaps it just seemed like he shrugged, or almost shrugged. . . .

"Excuse me, I think I will move the child to the back. He will be more comfortable if he lies across two seats, I think."

"Of course," said Mrs. García. She moved her bag with the purple and yellow stripes out of the way to say yes as the man picked up the child and spread him out across the two seats directly in back of the two women. The boy did not wake up. The man sat in the closest of the adjoining two seats so that he was still opposite the two ladies, but one row back.

"The child has slept for a long time," said Mrs. Sandoval to Mrs. García.

Mrs. García sighed. She wished she could sleep like that. "Yes, and isn't his face pale though? A little honey and lemon would surely help some. He must be very sick."

"Agustín was such a good man," said Mrs. Sandoval.

"Yes, yes he was." They both nodded up, and down. Yes.

The traveling was like an hour hand's and several more people got on the bus. They had been waiting along the road and had probably come from one of the ranches because the men wore cowboy hats and the women were not used to shoes. The hats were a cheaper quality of straw. The two widows had prayed the rosary again after mentioning Mrs. Sandoval's brother. They would soon be in Hermosillo. That would surely be like a drink of water. It had been a long time since she had eaten *quesadillas* at the El Yaqui, remarked Mrs. García. She put her hand on her stomach. Mrs. Sandoval said that she was not hungry. She put her hand flat on the top part of her chest.

The bus stopped in Hermosillo and almost everyone got out this time. One man was too fat, and did not find rising worth the trouble. He was so used to sitting now, he said, to Mrs. García, who asked, that standing felt unnatural, really. He slept sitting, too, because his stomach felt like a horse stepping on his chest when he stretched out on his back. Mrs. García's head said no, God, from side to side, it's too much to bear. But we're like that, aren't we, said her head. She decided she would not offer to bring him anything from the restaurant. She certainly would not eat if she were like that. The two ladies went out and were followed, patiently because he had no choice, by the man who was sitting now behind them.

"Are you going to bring the child?" asked Mrs. García, in all the ways she was capable. They were already outside the bus, and he did not have the boy with him.

"No, I don't want to wake him. He needs all the sleep he can get." The man crushed his cigarette on the ground.

"Yes, of course. By the way, I recommend very highly the quesadillas here. No place has quesadillas like El Yaqui." She smiled.

"So I have heard," said the man. Yes, nodding.

The ladies went into the restaurant. The man said that he would be right in, but that he had to stretch first, that he felt like crumpled paper. He pulled out one of his American cigarettes. Everyone in the restaurant ordered the *quesadillas* without exception. Rumor had made them larger than any of the other choices, had put more letters in their name. Mrs. García felt that it was the quality of the cream in the white cheese. The man came in a little later and ordered the same. Of course, nodded Mrs. García. He sat by himself at a table near the turquoise painted door.

Mrs. Sandoval ordered an orange soda, preferably a Mission if they had any. Mrs. García ordered an *agua de manzana* and a glass of water. The ladies finished quickly and commented on the tastiness of the food. Yes, yes. Mrs. Sandoval had ordered only one *quesadilla* and Mrs. García had ordered three. They finished eating at the same time.

"I think the agua de manzana will give you heartburn," said Mrs. Sandoval. "You ate too fast."

"It's very good for the stomach." She was sure.

"It has always given me heartburn. Why did you order the water when you haven't even tasted it?"

"I am going to take it to the boy. He should have lots of liquids." Certainly, on her face. The doctor, after all, had said so.

"Shouldn't you leave that to his father?"

"The poor man is dazed," said Mrs. García. "I don't think he knows what to do for the child. Anyway, a little water won't hurt, and the poor thing hasn't had any since we got on the bus. His throat must be like the road."

"Yes, yes, that is true," said Mrs. Sandoval. "But shouldn't you tell the man?"

"I told him the child needs lots of liquids but, like I said, he is in a daze. Let the poor man eat. Come on, a little water will be a big help for the boy." The two ladies paid their bill and took the water out. They told the *señora* of the restaurant that they would bring the glass back in a couple of minutes. Yes would have been the word in the *señora's* mouth, opened like a question, yes, of course.

The two widows got back on the bus. It was much easier for them since the bus was almost empty. They made their way past the few people, the far [fat] man, yes, hello, he was eating *quesadillas* someone had brought, and got to the back where the child was. Mrs. García saw that he was still sleeping.

"Do you think that you should wake him?" asked Mrs. Sandoval.

"It won't hurt him. He needs the water, especially in this heat." She reached for the covers and moved them from his face.

"Ah, this child is cold. His chills must be like ice," said Mrs. García. Her eyebrows.

"Here, let me see." Mrs. Sandoval's hands.

"Wait," said Mrs. García. She moved the blanket so as to rearrange it and stared at the white child. Vanilla ice cream. "Oh, oh my God!" she screamed, and moved like she had put her hands into the flames of a stove, like when she first learned to make tortillas. She was a young girl then. She moved back with the same kind of strength. Mrs. Sandoval caught her as she fell, fainted.

"¡Dios mío! Jesús? Help, ah, this child is dead, he is dead!" screamed Mrs. Sandoval in much the same voice as Mrs. García had screamed. Very high. All the people jumped to get over them. Everyone started screaming, and crying. The fat man came. Mrs. García was laid down in the adjoining chairs and Mrs. Sandoval sat with her, crying and clasping her rosary, squeezing it so that if it had been plastic. . . . A man with a cowboy hat— one of them, they were all mixed up—covered the child again with the blanket.

"Get the police, get the police, the Red Cross," yelled the man, too loudly. "Who is this, whose child is this?"

Mrs. Sandoval gasped. There was a loud implication not only in the question, but in the way he grabbed the seat to push himself, once he was aimed. "He's the man's, the man who ate alone." Mrs. Sandoval half stood. Her eyes went through the bus with sharp edges and fast.

By this time the bus driver was calling for the police. The man was nowhere to be found although everyone looked for him. Every person was asking what happened and the bus was an elevator full of voices. Too many, and they bounced into each other. Mrs. García was brought out and lay resting in a bedroom behind the restaurant. Mrs. Sandoval sat with her, praying out loud. The child was left where it was. Nothing moved it.

When the police arrived, the bus stop was much quieter. Too quiet like it had been too loud. Everyone was sitting in the restaurant. No one could believe it, and where was the father? The Red Cross ambulance arrived just after the police and took the child away. Just picked him up.

The head policeman was trying to get everyone's attention. "All right, all right, who can tell me what happened here? I am the Sergeant."

Mrs. García's name was mentioned by Mrs. Sandoval. The policeman asked where she was and Mrs. Sandoval led him to the bedroom in back where she was resting. The *señora* was fanning her. Mrs. Sandoval pointed with her eyes.

"Mrs. García?"

"Yes, yes, at your service." She would talk. Of course, if it would help.

"I understand that you can tell me something about what has happened here." It all came from his mouth, like a sergeant.

"Well, only that the man said that the child was sick, and when I tried to give it some water I saw that it was dead. The boy, I mean."

"Can you describe the man?"

"Oh, yes, of course." Her eyebrows went up, one a little more than the other. "He was . . ."

"Well, I would rather you tell me this at the station house. Is that all right with you?" Like a sergeant still.

"Well, we are going to a funeral." Her eyes looked at the floor.

"I'm sorry. It won't take too long, and there are a number of other busses. Where are you going?" Less like a sergeant. Funerals do that.

"To Nogales," replied Mrs. García.

"Ah, yes, certainly there are other busses going to Nogales today." Head up and down. He was a man after all. She felt better.

"Would I be able to telephone from the station in case something happens to keep me?" She kept her head down.

"Of course, yes of course." Not impatiently.

Mrs. García looked at Mrs. Sandoval. "You go on ahead. I should stay and help. All right?" She asked with all her body.

Mrs. Sandoval nodded her head. "Yes, if you'll be okay." She glanced at the Sergeant. "Try and get to Nogales in time. We will all be waiting for you. It's not too far, anyway."

"I will, I promise." Yes . . .

As Mrs. García goes off with the police, Mrs. Sandoval continues on her way to the funeral in Nogales, where she is besieged with questions about the little boy.

Mrs. Sandoval spoke. She spoke the words of Mrs. García, who had spoken the words of the Sergeant, who had spoken the words of the doctor. More truthfully, she carried the words.

The child was dead. It had been dead for a long time. That is true. But it had also been operated on. The boy's insides had been cleaned out and replaced with bags of opium. They had tested to be certain. Then the boy was sewn up again, put into clothes. Sometimes this happens. This was not the first.

Oh my God, Dios mío, Dios mío was all Mrs. Sandoval kept saying, maybe with words, saying just like Mrs. García. Their heads moved from side to side, but not fast enough.

Section 2

Stereotypes are born, not made.
Here are some of the best stereotypes aborning.

Shortly after graduating from Columbia University, the young poet took a long trip through Mexico. He spent his last hours in Baja California.

Mexicali, June 1954

Allen Ginsberg

My room on the garbage cliff overlooking the Casbah poor barrio, tin shacks and white roofs, and little dirty gardens down below bounded by the uptown hip cliff and superhighway nightmare 20th cent viaduct. To stand on my garbage cliff and see I am at the end of Mexican trip.

The town so noisy, dirty, streetfulls of wild boys all night, drunken wetbacks, restaurants, Chinese hotels, musicians, half american stores, jumping beans and tortilla concessions, Chinese Masonic lodges & barbers too. Big halls for restaurants and music, painted crudely with monolithic donkeys.

I walked thru the border at nite to get a map of California, a dead silent fairyland of U.S. dusk—deserted ghost streets and sad quiet air-cooled diners with white capped waitresses joking softly and no one on the streets.

from *Lonesome Traveler*

Jack Kerouac

When you go across the border at Nogales Arizona some very severe looking American guards, some of them pasty faced with sinister steelrim spectacles go scrounging through all your beat baggage for signs of the scorpion of scofflaw.—You just wait—patiently like you always do in America among those apparently endless policemen and their endless laws *against* (no laws *for*)—but the moment you cross the little wire gate and you're in Mexico, you feel like you just sneaked out of school when you told the teacher you were sick and she told you you could go home, 2 o'clock in the afternoon.—You feel as though you just come home from Sunday morning church and you take off your suit and slip into your soft worn smooth cool overalls, to play—you look around and you see happy smiling faces, or the absorbed dark faces of worried lovers and fathers and policemen, you hear cantina music from across the little park of balloons and popsicles.—In the middle of the little park is a bandstand for concerts, actual concerts for the people, free—generations of marimba players maybe, or an Orozco jazzband playing Mexican anthems to El Presidente.—You walk thirsty through the swinging doors of a saloon and get a bar beer, and turn around and there's fellas shooting pool, cooking tacos, wearing sombreros, some wearing guns on their rancher hips, and gangs of singing businessmen throwing pesos at the standing musicians who wander up and down the room.—It's a great feeling of entering the Pure Land, especially because it's so close to dry faced Arizona and Texas and all over the Southwest—but you can find it, this feeling, this fellaheen feeling about life, that timeless gayety of people not involved in great cultural and civilization issues—you can find it almost anywhere else, in Morocco, in Latin America entire, in Dakar, in Kurd land.—

The author, completing a ninety-mile bus trip, draws dangerously poetic conclusions.

from *The Mexican Night*

Lawrence Ferlinghetti

Ensenada to Tijuana to Mexicali by bus. Rode all day, contemplating the earth, saw nothing. Endless riprap of roads, hills, mountains, hopeless houses, trees, sagebrush, fences, dust, burros, dry land. Dry people stuck to it. . . . Passing through Tijuana, I see legless man at downtown dirt corner sitting in back of antique sedan from which doors have been torn. He has stained felt hat on center of head, rimless eyeglasses with cracked glass, a huge old typewriter propped up before him on wood box. Typing, he has butt of cigarette stuck to lower lip, burnt-out. Signs hung on car say

ESCRITOR PUBLICO

A campesino is speaking to him from the curb, he writes what he hears: a great writer, this Public Stenographer, Public Writer giving people back true images of themselves. Legless, he holds the mirror up. . . .

Tijuana to Mexicali, approaching the town of Tecate, but passes through hill country strewn thickly with rocks from road to horizon, nothing but rocks, rocks, millions of them covering the landscape, in place of trees. Nature has tried everything! There's beautiful country further on, other side of Tecate—rock mountains, Tibetan peaks (one of those border mountains north of Tecate, on U.S. side, inhabited by American translator of the *Tibetan Book of the Dead*). We roll on between hills of small rocks, pepper trees and sage and twisted fir growing out of rockhills, rock mountains beyond, sunset coming, bright sun flames close over, bright blue sky with rock holes in it, whole fantastic mountainous landscape of nothing but stone. Then suddenly, at turn of highway high up, a great brown plain stretched way below, Eastward and Northward for a hundred miles, North America. . . .

Arrived at Mexicali, another dusty town, only worse, in midst of flat brown plain I saw from above, at nightfall—bus station crammed with campesinos looking grim, tough and hungry, under enormous hats and ponchos, waiting for country buses and revolutions. These are the Front Teeth of Latin America. . . . I walk out into mud boulevard & vision of utter

Desolation, Dung & Death in the image of crowded streets and dark people. Everywhere I walk & look, the same! Enough to drive any voyeur back home. . . . Later found the tourist part of town, and the American border: big sign over it saying UNITED STATES. Showed my California Driver's license and went thru to the American Zone, saw an American movie with Bingo advertised with double feature. Went in. Bingo just starting, American on stage with mike announcing numbers drawn out of whirling basket, says numbers in American and in atrocious Spanish. . . . Came out at midnight, walked back through border station, no one on Mexican side to check—completely open in *that* direction. Sign said in English: "Narcotics addicts & Users Are Required by U.S. Law to Register Before Leaving Country." Also, "Warning: Cats & Dogs Leaving U.S. May Not Be Allowed to Re-enter." Do not pee on the wrong side of the fence. Show your dog tags. Borders must be maintained! An insane fluidity & deracination surely would prevail without them—no countries, no nations, nothing at all to stop us anywhere, nothing to stop the hordes of the world still starving and howling like Calibans at the gates, no customs, no wars, no protective tariffs, no passports, no immigration and naturalization papers, none of the old protective barriers protecting everyone from everyone else, even the oceans dried up eventually, leaving us no alternative but to recognize Indians as brothers, the whole earth only one continent, under it all, after all, all colors of skin at length into one skin with one tongue. It'll only take 5000 more years to do this, Indian, even after wasting 2000 mostly in the wrong direction. A very simple little revolution could accomplish it in no time: declare an immediate moratorium on all liaisons, partnerships and marriages between all people of the same color, everyone immediately to seek union with someone of a different color, all national flags made into snotrags or bandages to be used in maternity hospitals giving birth to nothing but a new generation of babies of nothing but mixed colors and races. . . .

The Shop Keepers (or Long Live Tourism!)

Oscar Monroy Rivera

TRANSLATED BY Alicia Garza

CHARACTERS

> Liberio Chásquez: 30 years old; proprietor of a small shop
> John: Tourist, older Anglo man
> Chris: Tourist, older Anglo woman

SETTING

Any town on the northern border of Mexico toward the end of the twentieth century. We see a main street tourist shop:

Yonny the King

Stacked on its shelves are sombreros, sarapes, belts, and trinkets made from bronze, tin, and onyx.

Act I

Scene 1

Liberio Chásquez drops an Alka Seltzer in a glass of water. He looks at the fizz.
LIBERIO: I am about to die from this hangover. I started to drink again because I felt as dry as the desert. I feel as if I'm spinning, my legs are wobbly. Work is about to start. I have to be strong. No one better notice this deathly hangover that I've got.

Scene 2

Two silhouettes appear from the side of the stage; John and Chris, an older couple dressed in summer clothes. John wears a pith helmet and Chris has her purse protectively tucked under her arm. Both have cameras around their necks. Liberio watches them at a distance.

Scene 3

LIBERIO: [yelling] Camon meester. Camon meester tekah luke.

(The couple ignores Liberio's broken English and laugh sweetly at him.)

LIBERIO: Camon beyootifool leddy. [in a low voice] Ay! Mamacita, you look so good, even at your age! [loudly] Plees see ebrebody, I have meny sorprais por you. [low, again] Oooh! Delicious blondie, come here to daddy so that I can show you a special surprise I've saved just for you.

(The tourists approach the store, glancing at the items for sale. John tries on a sombrero, while Chris looks at a pair of sandals. Liberio begins to caress Chris' arms. The two tourists look at each other and Chris realizes that Liberio has his hand on her ass. She smiles, feigning a surprised look.)

LIBERIO: [low voice] What a great cushion for a-pushin'. A few moments on this sweet pillow and I could forget all about my hangover.

JOHN: Mexican music—

LIBERIO: Yeah, meeusic mex-i-ca-na . . . meeusic charra . . . ass-kicking meeusic.

(Liberio begins to stamp his feet and dance to the music. John and Chris look at each other perplexed. Meanwhile, Liberio dances wildly as the mariachi music increases in volume. Suddenly there is silence.)

Act II

Scene 1

The stage is lit by a very dim light. The silhouettes of some of the merchandise are visible. Liberio Chásquez sits between two Mexican statues, resembling them in every way except they wear sombreros and he doesn't. He switches positions to a squat.

LIBERIO: Pinches gringos. I can't stand them. That's why I screw them by selling them things five times their worth. Or ten times if I can get away with it. That's why whenever they forget something in my store I keep it. That's why I enjoy putting my hand on those big gringa asses. Young or old, it doesn't matter what they looks like. When I see them and they are close by, I feel like saying: Camon mamacita . . . teka luke . . . take off your clothes! Go ahead! Now! I'm a little Mexican who is always ready to get laid. I'm like one of those shotguns that the Italians made famous: I shoot and immediately, I'm ready to shoot again. And when a mother and daughter come in I'll feel the both of them up. What do I have two hands for? What hands! Strong. Firm. Kick ass hands. That's why I have a cot in the back of my little shop. If something happens to drop by, I can attend to it immediately.

Scene 2

"El Son de La Negra" blasts from Liberio's boom box. He appears in silhouette and turns down the volume.

LIBERIO: What do I sell? Trash. Some pinches dishes. Some old sticks. Some polished rocks. Copper. Trinkets and nothing else. My prices are high because I don't believe in this shit. (Pauses.) That's why I have this little business, because I don't know how to do anything else. I don't have an education. In reality, in the reality of all realities: I don't know English or Spanish. I don't know who we are, us Mexicans. I don't know who the North Americans are. They come here, day after day, alone, to leave me their dollars. I don't like them. I don't know who they are, nor do I want to know. It doesn't matter to me, I only want their money. My god is the dollar. It guides me. With dollars I can screw the Mexicans that can't earn it or possess it.

Scene 3

LIBERIO: I wouldn't want to be me. Being here all day like a stupid shit. I spend the summer joking, making money, playing with a cup and ball toy, like a big dumbass. Like a retard. In the winter, as if I were a six year-old boy, I throw snowballs at the employees who work in the shop across from mine; I do this in front of the whole world, friends and acquaintances. I play the idiot. I do it alone or on a team. Thanks to easy money. I am becoming an alcoholic without much effort, like half of the other shop-keepers on the street.

What's my goal? Why am I taking these chances? How far am I going to get this way? It cost me so much work to go from a petty ripoff artist to a shop owner. From grammar school, to the store, to bullshitting. Here is where you bullshit people. The twenty words of English that I know make me feel as if my head is spinning. It's too much of an effort to speak English. That's why I don't like this job. I don't get along with the gringos, but I do like their money. . . .

Scene 5

Liberio Chásquez is dressed like the Mexican comedian Cantinflas. He cleans his store's merchandise with a feather duster while singing a popular song by the singer Tin Tan.

LIBERIO: Ta ta tira taraira tau

Ta ta tira tararira tauuu

Ta ta tira taraira tauuuuuuuu

(To the audience.) Camon meester. Camon, sir, nerd, turd, shithead. . . . Plees. Mees . . . lemme look at your teetees. Camon leddy. Wa ta tira tararira. Come in, pinches gringos, it's time for you to turn loose of that cash. Cabrones. Oh mamacita! Movie star! You are so beautiful. Damn, I started the day completely dominating Sha-ques-pier's language. I've noticed that when I drink Siete Machos mezcal, I'm less of a dumb ass, my capacity for speaking this language doubles. (He waves to a passerby.)

Goodbye, buddy, fuddy-duddy, cruddy, craphead. I got something for your mother, too! (He laughs, continues with the feather duster, and dances a few steps.)

Scene 6

LIBERIO: Ta ta tira tararila pau. Yes I have always been pretty chingón at dancing. Not too good at working, but when I am at the dance hall. . . . Yes I am very fucking good, like they say in Washington.

In this town they don't realize what they've got, but sooner or later they'll find out what a bad ass I am. They'll know. I em shure. It can't be hidden any longer.

(Yells.) Camon meesters. Leddies and yentelmens. Come one, evree-bodee. Teka luke. See tha merchandais. Don't act like mice. Yes, see, don't be such assholes. Here I am for the taking. I am the king, just twiddling my thumbs. [The song "Guadalajara" suddenly plays.] It sounds so damned good! Guadalajara! It's my city. The land of machos like myself. Of badasses like myself. Of mean motherfuckers like myself.

(The music stops abruptly; Liberio sets the feather duster down and looks sadly at the audience as he lights a cigarette.)

LIBERIO: I got sued again. I have forty lawsuits against me for unpaid bills, bad checks, late payments, fraud. . . . Now they want to fuck over the fucker. Now they want to screw me. I have to ask my family to help me, if I don't, I'll sink. Now I'm really in trouble.

Scene 7

Liberio Chásquez sprinkles holy water on the street to attract shoppers. He joins his hands in prayer.

LIBERIO: For the horns of the exported cows, bless my business, Father. For the trailers of produce, tomatoes, melons and watermelons, that are going across the border, protect us Father. For the cocaine and the marijuana that exists amongst us, save us Father. May they buy all of these pinches dishes, Father. Amen.

(Yells.) Now, ¡a chingar los gringos!

Camon meester! Tek a luke. Camon leddy. I haven somping por you. Mama! Gorgeous! Movie Star! Look at that long-legged gringa coming this way!

(John and Chris reappear and examine the merchandise. Some items distract John, and Liberio quickly moves close to Chris and begins to whisper in her ear. Curious, Chris follows Liberio to the back of the shop. John walks all over the stage looking for his wife.)

JOHN: Chris? Chris . . . Chris, where are you?

(Eventually Liberio Chásquez emerges from the back of the store with a nasty smile. Chris also appears, her hair is messed up and she is buttoning her shorts. She looks at her husband, then at Liberio.)

CHRIS: My goodness!

JOHN: Are you ready to go?

CHRIS: Yes. Now. Please.

(The couple leaves YONNY THE KING; Chris looks fearful and glances over her shoulder at Liberio. He waves and blows her a kiss.)

CHRIS: The border is terrible. It—it—it's a mystery. And surprising.

LIBERIO: (standing in front of a mirror running a comb through his hair, yelling) Camon meester. Tek a luke. Camon leddy, see the merchendaise. Pinches gringas, even the little old ladies have tough hides. The one today, though, she was tasty.

Denuncia!

Gilberto Maldonado Herrera

Meanwhile, the Ku Klux Klan was holding an urgent meeting.

Order, Brothers, Order!

I've called you here on a very urgent matter.
What's happened?
What's it about?
We are being threatened by an intolerable invasion.

The "wetbacks" cross the border by the thousands and come to take our jobs.
and to rob us
and to rape our white women.

We have to stop this situation ourselves since the government doesn't care.
What should we do?
How do we stop it?

We need to arm ourselves, bring attack dogs . . .
Patrol the border day and night, kill them if necessary
Yes, yes!
Kill them!
Damn right!

The following day, the Ku Klux Klan held another meeting.
You patrol the west with these pickups.
You young'ens, take dogs.

Terror was unleashed on the border that day.
Day and night they carried out their human hunt.

But the actions of the Ku Klux Klan provoked complaints from the Mexican Government.
This has got to stop.
Sí, Señor!

El Mordido

Gilbert Shelton and Dave Sheridan

Part 8

The glue that binds the two sides is made of symbiosis, not bitterness, vitality, not repulsion, though you might be hard-pressed to persuade these writers of that.

Corridista Vicente Macías

John Ross

We rode the Texas night,
Vicente Macías and me,
inside a Trailways Bus
with greyhounds on its sides.
91 long years here,
he doesn't distinguish
the darkness now,
the clouded corneas
let in little light,
these days as long
as the years are young
he said but couldn't hear
his own words sing.
Once he played on the avenidas
of Piedras Negras and Eagle Pass
with the great ciego
Blind Melquíedes,
now he himself is going blind,
deaf, food don't taste
too good to him no more,
his hand shakes
when he holds the big guitar
or tries to fly on the fiddle.
He showed me long elegant fingers,
the nails neatly manicured
the way the great players keep 'em,
they jigged with palsy
like brown weeds in a remolino.
I've written one hundred corridos,
a hundred of them, un centenario
he announced to no one
but me and the night,
that's enough, don't you think,
bastante, no señor?
I've sung about bandits and gunfights,

lovers who shot their ladies
for looking at the wrong guy
in the right cantina,
the way the Luna lights the river
so the contrabandistas can come across,
how green the green maíz grows.
Now my own voice is lost to me
and the darkness don't sing to me no songs,
these are the words
of an old corridista,
his last will and testimony.
as we careened through the Texas night
on the road to Piedras Negras.

Un mojado sin licencia / A Wetback without a License

FLACO JIMÉNEZ

All the way from Laredo to San Antonio
I've come to marry Chencha.
But I haven't been able to do it because I'm a wetback
And I keep being asked for my license.

I thought I'd buy a car
To take my love for a ride
And that night I wound up in the can
'Cause I didn't have any lights or a license.

Finally I got out of the clink
Looking forward to seeing my Chencha
I found her with a Gringo,
The head boss who gives out licenses.

I am also looking for a job.
I am an experienced carpenter and musician,
But what good is my job for
If they keep asking for my license?

I'm going back to Laredo
I've suffered enough shame.
These Gringos sure are sneaky
I lost my car and my Chencha.

"Un mojado sin licencia"
Desde Laredo a San Antonio
yo he venido a casarme con mi Chencha
y no he podido, por ser mojado.
Pues para todo me exigen la licencia.

Se me hizo facil comprar un carro
para sacar a pasear a mi cresencia
y por la noche fui a dar al bote
porque no traiba ni luces ni licencia.

Al fin de todo sali del bote
con muchas ganas de ver a mi Chencha.
La halle paseando con un gabacho,
el mero jefe que arregla las licencia

Ando buscando tambien trabajo
soy carpintero y mariachi de experiencia,
¿de que me sirve mi buen oficio
si para todo me exigen mi licencia?

Ya me regreso para Laredo
Aquí he sufrido
ya basta de verguenzá.
Estos, gabachos son abusados,
perdí mi carro y me quitarón a Chencha.

El Deportado

Los Hermanos Bañuelos

I'm going to sing to you, gentlemen,
I'm going to sing to you, gentlemen,
all about my sufferings,
Since I left my country,
Since I left my country
to come to this nation.

It must have been about ten at night,
It must have been about ten at night,
the train began to whistle.
I heard my mother say,
"Here comes that ungrateful train
that is going to take my son."

Goodbye my beloved mother,
goodbye my beloved mother,
give me your blessings.
I am going abroad,
I am going abroad,
where there is no revolution."

Run, run little train,
run, run little train,
let's leave the station.
I don't want to see my mother
cry for her beloved son,
for the son of her heart.

Finally the bell rang,
finally the bell rang,
the train whistled twice.
"Don't cry, my buddies,
Don't cry my buddies,
for you'll make me cry as well."

Right away we passed Jalisco,
right away we passed Jalisco,
my, how fast the train ran.
La Piedad, then Irapuato,
Silado, then La Chona,
and Agua Calientes as well.

When I remember these hours,
when I remember these hours,
my heart beats.
When I saw from afar,
when I saw from afar
that infamous city of Torreón.

When we passed Chihuahua,
when we passed Chihuahua,
we noticed great confusion,
The employees from the customhouse,
the empoloyees from the customhouse,
who were checking things out.

We arrived at Juárez at last,
we arrived at Juárez at last,
there I ran into trouble.
"Where are you going, where do
you come from?
How much money do you have
to enter this nation?"

"Gentlemen, I have money,
gentlemen, I have money
so that I can emigrate."
"Your money isn't worth anything,
your money isn't worth anything,
we have to bathe you."

Oh, my beloved countrymen,
oh, my beloved countrymen,

this is idle conversation.
They were making me feel,
they were making me feel,
like going right back.

At last I crossed the border,
at last I crossed the border,
and left in a group.
Oh my beloved countrymen,
oh my beloved countrymen
I suffered a lot.

The white skinned men are very wicked,
the white skinned men are very wicked,
they take advantage of the occasion.
And all the Mexicans,
and all the Mexicans,
are treated without compassion.

There comes a large cloud of dust,
there comes a large cloud of dust,
with no consideration.
Women, children and old ones
are being driven to the border.
We are being kicked out of this country.

Goodbye beloved countrymen,
goodbye beloved countrymen,
we are being deported.
But we are not bandits,
but we are not bandits,
we came to work.

I will wait for you in my homeland,
I will wait for you in my homeland,
there is no more revolution.
Let's leave my dear friends,
we will be welcomed
by our beautiful nation.

Voy a cantarles señores,
voy a cantarles señores
todo lo que yo sufrí,
Desde que dejé mi patria,
desde que dejé mi patria
por venir a este país.

Serían las diez de la noche,
serían las diez de la noche,
comenzó un tren a silbar.
Oí que dijo mi madre,
"Ahí viene ese tren ingrato
que a mi hijo se va a llevar."

"Adiós mi madre querida,
adiós mi madre querida,
héchame su benedición.
Yo me voy al extranjero,
Yo me voy al extranjero
donde no hay revolución.

Corre, corre maquinita,
corre, corre maquinita,
vámonos de la estación.
No quiero ver a mi madre
llorar por su hijo querido,
por su hijo del corazón.

Al fín sonó la campana,
al fín sonó la campana
dos silbidos pegó el tren.
"No lloren mis compañeros,
no lloren mis compañeros,
que me hacen llorar también."

Pasamos pronto Jalisco,
pasamos pronto Jalisco,
ay qué fuerte corría el tren.

La Piedad, luego Irapuato,
Silado luego La Chona,
y Aguas Calientes también.

Al recordar estas horas,
al recordar estas horas,
me palpita el corazón.
Cuando devise a lo lejos,
cuando devise a lo lejos
a ese mentado Torreón.

Cuando Chihuahua pasamos,
cuando Chihuahua pasamos
se notó gran confusión,
Los empleados de la aduana,
los empleados de la aduana
que pasaban revisión.

Llegamos por fin a Juárez,
llegamos por fin a Juárez,
y allí fué mi apuración.
"¿Que 'onde vas que de 'onde vienes?
¿Que cuanto dinero tienes
para entrar a esta nación?"

"Señores traigo dinero,
señores traigo dinero
para poder emigrar."
"Tu dinero nada vale,
tu dinero nada vale,
te tenemos que bañar."

Ay, mis paisanos queridos,
ay, mis paisanos queridos,
yo les platico no más.
Que me estaban dando ganas,
que me estaban dando ganas,
de volverme para atrás.

Crucé por fin la frontera,
crucé por fin la frontera,
y en un renganche salí.
Ay, mis queridos paisanos,
ay, mis queridos paisanos,
fué mucho lo que sufrí.

Los güeros son muy maloras,
Los güeros son muy maloras,
se valen de la occasión.
Y a todos los mexicanos,
y a todos los mexicanos,
los tratan sin compasión.

Ahí traen la gran polvadera,
ahí traen la gran polvadera,
y sin consideración.
Mujeres, niños y ancianos
los llevan a la frontera.
Nos hechan de esta nación.

Adiós paisanos queridos,
adiós paisanos queridos,
ya nos van a deportar.
Pero no somos bandidos,
pero no somos bandidos,
venimos a camellar.

Los espero allá en mi tierra,
los espero allá en mi tierra,
ya no hay más revolución.
Vámonos cuates queridos,
seremos bien recibidos
de nuestra bella nación.

The plight of Mexican workers in the United States has stimulated our best songwriters to lament the campesinos' fate. The following works span a quarter century; little has changed but the key of their songs.

Deportee

PLANE WRECK AT LOS GATOS

Woody Guthrie

The crops are all in and the peaches are rotting.
The oranges piled in their creosote dumps.
You're flying 'em back to the Mexican border,
To pay all their money to wade back again.

Good-bye to my Juan, good-bye, Rosalita,
Adios mis amigos, Jesús y María;
You won't have your names when you ride the big airplane,
All they will call you will be deportees.

My father's own father, he waded that river,
They took all the money he made in his life;
My brothers and sisters come working the fruit trees,
And they rode the truck till they took down and died.

Some of us are illegal, and some are not wanted,
Our work contract's out and we have to move on;
Six hundred miles to that Mexican border,
They chase us like outlaws, like rustlers, like thieves.

We died in your hills, we died in your deserts,
We died in your valleys and died on your plains,
We died 'neath your trees and we died in your bushes,
Both sides of the river, we died just the same.

Good-by to my Juan, good-bye, Rosalita,
Adios mis amigos, Jesús y María;
You won't have your names when you ride the big airplane,
All they will call you will be deportees.

The sky plane caught fire over Los Gatos Canyon,
A fireball of lightning, and shook all our hills,
Who are all these friends, all scattered like dry leaves?
The radio says they are just deportees.

Is this the best way we can grow our big orchards?
Is this the best way we can grow our good fruit?
To fall like dry leaves to rot on my topsoil,
And be called by no name except deportees?

Good-bye to my Juan, good-bye, Rosalita,
Adios mis amigos, Jesús y María;
You won't have your names when you ride the big airplane,
All they will call you will be deportees.

Bracero

Phil Ochs

Wade into the river through the rippling shadow waters,
Steal across the thirsty border, Bracero,
Come, bring your hungry body to the golden fields of plenty,
From a peso to a penny, Braccro.
Oh, Welcome to California, where the friendly farmers will take care of
    you.

Come labor for your mother, for your father and your brother,
For your sisters and your lover, Bracero.
Come pick the fruits of yellow, break the flowers from the berries.
Purple grapes will fill your bellies, Bracero.

And the sun will bite your body as the dust will dry you thirsty
While your muscles beg for mercy, Bracero.
In the shade of your sombrero, drop your sweat upon the soil,
Like fruit, your youth can spoil, Bracero.

When the weary night embraces, sleep in shacks that could be cages.
They will take it from your wages, Bracero.
Come sing about tomorrow with the jingle of the dollars,
And forget your crooked collars, Bracero.

And the local men are lazy, and they make too much of trouble.
'Sides we'd have to pay them double, Bracero.
Ah, but if you feel you're falling, if you find the pace is killing,
There are others who are willing, Bracero.
Oh, welcome to California, where the friendly farmers will take care of
    you.

Across the Borderline

Ry Cooder, John Hiatt, and James Dickinson

There's a place so I've been told
Every street is paved with gold,
And it's just across the borderline.
And when it's time to take your turn
There's a lesson that you must learn,
You may lose more than you ever hoped to find.

When you reach the broken promised land,
And all your dreams slip through your hand.
And you have learned it's too late to change your mind.

'Cause you've paid the price to come this far
Just to wind up where you are,
And you're still just across the borderline.

Up and down the Rio Grande,
A thousand footprints in the sand.
Reveal a secret no one can define.
The river flows on like a breath,
In between our life and death.
Tell me, who's the next to cross the borderline?

En la triste oscuridad
Hoy tenemos que cruzar
Este río que nos llama mas allá
But hope remains when pride is gone
and it keeps you moving on
Calling you across the borderline.

And when you reach the broken promised land.
Every dream slips through your hand.

And you'll know, it's too late to change your mind.
'Cause you've paid the price to come so far
Just to wind up where you are.
And you're still just across that borderline.

El Paso

Marty Robbins

Out in the West Texas town of El Paso
I fell in love with a Mexican girl.
Nighttime would find me in Rosa's Cantina,
Music would play and Felina would whirl.

Blacker than night were the eyes of Felina,
Wicked and evil while casting a spell.
My love was strong for this Mexican maiden,
I was in love, but in vain I could tell.

One night a wild young cowboy came in,
Wild as the West Texas wind . . .
Dashing and daring, a drink he was sharing,
With wicked Felina, the girl that I love.

So in anger I challenged his right for the love of this maiden;
Down went his hand for the gun that he wore.
My challenge was answered, in less than a heartbeat
The handsome young stranger lay dead on the floor.

Just for a moment I stood there in silence,
Schocked by the foul evel deed I had done.
Many thoughts ran through my mind as I stood there;
I had but one chance and that was to run.

Out through the back door of Rosa's I ran,
Out where the horses were tied . . .
I caught a good one; it looked like it could run,
Up on its back and away I did ride.

Just as fast as I could from the West Texas town of El Paso,
Out through the badlands of New Mexico.
Back in El Paso my life would be worthless;
Everything's gone in life; nothing is left.

But it's been so long since I've seen the young maiden,
My love is stronger than my fear of death.

I saddled up and away I did go,
Riding alone in the dark . . .
Maybe tomorrow a bullet may find me,
Tonight nothing's worse than this pain in my heart.

And at last here I am on the hill overlooking El Paso,
I can see Rosa's Cantina below.
My love is strong and it pushes me onward,
Down off the hill to Felina I go.

Off to my right I see five mounted cowboys,
Off to my left ride a dozen or more.
Shouting and shooting; I can't let then catch me.
I've got to make it to Rosa's back door.

Something is dreadfully wrong for I feel
A deep burning pain in my side . . .
It's getting harder to stay in the saddle.
I'm getting weary, unable to ride.

But my love for Felina is strong and I rise where I've fallen;
Though I am weary, I can't stop to rest.
I see a white puff of smoke from the rifle,
I feel the bullet go deep in my chest.

From out of nowhere, Felina has found me,
Kissing my cheek as she kneels by my side.
Cradled by two loving arms that I'll die for,
One little kiss and Felina good-bye.

What Money?

There was a fellow who knocked over a bank in Tucson and fled for the border with the FBI in hot pursuit. When he got to the border he wasn't real interested in formalities and he got through real fast and kept on moving. The FBI had to stop and *sacar* their *papeles* to get permission to pursue a fleeing malefactor across international boundaries. By the time they got across the border, the robber had disappeared. But the FBI always gets its man, and they got him this time, too. He was way up in the sierra in a little town called Bacadéhuachi. A beautiful little place.

When they caught him, he didn't have the money with him, and they didn't speak any Spanish, and he didn't speak any English. So they hired an interpreter. The FBI man said to the interpreter, "tell him to tell us where he hid the money."

The interpreter turned to the prisoner and said, "Dice el señor, ¿donde está el dinero?"

And the prisoner replied, "¿Dinero? ¿Dinero? Pues, claro que había dinero, y debe que estar por alguna parte, pero no me acuerdo precisamente que donde está.

The interpreter turned back to the head FBI man, and he said, "He's forgotten where he hid the money."

Entonces, the head FBI man *saquó la pistolota,* and he cocked it and he laid it up against the prisoner's head and he said, "Tell him that if he doesn't remember where he hid the money in two minutes, I'm going to blow his brains out."

The interpreter turned to the prisoner and said, "Dice el señor, que si no te acuerdas que donde está el dinero entre de dos minutos, te va a dar un balazo por la cabeza."

And the prisoner said, "Pues, en este caso, está el dinero atrás de la casita de mi hermana. Es una casita blanca en esta mera calle, al lado izquierda de la calle, tres cuadras distancia de aquí. Atrás de la casa, hay un arbol muy grande. Dos pasos al norte del arbol, hay una piedra blanca, y allí está enterado el dinero."

Whereupon the interpreter turned to the FBI man, removed his hat, and said, "He says he's willing to die like a man."

Lajitas and the NFL

Sam Shepard

This time of year, the Mexicans know a low spot on the Rio Grande where they can cross their skinny ponies and ride up to the trading post in Lajitas, on the U.S. side of the border. Nobody bothers them. Nobody asks to see papers or questions their motives. They're regular visitors. This same low spot is the reason General John J. Pershing established his little fort here in 1916, in his vain attempt to bring Pancho Villa to his knees. He never got close enough to even see the dust of Villa's army. The infamous Comanche trail also encountered this shoal in the river, where for more than a hundred years the Comanche raided like clockwork under the full moon and vanished with their booty into the vast plains of Chihuahua. Today these Mexican villagers have simply come to hear some cantina music on an old Wurlitzer jukebox, drink Bud Light, then return to San Carlos, seventeen miles into Old Mexico. As they arrive at the trading post, their eyes squint toward the patio, draped for some reason in black plastic sheets. Gringos in funny hats are crowded around a TV set in the center of a dusty old pool table. These gringos cheer in unison, then fall deathly silent, then cheer again. Their eyes are nailed to the tiny screen, watching the NFC playoff game between Dallas and San Francisco. They are totally oblivious to the ragged little band of men on mud-splattered ponies trotting up behind them. The Mexicans drop the reins of their bony horses into mesquite bushes and dismount. They don't even tie them. The horses know the routine. The men go directly into the grocery store and buy a case of beer, then shyly come back out to the plastic shade of the patio. They quietly seat themselves on a wood bench like a row of crows on a wire, their straight backs flat against the cool adobe wall of the store. Their eyes are careful not to meet the gaze of the gringos in funny hats. They care nothing about American football. They're only here for la música and Bud Light.

The black visqueen sheets ripple gently in the desert wind. Goats bleat from a pen devised from hubcaps and barbed wire at the back of the store. You can see their spotted legs through the gaps of the billowing plastic. The Mexicans pop their beers, and their dark eyes shift toward the TV image of Troy Aikman in close-up. His very white Viking face barking out the play pattern. He drops into a boot-leg left to Emmitt Smith, who darts through the 49er defense and is about to break into open field, when his chronic hamstring seizes him and he drops like he's been shot. The gringos in funny hats bolt to their feet in unison, an enraged, many-headed beast, curing and moaning in chorus as though Emmitt's sudden relapse was somehow deeply personal and beyond football; beyond a mere game. The moaning echoes out over the Rio Grande like the loss of manhood itself. The Mexicans are silent; absolutely still. Very slowly they sip their beer and smile at the gray caliche floor, almost embarrassed to be in the presence of such bewildering madness. The gringos are now angrily crushing their beer cans and throwing money on the picnic tables; punching garbage cans; stomping their funny hats in the dirt. The Mexicans say nothing. Not even in Spanish. They just stare at the floor. Their horses shift weight and twitch their ears toward the roar of the rankled Texans. A crow hops and struts through the dusty parking lot, then stops and pecks at a half-eaten hot dog.

The replay of Smith's injury in slow motion shows his massive piston legs stretched to their limit, then a freeze-frame reveals the exact moment of pain. His face contorts into a mask of agony, then the film continues into his sudden crash to the earth. Again, the Dallas gringos moan and groan, reliving their bad luck, cursing their mothers and sons. The Mexicans grow even more stoic and almost invisible, dissolving into the cool adobe wall until just their black Indian eyes float above the wooden bench. The TV goes into a spasm of static and horrible hissing, desperately trying to link up the immense distance between rainy San Francisco and this remote edge of the world. Territories that have nothing in common. Territories joined, only for a moment, by this game about territory. A national obsession. More than a river divides the dark men on the bench from the gringos in funny hats.

The sun begins to drop behind the jagged buttes of Chihuahua. The temperature takes a dip. Geese fly downriver, silhouetted black against the pink fading sky. The fourth quarter looks bleak for Dallas. Aikman's eyes now have the dull recognition of imminent defeat. His helmet is dripping with Candlestick mud, and swaths of slimy green turf are branded across his backside. It's too little too late for the Cowboys. Already, the humbled group of Dallas fans have begun to abandon their funny hats and shuffle off toward pickup trucks, casting last minute aspersions back toward the TV set. The Mexicans watch them leave. They don't get up from their bench until the last Texan has ground his angry tires in the gravel and disappeared over the sharp rise. They listen to the fading engines, waiting for the air to clear, then, suddenly, the whole line of men is on its feet and dancing. Spanish fills the space. They snap off the TV set, and the hyper, pumped-up enthusiasm of John Madden's voice is replaced by the ancient jukebox. Now all the Mexicans are laughing as the sun sinks deeper, forging broad crimson bands behind the black buttes of their homeland. A dog barks from the Mexican side of the Great River. A confused rooster crows. A pig squeals, and the laughter and music is gobbled up into a silence so complete a man can suddenly hear his own heart.

Credits

Acosta, Oscar Zeta. From *The Autobiography of a Brown Buffalo*. San Francisco: Straight Arrow Books, 1972. Reprinted with the permission of Marco Acosta.

Aguilar-Melantzón, Ricardo. "Cloister." *Puerto del Sol* 29 (Spring 1994):74–84. Reprinted with permission of the author.

Anda Jacobsen, Miguel de. "To Tijuana." From *Trípticos de la Baja California*. Mexico City: SEP, Programa Cultural de las Fronteras, 1988.

Angelou, Maya. From *I Know Why the Caged Bird Sings*, copyright © 1969 and renewed 1997 by Maya Angelou. Used by permission of Random House, Inc.

Anzaldúa, Gloria. From *Borderlands La Frontera: The New Mestiza*, copyright © 1987, 1999. Reprinted by permission of Aunt Lute Books.

Azuela, Mariano. From *The Underdogs: A Novel of the Mexican Revolution*. Trans. E. Munguía, Jr. New York: New American Library, Inc., 1962

Bowden, Charles. From *Blue Desert*, copyright © 1986 The Arizona Board of Regents. Reprinted by permission of the University of Arizona Press.

Brito, Aristeo. From *The Devil in Texas/El diablo en Texas*. Trans. David William Foster. Copyright © 1990 by Bilingual Press/Editorial Bilingüe. Tempe, Ariz.: Bilingual Press/Editorial Bilingüe, Arizona State University, 1990.

Burciaga, José Antonio. From *Undocumented Love/Amor Indocumentado*. San Jose, Calif.: Chusma House Publications, 1992.

Cantú, Norma Elia. From *Canícula: Snapshots of a Girlhood en la Frontera*. Albuquerque: University of New Mexico Press, 1995.

Cervantes, Lorna Dee. "Poem for the Young White Man Who Asked Me How I, an Intelligent Well-Read Person Could Believe in the War between Races" from *Emplumada*, by Lorna Dee Cervantes, © 1981. Reprinted by permission of the University of Pittsburgh Press.

Cisneros, Sandra. From *Woman Hollering Creek*. Copyright © 1991 by Sandra Cisneros. Published by Vintage Books, a division of Random House, Inc., New York and originally in hardcover by Random House, Inc. Reprinted by permission of Susan Bergholz Literary Services, New York. All rights reserved.

Cooder, Ry, John Hiatt, and James Dickinson. "Across the Borderline." Words and music by Ry Cooder, John Hiatt, and James Dickinson. © Copyright Universal-MCA Music Publishing, a division of Universal Studios, Inc., Sooland Inc., and Universal-Duchess Music Corp. (ASCAP/BMI). International copyright secured. All rights reserved.

Crane, Stephen. "Stephen Crane in Mexico (II)." From *The Work of Stephen Crane*. Charlottesville: University Press of Virginia, 1969. Reprinted with the permission of the University Press of Virginia.

Crawford, Cora Hayward. From *The Land of the Montezumas*. New York: John B. Alden, 1889.

Domecq, Brianda. "Two Faces, One Reality." *Voces y rostros del Bravo* Copyright © 1987 by Brianda Domecq. Mexico City: Casa de Bolsa Inverlat, 1987.

Ferlinghetti, Lawrence. From *The Mexican Night,* copyright © 1970 by Lawrence Ferlinghetti. Reprinted by permission of New Directions Publishing Corp.

Fuentes, Carlos. Excerpt from Chapter 3 from *The Old Gringo,* translated by Margaret Sayers Peden and Carlos Fuentes. Translation copyright © 1985 by Farrar, Straus & Giroux, Inc. Reprinted by permission of Farrar, Straus and Giroux, LLC.

Galeano, Eduardo. From *Memory of Fire,* vol. 2: *Faces & Masks,* and vol. 3: *Century of the Wind* by Eduardo Galeano, translated by Cedric Belfrage, translation copyright © 1988 by Cedric Belfrage. Used by permission of Pantheon Books, a division of Random House, Inc.

Gaspar de Alba, Alicia. "La Frontera." From *Three Times a Woman: Chicana Poetry,* by Alicia Gaspar de Alba, María Herrera-Sobek, and Demetria Martínez. Copyright © 1989. Tempe, Ariz.: Bilingual Press/Editorial Bilingüe, Arizona State University, 1989.

Ginsberg, Allen. "Mexicali, June 1954." From *Journals: Early Fifties Early Sixties* by Allen Ginsberg, edited by Gordon Ball. Copyright © 1977 by Allen Ginsberg. New York: Grove Press, 1977. Used by permission of Grove/Atlantic, Inc.

Gómez-Peña, Guillermo. "On U.S./Mexico Relations: From the Battle of El Alamo to the signing of NAFTA." From *The New World Border* by Guillermo Gómez-Peña. Copyright © 1996 by Guillermo Gómez-Peña. San Francisco: City Lights, 1996. Reprinted by permission of City Lights Books.

González, Genaro. Passage from *Rainbow's End* by Genaro González is reprinted with permission from the publisher (Houston: Arte Público Press—University of Houston, 1988).

Gonzalez, Ray. "Mi Tierra." From *Memory Fever: A Journey Beyond El Paso del Norte* by Ray Gonzalez. Copyright © 1993 by Ray Gonzalez. Seattle: Broken Moon Press, 1993.

Greene, Graham. From *Another Mexico (Lawless Roads)* by Graham Greene, copyright 1939, renewed © 1967 by Graham Greene. British title *Lawless Roads.* Used by permission of Viking Penguin, a division of Penguin Putnam Inc.

Guthrie, Woody. "Deportee: Plane Wreck at Los Gatos." Words by Woody Guthrie; music by Martin Hoffman. TRO © Copyright 1961 (renewed 1963) Ludlow Music, Inc., a division of The Richmond Organization (TRO). Reprinted with permission of TRO.

Guzmán, Martín Luis. From *The Eagle and the Serpent* by Martín Luis Guzmán, translated by Harriet de Onis, copyright © 1965 by Doubleday, a division of Random House, Inc. Copyright 1930 by Alfred A. Knopf, Inc., a division of Random House, Inc. Used by permission of Doubleday, a division of Random House, Inc.

Herrera-Sobek, María. "Surrender." From *Literatura Fronteriza.* San Diego: Maize Press, 1982. Used by permission of the author.

Hinojosa, Rolando. "When It Comes to Class: Viola Barragán." From *The Valley.* Copyright © 1983 by Bilingual Press/Editorial Bilingüe. Tempe, Ariz.: Bilingual Press/Editorial Bilingüe, Arizona State University, 1983.

Ibargüengoitia, Jorge. From *The Lightning of August* by Jorge Ibarguengoitia. Translated from Spanish by Irene del Corral. Published by Avon Books, copyright © 1979, 1986. Used by permission of the Wallace Literary Agency.

Islas, Arturo. From *The Rain God,* pp. 141–49, by Arturo Islas. Copyright © 1984 by Arturo Islas. Reprinted with permission of HarperCollins Publishers Inc.

Jacobs, Bárbara. "Rough Portrait," translated by David Unger. From *Doce Cuentos en Contra,* by Bárbara Jacobs. Copyright © 1982 Ediciones Era, S.A. de C.V. Mexico City: Ediciones Era, 1990.

Jiménez, Flaco. "Un mojado sin licencia/A Wetback without a License." © by Santiago Jimenez/Tradition Music Co. From Arhoolie CD 318 (Arhoolie.com). El Cerrito, Calif.: Arhoolie, 1975.

Jones, Robert L. "A Border Rose" copyright 1985 by Robert L. Jones. Reprinted from *Wild Onion* with the permission of Graywolf Press, Saint Paul, Minnesota.

Kerouac, Jack. From *Lonesome Traveler.* New York: Grove Press, 1960. Reprinted by permission of Sterling Lord Literistic, Inc. Copyright 1988 by Estate of Jan Kerouac.

Limón, Graciela. From *In Search of Bernabé.* Copyright © 1993 by Graciela Limón. Houston, Texas: Arte Público, 1993. Copyright © 1993 by Graciela Limón. Reprinted with permission of Arte Público Press.

López-Stafford, Gloria. From *A Place in El Paso: A Mexican-American Childhood.* Albuquerque: University of New Mexico Press, 1996.

Los Hermanos Bañuelos. "El Deportado," from Arhoolie booklet accompanying CD 7019/7020, *Corridos y Tragedias de la Frontera* (Arhoolie.com).

Los Pingüinos del Norte. "Jacinto Treviño." © arr. by Ruben Castillo; Juarez/Tradition Music Co., from Arhoolie CD 311 (Arhoolie.com).

Maldonado Herrera, Gilberto. "Denuncia!" Mexico City: 4 Editores, 1987.

Martínez, Demetria. "Crossing Over." From *Three Times a Woman,* by Alicia Gaspar de Alba, María Herrera-Sobek, and Demetria Martínez. Copyright © 1989 by Bilingual Press/Editorial Bilingüe Tempe, Arizona: Bilingual Press/Editorial Bilingüe, Arizona State University, 1989.

Martínez, Oscar J. "La Frontera." From *U.S.–Mexico Borderlands: Historical and Contemporary Perspectives.* Edited by Oscar J. Martínez. Wilmington, Del.: Scholarly Resources Inc., 1996.

Martínez, Rubén. From *The Other Side: Notes from the New L.A., Mexico City, and Beyond.* Copyright © 1992 by Verso. New York: Verso, 1992.

Mayakovsky, Vladimir. "Laredo, Texas," translated by Marian Schwartz. From *My Discovery of America* by Vladimir Mayakovsky. Moscow, 1926.

Méndez, Miguel. From *Pilgrims in Aztlán.* Copyright © 1992 by Bilingual Press/Editorial Bilingüe. Tempe, Ariz.: Bilingual Press/Editorial Bilingüe, Arizona State University. 1992.

Miller, Tom. "Sonoyta Interlude." From *On the Border: Portraits of America's Southwestern Frontier* by Tom Miller. Copyright © 1981 by Tom Miller. Tucson, Arizona: University of Arizona Press, 1985.

Monroy Rivera, Oscar. "The Shop Keepers (Long Live Tourism!)." From *Obras de Teatro: Teatro Fronterizo.* by Oscar Monroy Rivera. Copyright © 1988 by Oscar Monroy Rivera. Mexico City: Editorial Libros de México, 1988. Used by permission of the author.

Mora, Pat. "Legal Alien" is reprinted with permission from the publisher of *Chants* (Houston: Arte Público Press—University of Houston, 1984).

Moscona, Myriam. "Naturalization Papers," translated by Cynthia Steele. First publishied in *TriQuarterly* magazine. Reprinted with permission of Cynthia Steele.

Nabhan, Gary. "Raising Hell as Well as Wheat" from *The Desert Smells Like Rain* by Gary Nabhan. Copyright © 1982 by Gary Paul Nabhan. Reprinted by permission of North Point Press, a division of Farrar, Straus and Giroux, LLC.

Nelson, Eugene. From *Bracero.* Copyright © 1972 by Eugene Nelson. Culver City, Calif: Peace Press Publishing, 1975. Reprinted with permission of Tamar J. Solinger.

Ochoa, Victor. *Border Dictionary/Diccionario Fronterizo.* San Diego: Centro Cultural de la Raza, 1995.

Ochs, Phil. "Bracero." Copyright © 1966 Barricade Music Inc. (ASCAP), 1966. All rights administered by Almo Music Corp. (ASCAP)

Paredes, Américo. "The Mexicans Who Speak English." From *A Texas-Mexican Cancionero: Folksongs of the Lower Border* by Américo Paredes. Urbana: University of Illinois Press, 1976.

Poniatowksa, Elena. From *Guerrero Viejo.* Copyright © 1997 by Anchorage Press. Houston, Texas: Anchorage Press, 1997.

Quezada, Janet Arelis. "Speaking of My Tongue." From *Blue Mesa Review,* no. 9.

Rabasa, George. From *Floating Kingdom.* Copyright © 1997 by George Rabasa. Minneapolis: Coffee House Press, 1997.

Reed, John. "On the Border." From *Adventures of a Young Man: Short Stories from Life* by John Reed. Copyright © 1975 by City Lights Books. San Francisco: City Lights, 1975.

Ríos, Alberto Alvaro. "The Child." From *The Iguana Killer: Twelve Stories of the Heart* by Alberto Alvaro Ríos, copyright © 1984 by Alberto Alvaro Ríos. Lewiston, Idaho: Blue Moon and Confluence Press, 1984.

Robbins, Marty. "El Paso." © Copyright 1959. Renewed 1987. Mariposa Music, Inc./ BMI (admin. by ICG). All rights reserved. Used by permission.

Rodríguez, Luis J. From *Always Running—La Vida Loca, Gang Days in L.A.* by Luis J. Rodríguez. Curbstone Press, 1993. Reprinted with permission of Curbstone Press. Distributed by Consortium.

Rodriguez, Richard. "I Will Send for You or I Will Come Home Rich." Copyright © 1988 by Richard Rodriguez. Reprinted by permission of Georges Borchardt, Inc.

Ross, John. "Corridista Vicente Macías." From "Tres Corridistas" in *Whose Bones* by John Ross. Mexico City, 1990.

Sáenz, Benjamin Alire. "Journeys: El Paso/Juárez, 1984." From *Calendar of Dust.* Copyright © 1991 by Benjamin Alire Sáenz. Seattle: Broken Moon Press, 1991. Used by permission of the author.

Sánchez, Ricardo. "Nos Sentamos, Part 6: El Paso." From *Eagle-Visioned/Feathered Adobes* by Ricardo Sánchez. Copyright © 1990 by Ricardo Sánchez. El Paso, Texas: Cinco Puntos Press, 1990.

Sánchez, Trinidad V. "To My Fatherland." Used by permission of Trinidad Sánchez Jr.

Sheehan, Edward R. F. From *Innocent Darkness.* Copyright © 1993 by Edward R. F.

Sheehan. Used by permission of Viking Penguin, a division of Penguin Putnam Inc.

Shelton, Gilbert, and Dave Sheridan. "El Mordido." From *The Fabulous Furry Freak Brothers Library,* vol. 2. Copyright © 1988 by Rip Off Press Inc. Used by permission of InterLicense, Ltd.

Shepard, Sam. From *Cruising Paradise.* Copyright © 1996 by Sam Shepard. Used by permission of Alfred A. Knopf, a division of Random House, Inc.

Shorris, Earl. From *Under the Fifth Sun: A Novel of Pancho Villa.* Copyright © 1980 by Earl Shorris. New York: Delacorte Press, 1980. Reprinted by permission of the author.

Spota, Luis. From *Murieron a mitad del río* (They Died in the Middle of the River). Copyright © 1948, 1985 by Luis Spota. Mexico City: Editorial Grijalbo, S.A., 1987.

Stilwell, Hart. From *Border City.* Copyright © 1945 by Hart Stilwell. Garden City, N.Y.: Doubleday, Doran and Company, Inc., 1945.

Taibo, Paco Ignacio, II. From *Frontera Dreams.* Used by permission of Cinco Puntos Press, El Paso, Texas.

Trujillo Muñoz, Gabriel. "Lucky Strike." Reprinted with permission of the author.

Urrea, Luis Alberto. From *Across the Wire: Life & Hard Times* copyright © 1993 by Luis Alberto Urrea. Photographs © 1993 by John Lueders-Booth. Used by Permission of Doubleday, a division of Random House, Inc.

Vasconcelos, José. From *A Mexican Ulysses: An Autobiography.* Translated and abridged by W. Rex Crawford. Bloomington. Indiana University Press, 1963. Reprinted with the permission of Indiana University Press.

Villaseñor, Victor. Pages 225–227 from *Rain of Gold* by Victor Villaseñor are reprinted with permission from the publisher of *Rain of Gold* (Houston: Arte Público Press —University of Houston, 1991).

Wambaugh, Joseph. From *Lines and Shadows* copyright © 1984 by Joseph Wambaugh. Used by permission of Bantam Books, a division of Random House, Inc.

Weisman, Alan. From *La Frontera: The United States Border with Mexico* by Alan Weisman. Photographs by Jay Dusard. Copyright 1986, 1984 by Jay Dusard and Alan Weisman. San Diego, California: Harcourt Brace Jovanovich, Publishers, 1986. Used by permission of the author.

Williams, William Carlos. "Desert Music" from *Collected Poems, 1939–1962,* volume II, copyright © 1953 by William Carlos Williams. Reprinted by permission of New Directions Publishing Corp.

Yáñez, Agustín. From *The Edge of the Storm.* Translated by Ethel Brinton, copyright © 1963. Courtesy of the University of Texas Press.

About the Contributors

Oscar Zeta Acosta (1935–1974?) was an emotionally charged friend of the people whose larger-than-life activities culminated in his disappearance in Mexico. Lawyer, writer, and activist, El Paso native Acosta enlisted in the Air Force after high school and subsequently earned a law degree in 1966. He worked for an antipoverty agency, represented Chicano defendants in political cases, and eventually ran for sheriff of Los Angeles County, a race in which more than 100,000 voters supported him. His books *Autobiography of a Brown Buffalo* and *The Revolt of the Cockroach People,* from the early 1970s, were seen as integral to the Chicano literary renaissance. Acosta was the model for the Samoan attorney in Hunter Thompson's *Fear and Loathing in Las Vegas*.

Ricardo Aguilar-Melantzón, who was born in El Paso in 1947 and raised in Ciudad Juárez, is a professor in the Languages and Linguistics Department at New Mexico State University at Las Cruces. He has published throughout the Americas on borderland vernacular and literature, and was awarded a literature fellowship from the National Endowment for the Arts. His fiction about growing up in Juárez, *Cloister,* was published in full in *Puerto del Sol,* the literary journal of New Mexico State University.

Maya Angelou, author of numerous books, including *I Know Why the Caged Bird Sings* and *Even the Stars Look Lonesome,* is a professor of American Studies at Wake Forest University. Ms. Angelou has participated in civil rights struggles and has worked in film and on the stage. She delivered a poem at the 1993 presidential inauguration and has received scores of honorary degrees and awards. She was born in 1928 in St. Louis.

Gloria Anzaldúa was born in 1942 into a family that worked the fields in the Rio Grande Valley of Texas. Eventually Anzaldúa attended college and earned a masters degree from the University of Texas. Her best-known book, *Borderlands/La Frontera: The New Mestiza,* has been praised for its poetic articulation of the border's cultural anomalies. She has been awarded a National Endowment for the Arts fellowship, a Before Columbus Foundation award, and a Sappho Award of Distinction.

Mariano Azuela, born in a small Jalisco town in 1873, served as a doctor during the tumultuous Revolution of 1910 for various factions, including that of Pancho Villa. When the *villistas* fell, Azuela moved to El Paso, Texas, where he wrote and published the initial draft of his classic novel of the revolution, *The Underdogs*. Back in Mexico, he continued his medical activity, establishing free clinics for the poor, and lectured on literature. He died in Mexico City in 1952.

Charles Bowden's many books of nonfiction reflect revulsion at the trajectory of the social and political order. Born in Joliet, Illinois, in 1945, Bowden has lived in Tucson for many years and writes with dark moral vision about the fragile land and mankind's misguided efforts to improve and build upon it. His titles include *Blue Desert, Blood Orchid: An Unnatural History of America, Blues for Cannibals: The Notes from Underground,* and *Down by the River.* He is a recipient of a Lannan Foundation Literary Award for Nonfiction.

Aristeo Brito was born in Ojinaga, Chihuahua, across the Rio Grande from Presidio, Texas, in 1942 and grew up along the border. Brito, who worked the fields in his youth, eventually earned a doctorate from the University of Arizona. He teaches Spanish at Pima Community College in Tucson. As a delegate to the Modern Language Association in the early 1970s, he was instrumental in introducing Chicano literature into higher education. His novel *El diablo en Texas* was first published in 1976, then republished with an English translation in 1990, when it won the Western States Arts Award for fiction. *The Devil in Texas* is a dark and despairing look at the social structure of Presidio and the inextricable decline it has suffered through the generations. Brito has won grants from the National Endowment for the Humanities and the National Endowment for the Arts.

José Antonio Burciaga (1940–1996), born in El Chuco, Texas, was an illustrator, essayist, and poet. A co-founder of the comedy group Culture Clash, Burciaga attended the Corcoran School of Art and the San Francisco Art Institute. While he was growing up in El Paso, Burciaga's family lived in the basement of a synagogue where his father worked as a caretaker. As a child he sometimes wore tortillas on his head like yarmulkes, and he and his friends were known as the Temple Gang. He is best known for his whimsical and prideful writing about Chicano life and identity. Burciaga's books include *Drink Cultura: Chicanismo; Undocumented Love,* which won a Before Columbus Foundation American Book Award; *Spilling the Beans;* and *Weedee Peepo.* For many years he served as a Resident Fellow at Stanford University. His poetry and essays can be found in numerous collections.

Norma Elia Cantú was born in Nuevo Laredo, Mexico, in 1947 within a couple of miles of the border. When she was one year old, the family moved just north of the same stretch of frontier. Cantú was schooled in South Texas except for her doctorate, which she received from the University of Nebraska at Lincoln. Her research efforts over the years have been supported by Ford, Rockefeller, and Fulbright-Hays grants, and she has worked at the National Endowment for the Arts and has taught at colleges throughout South Texas and in Nebraska. Her book *Canícula: Snapshots of a Girlhood en la Frontera* won the Premio Aztlán and placed her in the Laredo Women's Hall of Fame. She is currently a professor of English at the University of Texas, San Antonio.

Lorna Dee Cervantes, born in California in 1954, has written two collections of poetry, *Emplumada* and *From the Cables of Genocide: Poems on Love and Hunger,* and has been widely anthologized. Cervantes has twice won fellowships from the National Endowment for the Arts. Currently she is a professor of English at the University of Colorado, Boulder.

Sandra Cisneros was born in Chicago in 1954 but often visited Mexico with her family for extended stays. A graduate of the Iowa Writers Workshop, Cisneros's best-known works are *The House on Mango Street* and *Caramelo*. She has received two fellowships from the National Endowment for the Arts, as well as a Before Columbus Foundation award. Her other awards include a Paisano Dobie Fellowship, a Lannan Foundation Literary Award, and a MacArthur Fellowship. Cisneros is a member of PEN and Mujeres por la Paz.

Ry Cooder, born in Los Angeles in 1947, has developed a unique niche in world music as a guitarist, producer, song and soundtrack writer, session man, and musicologist. He is known for broadening the appeal of authentic music, such as Tex-Mex accordion work by Flaco Jiménez and traditional Cuban melodies by the Buena Vista Social Club.

Stephen Crane, was born in Newark, New Jersey, in 1871. He traveled and wrote extensively during his brief life. His writing includes novels, news stories on the Spanish-American War in Cuba, parodies of better-known authors, and numerous short stories. In 1895 he filed a series of newspaper dispatches during a train trip into Mexico that were posthumously collected as *Stephen Crane in Mexico*. His best-known works are *Maggie: A Girl of the Streets* and *The Red Badge of Courage*. Crane died in 1900.

Cora Hayward Crawford's journey through the southwestern territories of the United States and south into Mexico, recorded in *Land of the Montezumas,* took place in the 1880s. Ultimately she published eight volumes of travel accounts.

Miguel de Anda Jacobsen (1927–2001) was born in Jalisco, Mexico, and spent most of his professional life in Baja California, where he served as the state's director of cultural affairs in the 1980s. A journalist and teacher, de Anda Jacobson was a member of the Baja California Association of Writers. His books of poetry include *Canto a Juárez* and *Triptich to Baja California*.

James Dickinson (born in Little Rock, Arkansas, in 1941) is a producer and pianist and is best-known for his group, The Dixie Flyers. He is identified internationally with Memphis music and has recorded with Arlo Guthrie, the Rolling Stones, and Los Lobos, among other artists.

Brianda Domecq was born in New York in 1942 and moved to Mexico at age nine. She studied at the Universidad Nacional Autónoma de México and El Colegio de México, where she earned a doctorate. She has worked for and contributed to numerous Mexican publications, from the *Revista de Bellas Artes* to *Excelsior*. Her books of short stories, novels, and essays include *Bestiario domestico, The Astonishing Story of the Saint of Cabora, Mujer que publica—mujer pública,* and *Eleven Days*. She currently lives in Spain.

Lawrence Ferlinghetti was born in Yonkers, New York, in 1919, earned a Ph.D. in poetry from the Sorbonne, and served in the U.S. Naval Reserve during World War II, during which time he was sent to Nagasaki shortly after it was bombed. He settled in San Francisco to begin a magazine called *City Lights,* along with a bookstore of the same name. A genial pacifist, Ferlinghetti befriended and published many Beat poets, though his own work has reflected a broader vision and more upbeat countenance. His extensive oeuvre includes novels, translations, and plays. His many books and chapbooks of poetry include *A Coney Island of the Mind, The Mexican Night,* and *Mule Mountain Blues.* He has won lifetime achievement awards from the National Book Critics Circle and the Robert Kirsch Award from the *Los Angeles Times.*

The wide-ranging career of Mexican author **Carlos Fuentes** (born in Panama City in 1928) has been shaped by international relations. Raised in a diplomat's family, Fuentes lived in Washington, D.C., for part of his youth, entered his country's foreign service, and eventually became Mexico's ambassador to France. His extensive writings, translated for readers throughout the world, include the novels *Terra Nostra, Holy Place, The Old Gringo,* and *The Years with Laura Díaz.* His nonfiction themes include Don Quixote, human rights, and Latin America's changing identity. Fuentes was one of the Latin American boom writers and has been honored worldwide with awards and visiting faculty positions at major universities.

Eduardo Galeano was born in Montevideo, Uruguay, in 1940, where at a young age he began his print career as a cartoonist, soon taking on editorial posts at a number of publications. He sought exile in Argentina after a coup, and when another coup forced him to leave Argentina, he moved to Spain, finally returning to his patria at age forty-four. Galeano has brought out more than thirty books, many of them in translation in English. His informal literary style is militant, compassionate, witty, and wise. His three-volume *Memory of Fire,* at once fictional and journalistic, traces the painful growth and scorching conflicts that have shaped the American hemispheres. Among his other books are *The Open Veins of Latin America: Five Centuries of the Pillage of a Continent, La canción de nosotros,* which won the Casa de las Américas prize, as did his *Days and Nights of Love and War.* He has also won an American Book Award and a Cultural Freedom Prize from the Lannan Foundation.

Alicia Gaspar de Alba, professor of Chicana/o Studies at the University of California, Los Angeles, was born in El Paso, Texas, in 1958. She earned her doctorate in American Studies at the University of New Mexico. De Alba is the author of *Sor Juana's Second Dream* and many other works, and the editor of *Velvet Barrios: Popular Culture and Chicana/o Sexualities.* De Alba, whose poetry, short stories, and scholarly works have been widely published, has been honored with numerous awards, including the Premio Aztlán and a Rockefeller Fellowship. Currently she is working on a mystery novel about the maquiladora murders in Juárez.

Born in Newark, New Jersey, **Allen Ginsberg** (1926–1997) was the best-known and most accomplished of the Beat poets. His many books of poetry include *Howl, Kaddish, The Fall of America,* and *Reality Sandwiches.* Ginsberg identified strongly with progressive and experimental cultural activities, participated in the movement against the Vietnam War, and advocated gay rights. Ginsberg was a student of Zen philosophy and helped start the Jack Kerouac School of Disembodied Poetics at the Naropa Institute in Colorado. He later taught poetry at Brooklyn College. His papers are housed at Stanford University.

Guillermo Gómez-Peña was born in Mexico City in 1955, immigrated to the United States at age twenty-three, and as an interdisciplinary artist and writer has exploited perceptions of the border in print, on stage, in film, and on radio. His best-known performance piece is "Border Brujo," and his books include *The New World Border, Warrior for Gringostroika,* and *Dangerous Border Crossers*. He has been a MacArthur Fellow and has been awarded prizes from the National Latino Film and Video Festival, the Corporation for Public Broadcasting, and the Before Columbus Foundation. He was a founding member of the San Diego-based Border Arts Workshop.

Genaro González, born in McAllen, Texas, in 1949, is the author of the novels *The Quixote Cult* and *Rainbow's End* (selected as a *Los Angeles Times Book Review* Critics' Choice) and the short-story collection *Only Sons*. He teaches psychology at the University of Texas–Pan American, in Edinburg.

El Paso–born **Ray Gonzalez** (1952) is a well-published poet, essayist, short-story writer, and anthologist. His books include *The Ghost of John Wayne, Memory Fever, and Turtle Pictures,* among others. He currently holds the McKnight Land Grant Professorship at the University of Minnesota. In 1991 he was elected to the Texas Institute of Letters, and in 1993 he won an award from the prestigious Before Columbus Foundation. He serves as poetry editor of the *Bloomsbury Review*.

Graham Greene (1904–1991) was born in Berkhamsted, England. At twenty-one Greene converted to Catholicism, a religion that provided the theme for many of his writings. A trip to Mexico in 1938 to look into the treatment of Catholics there provided material for *The Lawless Roads* and *The Power and the Glory*. Greene worked in British intelligence during World War II, service that provoked many literary devices he later used in his prodigious output. His books include *The Heart of the Matter, The Quiet American, Our Man in Havana,* and *Travels with My Aunt*. He also wrote screenplays and film criticism, as well as children's stories.

Woody Guthrie (1912–1967) was born in Okemah, Oklahoma, and early in his youth he traveled the hobo route through the West, composing and performing songs of working people. At the dawn of World War II he went east, where he joined a fertile left-wing group of creative activists. Although not a joiner himself, he advocated unionism and sang songs of protest and optimism with the Almanac Singers. During the war he served in the army and the merchant marine, and afterward continued his coast-to-coast travels. His thousands of songs include "This Land Is Your Land," "Roll on Columbia," and the Dust Bowl ballad "Goin' Down the Road Feelin' Bad."

Born in Chihuahua, **Martín Luis Guzmán** (1887–1976) wrote some twenty books, most of which drew on his participation in and observation of the Mexican Revolution, in which he fought as a *villista*. His titles include *The Eagle and the Serpent, La sombra del caudillo,* and *Javier Mina: Heroe de España y de México*. He edited Pancho Villa's memoirs and served his country as its ambassador to the United Nations in 1951.

María Herrera-Sobek was born in 1943. Her writing, both academic and popular, has focused on Mexican and Chicano culture and folklore. She has taught at Harvard and Stanford, and at the University of California, Santa Barbara, she has chaired the Chicano Studies Department, where she has taught since 1997 and held several administrative posts. Her prodigious output includes *The Bracero Experience: Elitelore versus Folklore, The Mexican Corrido: A Feminist Analysis,* and *Northward Bound: The Mexican Immigrant Experience in Ballad and Song*.

John Hiatt (born in Indianapolis in 1952) is a singer and songwriter whose tunes have been recorded by many performers, such as Bob Dylan, Eric Clapton, the Neville Brothers, and Jewel.

Born in Mercedes, Texas, in 1929, **Rolando Hinojosa** taught high school for a few years before beginning his college teaching career at Trinity University in San Antonio. He spent many years as a professor at the University of Texas, Austin. Hinojosa is best known for the Klail City Death Trip series, some ten novels that portray ongoing characters in a small Rio Grande Valley town. The first of these won a Casa de las Américas Award, which cited the book for the "richness of imagery, the sensitive creation of dialogues" and "the masterful control of the temporal element and its testimonial value."

Jorge Ibargüengoitia (1928–1983)—newsman, playwright, and novelist—was born in Guanajuato, Mexico, and lived in Paris at the time of his death. During his career, he won a Guggenheim Fellowship and the Casa de las Américas Award for *El atentado,* a play dwelling on the 1928 assassination of President-elect 'lvaro Obregón. His books include *The Lightning of August, The Dead Girls,* and *Estas ruinas que ves*.

El Paso native **Arturo Islas** (1938–1991) earned three degrees from Stanford, then taught English at the same university. His award-winning novel *The Rain God* and its sequel, *Migrant Souls,* followed the Angel family in their lives in Del Sapo, Texas. "We are on the border," says one family member in the latter book, "between a land that has forgotten us and another land that does not understand us."

Bárbara Jacobs, born in Mexico City in 1947, is a fiction writer and essayist. She is the author of *Dead Leaves,* which won the Xavier Villaurrutia Prize in fiction in 1987. Her other books include *Doce cuentos en contra, Escrito en el tiempo, Vida con mi amigo,* and *Juego limpio*.

Flaco Jiménez (born in San Antonio, Texas, in 1939), **Los Pingüinos del Norte,** and **Los Hermanos Bañuelos** are all contemporary Tex-Mex and *norteño* interpreters of *corridos*—Mexican folk ballads that tell a story of topical or historical significance.

Robert L. Jones (1945–1996) was born in Fresno, California, and taught at San Diego State University. He translated the works of many Tijuana poets into English, and in 1979 he co-founded *El último vuelo,* a transborder literary journal. His poetry collection *Wild Onions* was published in English in 1985 and subsequently in Spanish in Mexico. His ambition in life was to translate the complete works of the Mexican poet José Carlos Becerra (1937–1970).

Jack Kerouac (1922–1969) was born Jean-Louis Lebris de Kerouac in Lowell, Massachusetts, and grew up in a French-Canadian Catholic family, served in the U.S. Navy and merchant marine during World War II, and held odd jobs as a sports writer, mechanic, railroad brakeman, and fire lookout. He is best known for the book *On the Road,* a manic, barely fictionalized account of his adrenaline-fueled travels through the United States with a host of friends. He was the first to label free verse of his era as "beat" writing, a style of literature and life of which he was the best-known proponent. His many other books of prose and poetry include *Lonesome Traveler, The Dharma Bums,* and *Mexico City Blues.* He was awarded a grant from the American Academy of Arts and Sciences in 1955 and was a member of the Authors Guild.

Graciela Limón was born in Los Angeles in 1938 and received her bachelor's, master's, and doctoral degrees from Marymount College, the University of the Americas in Mexico City, and UCLA, respectively. She chaired the department of Chicana/o studies at Loyola Marymount University in Los Angeles, where she taught for thirty-five years. Limón's many books include *The Memories of Ana Calderón, Song of the Hummingbird,* and *In Search of Bernabé,* which won the 1994 Before Columbus Foundation American Book Award and other prizes. One critic described Limón as an author who places her work in "a transborder experience of the Americas" that links the people of Central America, Mexico, and Los Angeles.

Born in Ciudad Juárez in 1937, **Gloria López-Stafford** moved with her family across the river to the United States when she was two years old. Her memoir of her youth, *A Place in El Paso: A Mexican American Childhood,* tells of innocence and turmoil in the author's life and that of El Paso. López-Stafford worked for the Gadsden Independent School District in the part of New Mexico that adjoins El Paso, was a professor of social work, and is now retired.

Alberto Maldonado Herrera was an illustrator, and perhaps the writer, for *Denuncia,* a popular weekly Mexican novela in the 1970s that took the week's most notorious news and rendered it in a simple comic format.

Albuquerque-born **Demetria Martínez** (b. 1960) has taught at the Naropa Institute, has been a columnist for the *National Catholic Reporter,* and has been active with the Arizona Border Rights Project, a group that documents abuses by the U.S. Border Patrol. Her books of poetry are *Breathing Between the Lines* and *The Devil's Workshop*. Her novel *Mother Tongue* won the Western States Book Award for Fiction. She is a graduate of Princeton University's Woodrow Wilson School of Public and International Affairs and frequently speaks on legal and human rights for immigrants.

Oscar J. Martínez was born in San Francisco del Oro, Chihuahua, in 1943 and emigrated to the United States at age fourteen. He is Regents Professor of History at the University of Arizona, where his research and teaching have focused on the social and political development of Mexicans and Mexican Americans in the borderlands, especially the Juárez–El Paso area. Among his books are *Border Boom Town: Ciudad Juárez since 1848; Troublesome Border; Border People: Life and Society in the U.S.–Mexico Borderlands;* and *Mexican-Origin People in the United States: A Topical History*. He is a past president of the Association of Borderland Scholars and has received grants from the Ford, Rockefeller, and Mellon Foundations, as well as the National Endowment for the Humanities.

Rubén Martínez, born in Los Angeles in 1962, is an Emmy Award–winning journalist, poet, and performer. He has written *Crossing Over: A Mexican Family on the Migrant Trail* and *The Other Side: Notes from the New L.A., Mexico City and Beyond*. Martínez has served as an editor for the Pacific News Service and a Loeb Fellow at Harvard University. As a commentator, he has appeared on ABC's *Nightline* and *Politically Incorrect*, PBS's *Frontline*, on National Public Radio's *All Things Considered*, and on CNN. His work has also been published in the *New York Times, Washington Post, Los Angeles Times, La Opinión, The Nation, La Jornada Semanal, Reforma,* and *Mother Jones,* among other outlets. In 2002 he was awarded a Literary Fellowship from the Lannan Foundation.

Vladimir Mayakovsky (1893–1930), was born in the Russian town of Bagdadi in Georgia. After training at the Moscow Institute for the Study of Painting, Mayakovsky turned his creative energy to writing and became a well-known avant-garde poet and playwright who embraced Communism. While in favor with his government, he traveled abroad, including a 1925 trip that took him from Mexico into the United States. Eventually disillusioned with the Stalin regime, his works became overtly antigovernment, for which he was officially criticized and run out of the party. Much of his poetry has been translated into English, as well as the plays *The Bedbug* and *The Bathhouse*. He committed suicide at age 36.

Miguel Méndez was born in Bisbee, Arizona, in 1930 and spent his formative years in the borderlands as a construction worker and field worker. His many books—all written in Spanish, many with English translations—reflect an intimate understanding of the struggle by those who earn less than their daily bread. Now a professor at the

University of Arizona, Méndez's widely praised works include *Pilgrims in Aztlan, The Dream of Santa María de Las Piedras,* and *From Labor to Letters: A Novel Autobiography*.

Nogales, Sonora, native **Oscar Monroy Rivera** (b. 1933) has self-published his poetry, essays, fiction, and plays. A prolific, rebellious, and occasionally bombastic scribe, Monroy has enjoyed attacks from the establishment press and politicians, and wide support from the literary and the powerless. Two of his best-selling books are *El mexicano Enano III* and *El profeta de silencio.* He subscribes to José Vasconcelos's theories and has written of them in *México y vivencia dramática en el pensamiento vasconcelista* and other works.

Pat Mora (b. 1942), an El Paso native, is best known for poetry that articulates Chicana heritage and experiences. Her many books of poetry include *Chants, Borders,* and *Communion.* Among Mora's numerous children's books are *The Rainbow Tulip, The Desert Is My Mother,* and *The Race of Toad and Deer.* Mora has won many awards for her work, and she gives dozens of readings and workshops annually. Many of her books are published in bilingual editions.

Myriam Moscona, born in Mexico City in 1955, has a degree from the Universidad Iberoamericana and has worked in radio and television, bringing literary works to a wide audience. Her books of poetry include *Último jardín* and *Las preguntas de Natalia*.

Gary Paul Nabhan was born in Gary, Indiana, in 1952. A naturalist and an ethnobiologist, Nabhan's work dwells on the preservation of plant cultivation methods that have served mankind for millennia and the cultures that have nurtured them. Now the director of the Center for Sustainable Environments at Northern Arizona University, Nabhan was a founder of Native Seeds/SEARCH and worked at the Arizona-Sonora Desert Musuem. His books include *The Desert Smells Like Rain: A Naturalist in Papago Indian Country; Enduring Seeds: Native American Agriculture and Wild Plant Conservation; Songbirds, Truffles, and Wolves: An American Naturalist in Italy,* and *Coming Home to Eat: The Pleasures and Politics of Local Foods.* He is the recipient of a John Burroughs Medal and a MacArthur Fellowship.

Eugene Nelson (1929–1999) was born in Modesto, California, and gained a reputation as an activist writer for his passionate militancy on labor matters. A staunch member of the Industrial Workers of the World, Nelson worked as an organizer for the United Farm Workers in California and Texas, and wrote *Huelga: The First Hundred Days of the Delano Grape Strike.* After years of research and interviews, he wrote his classic novel *Bracero,* which has been translated into Swedish and Russian. Among his final literary works was the self-published *Tales of Crapitalism,* a collection of short stories, some of which were initially published in *Industrial Worker*.

Victor Ochoa was born in Los Angeles in 1948 and has since made the borderlands of Southern California and Northern Baja California his home. An artist and educator, in the late 1960s Ochoa was a founding director of San Diego's Centro Cultural de la Raza, a multidisciplinary community-based arts center devoted to producing and preserving Indian, Mexican, and Chicano art and culture. For many years the Centro's artist-in-residence, Ochoa has been an internationally recognized proponent of community murals as public and political art. He was also co-founder of the Border Arts Workshop/Taller de Arte Fronterizo arts collective. His paintings, graphic art, and installation pieces have been widely exhibited in Mexico, the United States, and Europe, and his work is archived in the Special Collections of the University of California, Santa Barbara, Library.

Phil Ochs (1940–1976), born in El Paso, was a major American folksinger and songwriter of the civil rights and anti–Vietnam War era. His poetic songs—among them "I Ain't Marchin' Any More," "I Declare the War Is Over," "Love Me, I'm a Liberal," and "Power and the Glory"—drew on daily journalism and ridiculed national hypocrisy.

Born in Brownsville, Texas, **Américo Paredes** (1915–1999) served in the infantry in World War II and as a journalist for *Stars & Stripes*. Back in the States, his studies culminated in a doctorate in English and folklore, subjects that dominated his teaching and writing for his entire career at the University of Texas. Don Américo was awarded major prizes from both the United States and Mexican governments for his studies of borderland culture. Credited with according academic vigor and respect to border ballads, humor, and oral tradition, Paredes's doctoral dissertation on Gregorio Cortez grew into his classic study, *"With His Pistol in His Hand": A Border Ballad and Its Hero*.

Elena Poniatowska was born in Paris in 1932 to a Mexican mother and a Polish-French father and moved with her family to Mexico when she was nine years old. The breadth of her writing reveals a passion for justice, as well as the subtleties of personality and achievement. Her books include *Tinísima*, about the photographer Tina Modotti; *Massacre in Mexico*, about her adopted country's brutality against student demonstrators in 1968; and *Dear Diego*, a novel about the artist Diego Rivera and his first wife. In all, she has written more than forty books and has received numerous awards, including a Guggenheim Fellowship. She lives in Mexico City.

Janet Arelis Quezada born in New York in 1975 is a poet, performer, and playwright of Dominican heritage. She has been published in the University of New Mexico journal *Blue Mesa Review* and in a chapbook for San Francisco Women Against Rape. Her short story "La fiesta de los Linares" appears on womenwriters.net, and she studied playwriting at the U.S.–Cuba Writers Conference in 2001. Quezada has been active in the effort to evict the U.S. Navy from Vieques, Puerto Rico, and takes her inspiration from the Caribbean-American poet and professor Audre Lorde.

Prize-winning author **George Rabasa,** born in Biddeford, Maine, in 1941, wrote the short-story collection *Glass Houses* and the novel *Floating Kingdom,* which won the

Writer's Voice Capricorn Award for Excellence in Fiction. He has lived in Minnesota since the mid-1980s.

John Reed (1887–1920) was a leading contributor to leftist magazines in the early twentieth century and agitated on behalf of striking workers and other radical causes. His coverage of Mexico's Revolution of 1910, *Insurgent Mexico*, described the *villista* effort in the north. He also wrote a few short stories drawn on these experiences. A confirmed rebel, when in Russia he identified with the Bolsheviks, sentiments found in *Ten Days That Shook the World*. He also wrote poetry and a play.

Born on the U.S. side of Ambos Nogales in 1952, **Alberto Alvaro Ríos** has mined his upbringing along the Arizona-Sonora border to bring forth fiction and poetry that represents, as one critic called it, "the baroque in the Southwest." His many titles include *Pig Cookies, Capirotada: A Nogales Memoir,* and *The Iguana Killer*. Ríos has been awarded fellowships from the National Endowment for the Arts and the Guggenheim Foundation, a Walt Whitman Award from the National Academy of American Poets, a Western States Book Award for fiction, and a Community Appreciation Award from Chicanos Por La Causa. He is a Regents Professor at Arizona State University, where he teaches in the Creative Writing Program.

Marty Robbins (1925–1982), a country music singer/songwriter born Martin Robinson near Glendale, Arizona, is best known for his *Gunfighter Ballads*. Many of his songs evoked a mythic western borderland, including "El Paso," "Saddle Tramp," "Bend in the River," and "She Was Young and She Was Pretty." Robbins, a member of the Grand Ole Opry, won two Grammys and was inducted into the Nashville Songwriter's International Hall of Fame. He was also a race-car driver and competed on the NASCAR circuit.

Luis J. Rodríguez was born in El Paso in 1954 and was raised in Los Angeles, where his gang-filled youth resulted in his memoir *Always Running: La Vida Loca—Gang Days in L.A.* Most recently he published a collection of short stories, *The Republic of East L.A.* In addition to writing, Rodríguez has worked as a bus and truck driver, a foundry worker, and a carpenter. He has written children's fare and poetry such as *It Doesn't Have to Be This Way: A Barrio Story* and *The Concrete River*. He is co-founder of the Tía Chucha Cultural Center in San Fernando, California. His many literary prizes include the Carl Sandburg Literary Award for nonfiction, the Hispanic Heritage Award for literature, and the Unsung Heroes of Compassion award.

Essayist and commentator **Richard Rodriguez** was born in San Francisco in 1944 and was educated in California, New York, and London. His three books, *Hunger of Memory, Days of Obligation: An Argument with My Mexican Father,* and *Brown: The Last Discovery of America,* are meditations on ethnic identity, social conditions, and the author himself. Rodriguez has worked as a janitor, reporter, and editor, and holds in highest esteem writing that joins journalism and literature. He is best-known for his essays on the PBS *NewsHour,* and has published in numerous outlets, including the Pacific News Service, where he works as an editor. He has received Fulbright and National Endowment for the Humanities fellowships, and many other prizes for articulating his vision of a moral and humanitarian society.

John Ross, born in Greenwich Village in 1938, has been writing vigorous and poetic accounts of insurgency and culture in Mexico for decades. Ross's extensive coverage of the Zapatista uprising prompted the Mexico City daily *La Jornada* to call him "a new John Reed covering a new Mexican revolution." His books include *The War against Oblivion: Zapatista Chronicles, 1994–2000; Rebellion from the Roots,* which won an American Book Award; *The Annexation of Mexico from the Aztecs to the IMF; Tonatiuh's People: A Novel of the Mexican Cataclysm;* and most recently *Mexico in Focus: A Guide to the People, Politics, and Culture.* He is also coeditor of a collection of basketball writing, *We Came to Play.* Ross regularly appears in the *Los Angeles Weekly* and the *San Francisco Bay Guardian* and outlets on five continents.

Benjamin Alire Sáenz born in Old Picacho, New Mexico, near Las Cruces in 1954, teaches in the creative writing program at the University of Texas, El Paso. Sáenz earned a masters in theology from the University of Louvain in Belgium and served in the priesthood for a few years. His poetry, fiction, and children's stories reflect the moral and tangible incongruities of the borderland and have won him many literary prizes, among them the American Book Award of the Before Columbus Foundation, a Lannan Poetry Fellowship, and a Wallace E. Stegner Fellowship in Creative Writing from Stanford University. Sáenz's books include *Calendar of Dust, Carry Me Like Water, Elegies in Blue,* and *A Gift from Papa Diego/Un regalo de papá Diego.*

Ricardo Sánchez (1941–1995) was the youngest of thirteen children born into an El Paso family. Raised both street and smart, the poetic Sánchez enlisted in the army before finishing high school and within a matter of years served time in California and Texas for separate armed robbery convictions. Not long after his second prison release, he published *Canto y grito mi liberación: The Liberation of a Chicano Mind,* a book that attracted wide attention for its gritty and intimate observations. At various times Sánchez held positions at colleges and universities in Texas, Wisconsin, Alaska, Utah, and Washington, and received support from the Ford Foundation. He published more books of verse, including *Eagle-Visioned/Feathered Adobes: Manito Sojourns and Pachuco Ramblings,* and *Selected Poems.* He was part of International PEN and the Southwest Poets Conference, worked for VISTA, and directed an itinerant migrant health project in Colorado. Sánchez was posthumously inducted into the El Paso Writers Hall of Fame.

Trinidad V. Sánchez (1898–1965) emigrated to Texas from his native Piedras Negras, Coahuila, at age sixteen, eventually settling in Michigan. A factory worker and poet, Sánchez contributed to publications in Texas and Michigan. Many of his poems were published posthumously in *Poems by Father & Son.* In retirement, Sánchez owned the Monterrey Poolroom in Pontiac, Michigan.

Edward R. F. Sheehan, born in Boston in 1930, has worked as a U.S. diplomat, a novelist and journalist, a playwright, and a teacher. His books include *Agony in the Garden: A Stranger in Central America, Kingdom of Illusion*, and *Innocent Darkness,* set along the border. He is also the author of *The Arabs, Israelis, and Kissinger: A Secret History of American Diplomacy in the Middle East* and has written for the *New York Times, Foreign Affairs,* and the *New York Review of Books*. His play *Kingdoms* was about the conflict between Napoleon and Pope Pious VII.

Dallas-born **Gilbert Shelton** (1940) first published the Fabulous Furry Freak Brothers comic strip in 1968. **Dave Sheridan** (1943–1981), born in Cleveland, began collaborating with him a few years later. The Freak Brothers, enormously popular in the underground press and outside mainstream America, were three inventive down-and-out San Francisco hippies whose slapstick misadventures usually involved illicit drugs. Both Sheridan and Shelton were part of the fertile 1960s underground comix scene in San Francisco, and Sheridan leant his talents to antiwar and other progressive causes. Shelton now lives in Europe, where the Freak Brothers remain beloved, and he still publishes a Freak Brothers book every few years with co-artist Paul Mavrides.

Sam Shepard was born in Ft. Sheridan, Illinois, in 1943, and shortly after his arrival in New York at age nineteen began an extraordinary career as a playwright, screenwriter, actor, and author. He has won numerous Obies for his Off-Broadway plays, the New York Drama Critics Award, and the Pulitzer Prize for Drama. He is a member of the American Academy and Institute of Arts and Letters, and in the late 1960s he was a member of the rock band the Holy Modal Rounders. Most of his plays—such as *Curse of the Starving Class, Fool for Love,* and *True West*—have been published in book form, and his collection of short stories, *Cruising Paradise,* was critically acclaimed on its release.

Earl Shorris, born in Chicago in 1936, has written social commentary for major American journals and is the author of fiction and nonfiction about Latinos, corporate culture, and education. His titles include *New American Blues: A Journey through Poverty to Democracy, Under the Fifth Sun: A Novel of Pancho Villa, Latinos: A Biography of the People,* and *Power Sits at Another Table and Other Observations on the Business of Power*. His book *Riches for the Poor: The Clemente Course in the Humanities* outlines the rationale for and development of a course for teaching the classic humanities to impoverished students.

Luis Spota (1925–1985), a major Mexican author of the mid twentieth century, found work selling encyclopedias and razor blades and waiting on tables before his writing career took off. His many titles include *La carcajada del gato, Vagabundo,* and *Los sueños del insomnio*. Many of his books were adapted for the screen by Spota or others. Early in his career he distinguished himself as a journalist, later tried his hand at bullfighting, and to research *Murieron a mitad del río* he lived among Mexicans who crossed into the United States. In his nonliterary life he served as president of the World Boxing Council. A Casa de Cultura is named for him in Mexico City.

A life-long Texan raised close to the Mexican border, **Hart Stilwell** (1902–1975) was the son of a Texas Ranger. After earning a degree in journalism from the University of Texas, Stilwell worked for the *Brownsville Herald* and then began a career in freelance writing for Texas newspapers (in San Antonio, Houston, and Austin) and national magazines (*Field and Stream* and *Outdoor,* among others). His three novels— *Campus Town, Border Town,* and the highly acclaimed *Uncovered Wagon*—were semi-autobiographical. Stilwell also wrote books about hunting and fishing in Texas and Mexico.

Paco Ignacio Taibo II (b. 1949) was born in Gijón, Spain, where he stages a mystery writers' festival called Semana Negra every summer. He moved to Mexico at age nine, grew up in the capital observing his government's corrupt ways, and incorporated them into his popular fiction. Best known for his philosophical detective, Hector Belascoarán Shayne, who is featured in some dozen books, Taibo has written history (*La huelga del verano de 1920 en Monterrey* and *Los Bolshevikis: Historia narrativa de los origenes del comunismo en Mexico, 1919–1925,* among other works), biography *(Guevara, Also Known as Che),* and journalism. His detective books in English include *Frontera Dreams, Life Itself, Return to the Same City,* and *Four Hands*. Taibo is a founding member of the International Association of Crime Writers.

Gabriel Trujillo Muñoz born in Mexicali in 1958, is the author of *Mercaderes,* a collection of short stories; *Rastrojo,* his selected poetry; *Lengua franca,* a book of essays; and numerous other titles. He has also compiled a number of collections, including *Un camino de hallazgos* (an anthology of the poetry of Baja California) and the *Diccionario bibliográfico de escritores de Baja California*. He won the binational Pellicer-Frost poetry prize in 1996, and two years later was awarded the Excelencia Frontera prize. He is a professor at the Universidad Autónoma de Baja California in Mexicali.

Luis Alberto Urrea (1955) was born in Tijuana, Baja California, in 1955 and moved a few miles north to San Diego at age three. His fiction, nonfiction, and poetry dwell on the western edge of the border and the American Southwest. After graduating from the University of California, San Diego, Urrea wrote lyrics for the prog-rock band Harlequin and began working with "Pastor Von" and a missionary group that ministered to the poor of Tijuana. These experiences were recounted in *By the Lake of Sleeping Children* and *Across the Wire,* chosen as a *New York Times* Notable Book of the Year. Urrea has worked in the Chicano Studies Department at San Diego Mesa College and Harvard University. He is now an associate professor at the University of Illinois– Chicago. He won the Before Columbus Foundation American Book Award for *Nobody's Son: Notes from an American Life*. His other books include *Wandering Time, Ghost Sickness,* and *In the Fever of Being*.

Writer, philosopher, and educator **José Vasconcelos** (1882–1959) was born in Oaxaca, came of age with the Revolution of 1910 during the regime of Porfirio Díaz, and served subsequent administrations in various posts, most notably minister of education. Best-known among his many books of philosophy, memoir, and pedagogical reform is *La raza cósmica* (The Cosmic Race), in which he forecasts racial qualities for all Latin America.

Victor Villaseñor was born in Carlsbad, California, in 1940 and was raised on nearby family land farmed by his Mexican immigrant parents. A lengthy foray into Mexico at age nineteen introduced him to literature, and when he returned he earned a living with seasonal labor and construction, all the while writing. His best-known work, *Rain of Gold,* tells of the hardships generations of his family endured in Mexico and after settling in the States. His many other works of fiction and nonfiction include *Macho!, Jury: The People vs. Juan Corona, Thirteen Senses: A Memoir,* and the screenplay for *The Ballad of Gregorio Cortez.* Villaseñor, who incorporates spiritualism and my thology into his works, appears frequently as a public speaker.

Joseph Wambaugh (1937) was born in East Pittsburgh, Pennsylvania, the son of a policeman. After serving in the marines, Wambaugh became a patrolman and detective sergeant for the Los Angeles Police Department, a job that afforded him material for his fiction and nonfiction about police officers and their considerable and often unlawful failings. Among his books have been *Lines and Shadows, The Onion Field, The New Centurions, The Choirboys,* and *The Fire Lover.* Wambaugh has won awards from the Mystery Writers of America and the International Association of Crime Writers. He has written screenplays of his own books and has created and worked as a consultant for police dramas on television.

Alan Weisman, born in Minneapolis in 1947, has covered the globe in pursuit of stories about displaced and disappearing cultures, energy sources both efficient and dangerous, and rank exploitation. His books include *Gaviotas: A Village to Reinvent the World,* which won a Social Inventions Award from the London-based Global Ideas Bank, *La Frontera* (with photographer Jay Dusard), and *An Echo in My Blood.* Weisman has been a Fulbright Senior Scholar in Colombia and a writer-in-residence at the Altos de Chavón Escuela de Arte y Diseño in the Dominican Republic. His work has appeared in *Harper's,* the *New York Times Magazine,* the *Atlantic Monthly,* the *Los Angeles Times Magazine,* and on National Public Radio and Public Radio International. The MacArthur Foundation is funding his research for a book about the future of energy.

William Carlos Williams (1883–1963) was born in Rutherford, New Jersey. A poet who has been called a modernist, Williams earned a medical degree from the University of Pennsylvania, served an internship in New York's Hell's Kitchen, and set up a private practice in his hometown, where he lived the rest of his life. He was considered part of the Imagist movement and was greatly influenced by his friend and mentor

Ezra Pound. His twenty-three books of poetry include *Spring and All, The Desert Music and Other Poems,* and the epic five-volume *Paterson*. He won just about every prize afforded a poet, including a Pulitzer and the National Book Award. His prose, plays, and translations were also well-received. Williams was a member of the American Academy of Arts and Letters, the National Institute of Arts and Letters, the Academy of American Poets, and the Bergen County (N.J.) Medical Association.

Agustín Yáñez (1904–1980) wrote literary criticism as well as novels and short stories. He held a degree in law and, like many cultural figures of his era, held political posts as well. His books include *The Edge of the Storm, La creación,* and *The Lean Lands.*

About the Editor

Photo by Jay Rochlin

Tom Miller was born in Washington, D.C., in 1947 and moved to the borderlands in 1969. Since that time, as a journalist and author he has brought us extraordinary stories about ordinary people from the American Southwest and Latin America. Miller, a veteran of the underground press of the 1960s and early 1970s, has written for *Smithsonian, Life, Natural History, Rolling Stone,* and the *New York Times,* among other outlets. He has worked as a consultant for network television and public radio, where his occasional commentaries have been heard on *Latino USA* and other programs. His collection of some eighty versions of the song "La Bamba" led to his Rhino Records release, "The Best of La Bamba."

Miller's nine books include *Jack Ruby's Kitchen Sink: Offbeat Travels through America's Southwest,* which won the prestigious Lowell Thomas Award for Best Travel Book of the Year, *The Panama Hat Trail, Trading with the Enemy: A Yankee Travels through Castro's Cuba,* and *On the Border.* An essay by Miller accompanies the photographs of Alex Webb in *Crossings: Photographs from the U.S.–Mexico Border.*

In addition to his published work, Miller has led educational trips through Cuba on behalf of the National Geographic Society and the American Museum of Natural History, and since 1990 he has been affiliated with the University of Arizona's Latin American Area Center. Miller, whose papers have been acquired by Special Collections of the University of Arizona Library, makes his home with his wife in Tucson.